THE REDISCOVERERS

THE REDISCOVERERS

Major Writers
in the Portuguese Literature
of National Regeneration

Ronald W. Sousa

The Pennsylvania State University Press
University Park and London

Library of Congress Cataloging in Publication Data
Sousa, Ronald W. 1943-
　　The rediscoverers, major writers in the Portuguese literature of national regeneration.
　　Includes bibliography and index.
　　1. Portuguese literature—History and criticism.
2. Portugal in literature. I. Title
PQ9018.S66　　　869'.09　　　80-21453
ISBN 0-271-00300-6

Copyright ©1981 The Pennsylvania State University
All rights reserved
Designed by Glenn Ruby
Printed in the United States of America

Contents

Introduction	1
Camões: The Noble Poet	11
Vieira: The Prophet	47
Garrett: A Poet Returned, Rebirth of a Nation	77
Eça de Queiroz: The Social Critic and the End of Social Criticism	101
Pessoa: The Messenger	131
The Rediscoverers: A Retrospect	161
Notes	169
Bibliography	183
Index	191

Introduction

The Spanish historian Américo Castro, in the chapter of *La realidad histórica de España* that he dedicates to Portugal, argues that Portugal's concept of its past is "a great work of art," "human poetic reality." He adds, underscoring the created nature of that concept: "A great novelist does not work differently."[1] While I do not agree with many of the reasons that Castro adduces to substantiate that analysis, its accuracy seems to me indisputable: for a substantial portion of its history Portugal has indeed, in various media, treated its past—and, as well, the nexus of that past with the present—in a manner that is properly described as "artistic."

To my mind, the propensity to approach history "artistically" has much to do with the susceptibility of the Portuguese past to dramatic interpretation—in service of the intellectual and psychological needs of a present that, during most of the past four centuries, has not in itself provided much room for optimism about national fortunes. The basic events in that history are as follows. The Portuguese expansion began early in the fifteenth century under the guidance of King John I, the first monarch of the newly established royal house of Aviz. Ceuta, an Arab port city on the African side of the Straits of Gibraltar, represented the first step. It fell to the Portuguese in 1415, and the so-called "Age of the Discoveries" was under way. In ensuing years Portuguese navigators explored the West African coast and areas in the Atlantic Ocean west of the mouth of the Mediterranean Sea, establishing Portuguese influence in those areas. The Madeira Islands were colonized in the 1420's; the Azores in the 1440's. National expansion may be said to have reached its culmination in 1498 with Vasco da Gama's voyage to Calicut, which established a Portuguese sea route, via the South African cape, to India and the Orient. In the first half of the sixteenth century, Portugal, then a nation of little more than one million people, maintained control of, or primary trade influence over, vast areas along the route of that expansion—in essence, it maintained a commercial empire. At its height, that empire included almost all of the African and Arabian coasts, large sections of India, parts of Indo-China, China, and Japan, much of the Malay Archipelago, and the northeastern coast of South America. The Portuguese of that time could justifiably view their nation as an international power, the discoverer and explorer of regions of the world theretofore unknown to Europeans. And they were quite aware that their many achievements were the more remarkable as their nation was small—in essence, a medieval holdover at the dawn of the age of modern nation states.

By the end of the era, however—that is, by the mid-1500's—the Portuguese international position clearly had weakened. The reasons for that weakening are unclear. We know that competition was growing from other European nations for the trade routes and trade areas that Portugal had established for itself and that smuggling and official corruption flourished. And, while prices brought by goods that the Portuguese were trading had considerably diminished, expenses for both trading ventures and other Crown undertakings continued to grow, in part in concert with the general European inflation of the era. Consequently, the sense of unlimited wealth to be derived from the nation's established mercantile system was negated. Nonetheless, the conclusion that the mid-sixteenth-century sense of decline within the nation derived directly from strictly tangible economic factors remains mere speculation, especially since throughout that era the empire remained more than solvent—though, to be sure, not as spectacularly prosperous as had been expected.

What may be more to the point is that various of the intellectual currents of the age—late medieval Christian thought and nobiliary ideology, Renaissance Humanism, and a tendency, probably of popular origin, toward prophecy—involved an approach to experience that can be characterized by the blanket term "idealistic." And that dominant idealism was susceptible of frustration. For example, it has been suggested that the implications, for religious faith, of the discoveries themselves and of the consequent efforts to spread Christianity into previously unknown lands led, for a variety of reasons, to a mixture of visionarism on the one hand and a sense of anxiety on the other.[2] Specific economic, military, political, social, and religious problems involved in the maintaining and Christianizing of an empire thus may have provided the concrete stumbling blocks that crystallized a general sense of frustration and failure—especially on the part of figures at the top of the social scale. As the Portuguese historian António Oliveira Marques points out,[3] while in the fifteenth and sixteenth centuries a small nation like Portugal could sustain imperial expansion, it could do so only by dint of such qualities as strength of purpose and national cohesiveness. Surely, then, it is a telltale sign that a feeling of frustration and a sense of failure—present or imminent—mingle with a sense of pride in the Portuguese achievements within writings of the time, from the verse letters of Francisco de Sá de Miranda (1481?–1558) and the lyrics António Ferreira (1528–1569) to the national epic poem, *Os Lusíadas*, of Luís de Camões (1525?–1580).[4] It clearly is significant too that all three authors, as well as other, less famous writers working in a variety of genres, recurringly express a wish to return to what is perceived as a stable past existence, although each casts that past in his own terms.

A headstrong, unstable young king, undeniably to a great degree the product of those intellectual and spiritual anxieties—he was advised and educated in accordance with them[5]—attempted to rekindle a feeling of national direction in 1578 by leading an army on an ill-conceived attempt to reconquer areas of North Africa. That attempt ended in the Moors' defeat of the Portuguese at Alcácer-Kebir(Ksar al-Kebir), in present-day Morocco. The king, Sebastian, perished in the battle, as did the cream of the nation's nobility and men-at-arms. The defeat, and the Spanish king's consequent accession to the Portuguese throne, while not representing the end of Portuguese empire in a political or economic sense, marks the definitive end, as far as the Portuguese consciousness is concerned, of an era of greatness. The artistic handling of the national past that Américo Castro describes consistently involves elements of that era or events that led to it. The basic pattern normally ascribed to the national history includes an era of glory, a dramatic fall, and, thereafter, successful revolution against Spain in 1640, reclaiming of independence, and continual struggle to regain international respectability. The truth, as I suggest above, and as virtually all modes of evaluation suggest, is more complex and far less dramatic. Nevertheless, the pattern of preeminence, fall, and then the occupying of a position from which attempts at reascendance can be made—fitting, as it does, various common mythological paradigms —seems to have been indelibly stamped upon their national history by the Portuguese.

Into that pattern—in different ways in different eras—notions of the very nature of history, evaluations of current changes in social structure, and even indices of individuality have been inserted. Indeed, the pattern has become, to my mind,[6] something of a constant in Portuguese culture, continually reelaborated over the years. The reelaborations regularly involve redefinition of elements from a set of symbols of the "pre-fall" national past: the concept of success against great odds; the notion of Portugal as initiator of a cultural era; the characteristics of various kings, heroes, and other figures seen as indicative of the past glory; and the sense of a fate at work in the history of the nation. Such redefinition occurs, as I hint in the metaphor to be seen in my title, in an effort to "rediscover" the vigor that characterized the "discoverer" nation at the height of its glory. The metaphor is, I think, accurately descriptive of some of the complexities that the situation can assume, for a "rediscovery" can be seen by the person or persons formulating it as, in any number of ways, a recapitulation of the original "discoveries," the "rediscoverer" as, in any number of ways, himself a new "discoverer." I shall return to concrete exemplifications of that complex of implications in the Retrospect at the end of this study. In any case, redefinitions of such items as those mentioned above are found in various areas of national cultural life, from political rhetoric to artistic production, and regularly appear in eras of major social change, a fact in itself indicative of the ascendancy of regenerationist thought in the minds of many Portuguese. The presence of such thought has often been remarked on in general terms, but there have been few systematic treatments of its function in any specific area.

The present study is directed to the area of literature and is the product of twelve years of investigation into the issue and thought about it. During that period I have spoken, both in public and also with other students of Portuguese literature, about aspects of the subject and have published writings that relate to it—some of which are neccessarily cited in this study, for they provide detailed substantiation for some of the analyses carried out in the ensuing chapters. I have also seen the need to incorporate into my thinking facets of Portuguese literature that I first thought at best marginal to the national-regeneration issue. Also during that time it has been suggested to me more than once that I attempt a history of modern Portuguese literature centered on that issue. After some thought I have rejected the idea, concluding that it is not possible to account for many of the important literary phenomena solely through recourse to the complex of notions involved in regenerationism as I see it. However, another sort of study *is* possible: a study of the history of Portuguese regenerationism in all its cultural manifestations. Such a study would be very valuable in mapping major currents in Portuguese cultural history, down to the artistic production and political rhetoric of the post-1974 era. To a limited extent the present study attempts to sketch some of the bare outlines of such a work, but only within the field of literature.

I go no further than that basic outlining because the guiding principle of the present endeavor runs in another direction: I wish not to *map* regenerationism, even within the literary sphere alone, but rather to show in moderate detail how it has worked in the production of given pieces of literature. It is not my intent here to formulate summary readings of the production of an author or of a movement and then to insert those readings into a chronology, but rather to show, through detailed analysis of a few key literary pieces, the complexity that regenerationism can attain in the literary sphere and the nature of the impingement of social reality upon literature (and of literature upon social reality) inherent to literary regenerationism, leaving little more than the juxtaposition of those analyses to suggest wider historical movement. I wish to deal with, among others, such matters as the nature of the interpretation of history implicit in an author's work, his notion of the relationship of past and present, the understanding that he has of his artistic endeavor and of himself as artist in the light of his view of the relationship between past and present, and the pretensions of his language to performative status within the society of his day. In short, I shall try to treat important aspects of the texture of regenerationist literature through examination of a few selected examples.

To that end I deal with five writers, each of whom has created regenerationist literature of considerable complexity, and I focus on only one of the works of each—the one that I think lends itself best to the task I have set. To be sure, I link some facets of my analysis of that work to other works of each author and, on occasion, to those of other contemporary writers, but more often than not I do so to firm up a point in my analysis rather than to introduce a wider scope for its own sake.

The writers and works to be dealt with are Luís de Camões (1525?–1580) and his epic poem *Os Lusíadas* (1572); Padre António Vieira (1608–1697) and his expository *História do Futuro* (1647–1663); Almeida Garrett (1799–1854) and his lyric-narrative poem *Camões* (1825); Eça de Queiroz (1845–1900) and his novel *A Ilustre Casa de Ramires* (1900); and Fernando Pessoa (1888–1935) and his volume of lyric poetry entitled *Mensagem* (1934). Each is a major figure in Portuguese literary history, and each can be seen as indicative of many of the directions taken in literary movements of his time. Moreover, each, as I shall show, in carrying out his regenerationist analysis and prescription, does reveal major tensions within the social structure of Portugal at his time and speaks to those tensions in his work. Indeed, while it has not necessarily been my intent to arrange it in this fashion, the study involves five prominent figures—"classics" in Portuguese literature, read and reread by the Portuguese as well as by others interested in Portuguese literature, though not primarily from the point of view of their literary regenerationism—who each can be viewed as indicative of a discrete era in the social and cultural history of his nation.

I intend, then, first that each of the ensuing chapters constitute a brief and somewhat schematic critical examination, oriented to illustration of the literary phenomena outlined in this Introduction, of a major literary piece by a major literary figure, and second, that the seriatim arrangement of the chapters say something about the changing forms into which regenerationist thought has been shaped as the nature of Portuguese society has evolved. The reader will be the judge of my success or failure in that undertaking.

A few matters of procedure and form should be clarified here at the outset. First—in the area of footnotes and bibliography—since little work has been done on literary regenerationism in Portugal, allusions to the work of others will be few. I believe that I include all works that touch on the subject in any substantial way. In any case, it is not my purpose here to argue perspectives on the overall question but rather to set forth my viewpoint through detailed examination of specific texts. As regards references to general criticism on each of the authors examined, since mine is a narrowly directed study, I note such only when I actually touch on, refer to, or seek substantiation from, perspectives developed by another investigator. My Bibliography is a listing of only the sources that have had orienting force upon my analysis, rather than a compilation that has any pretension of completeness. Further, even though it is made select in the ways herein described, it is beyond the scope of the Bibliography to suggest the nature of the orientation provided by every item. The same course is taken with the several works on Portuguese culture and history, else the list would become an unmanageable, unfocused exercise in bibliography; I merely list such sources in the first section of the Bibliography—to which the reader is herewith directed—instead of inserting repeated references to them in the bibliographies to my various chapters. Only when I refer to discrete information from them within a given chapter do I make footnote acknowledgment. Further, I should make it clear that my listing of a title does not always imply my agreement with its content; to the contrary, quite often a given work has had the primary value for me of providing data or analyses on the basis of which I have then come to different conclusions about a given topic. Finally, I have taken the position that notions of general European cultural history and of historical and literary-critical methods represent a part of the baggage that both the reader and I bring with us to the task of our communication in the pages that follow, and therefore do not include bibliographical references for them.

There are also several important editorial matters of which the reader of this study should be made aware. 1) All Portuguese quotations and texts, except some bibliographical information, a few archaic forms found in the earlier writers, and the poems of Fernando Pessoa's book *Mensagem*, appear in a form consonant with modern Lusitanian usage. When I draw material from a source in which spelling and accentuation conform to other conventions, I alter the material to modern Lusitanian standards. 2) In the case of *Mensagem*, editors since its first publication have usually preferred to retain the antiquated and often idiosyncratic form cultivated by Pessoa in its composition; I carry on that practice, generally following the third edition of the Galhoz compilation of Pessoa's verse (Rio de Janeiro, 1969). When readings in that edition vary from those found in the Ática editions (Lisbon, 1945 and various reprintings and reeditions) and from the first edition (Lisbon, 1934)—an edition which, unfortunately, is not definitive—editorial decisions have been made with an eye to obtaining as consistent and accurate a reading as possible. The whereabouts of the only definitive source for the text of *Mensagem*, a copy of the first edition corrected and amended by Pessoa, is no longer known. 3) Three unspaced periods (...) included in Portuguese texts represent punctuation reproduced from the original. Three spaced periods (. . .) represent an editorial notation—on either my part or the part of the editor of the material in question—indicating an omission or a lacuna.

In a project that has endured so long, there are, inevitably, many people to thank and many organizations to acknowledge. In the former area, to list all those who have expressed interest, given support and encouragement, and contributed ideas would be a task of considerable dimensions. To all those people I herewith give this general expression of my deepest appreciation.

Specifically, I should like to thank the Hispanic Society of America for generously allowing me to reproduce material from Leonard Bacon's translation into English of Camões's *Os Lusíadas*. And I should like to thank as well the Ohio University Press for its permission to reproduce passages from Ann Stevens's translation of Eça de Queiroz's novel *A Ilustre Casa de Ramires*. Thanks go too to Professor Edgar C. Knowlton, Jr. for permission to reproduce portions of his translation of Garrett's *Camões*.

And I should like to acknowledge the aid of the University of California and of the Ford Foundation, both of which provided financial support for my graduate education and ultimately for initiation of this project, and the assistance of the Fundação Calouste Gulbenkian in providing travel expenses to and from Lisbon. I should like to thank as well the Institute of Latin American Studies of the University of Texas at Austin for financial support that enabled me to finish the Camões chapter, and the University of Texas Research Institute for funds necessary to the gathering of materials. Also to be thanked are the National Endowment for the Humanities and the American Philosophical Society for aiding me in my work on Eça de Queiroz.

I should also like to thank the Staff of the Biblioteca Nacional de Lisboa—especially Srs. João Bernardo dos Santos and Fernando Nunes—for kind and invaluable help. I wish to express appreciation to three individuals: Professor James T. Monroe, of the University of California at Berkeley, for his willing help and pertinent suggestions; Professor Arthur L-F. Askins, of the University of California at Berkeley, for instruction and advice both on the present project and on preparatory studies; and Professor Benjamin M. Woodbridge, Jr., of the University of California at Berkeley, not only for his tireless work on this project but also for what must seem to him a lifetime of attempting to educate me. Finally, I should like to thank my students at the University of Texas, the University of California at Berkeley, and the University of Minnesota, whose reception of my formulations in regard to the concept of regenerationism in Portuguese literature—ranging, as it has, from overblown enthusiasm to critical incredulity—has helped immeasurably in the development of the ensuing pages.

Portrait of Camões painted by Fernando Gomes, probably in the 1570's. Because of the relatively individualistic face—within the stereotyped artistocratic mode of the era—it is presumed to have been posed for, giving us our only real glimpse of the poet.

Camões: The Noble Poet

The Portugal of the Discoveries, like the feudal society that preceded it, was dominated by the hereditary nobility, the traditional upper class of the social system. All the while continuing to conceive—and ideologize—itself as the warrior class deserving of the bulk of the wealth and prestige of society, it nonetheless underwent considerable change during the fifteenth and sixteenth centuries. The changes came as a response to changing material realities in the country; wealth increasingly derived not from the holding of land, as it had before, but rather from participation in the national mercantile undertaking that was part and parcel of the discoveries. At the beginning of the sixteenth century, the focus of the principal Portuguese noble families had transferred to the court and to Lisbon, the emporial center, attracted by the control of wealth and power situated there. Indeed, most of those families came to live at the court. To be sure, they continued to hold and cultivate their traditional lands, but, in the new financial structure, to limit oneself to only that activity would have amounted to a great loss in relative wealth and social standing. The new mercantilism was loosely but definitely centered on the king, who gained considerable power from the situation, through the central fiscalizing agency, the Crown. Members of the noble families, according to their relative prominence, held such positions as captains of ships or of fleets, colonial governors, emporial administrators, and—in the inevitable expansion of international relations—envoys, ambassadors, and the like. In this way the nobility, while suffering a great loss of power with respect to the king, continued to monopolize the national economic system.

The changed economic structure of Portugal also produced an increase in social mobility in comparison with feudal times. For the first time, a middle group—composed of individuals in an entire spectrum from small-scale merchants to bureaucrats, technicians of several sorts, purchasers of monopolies over some aspects of trade, and high-level financiers, a considerable portion of the latter three categories being composed of foreigners—entered the system in significant numbers. Some had influence at decision-making levels. The fact that many accepted (or bought) titles is an indication of the continued material and ideological ascendancy of the noble class. At the same time, however, this creation of a "new nobility" indirectly threatened the postion of especially the less powerful of the old noble families, thus producing tensions within that class.

The upper social level served not only as the primary organizing agent of the expansion, and primary recipient of the economic return therein produced, but also as the arena for reflection upon that undertaking. In fact, because of the need for educated men to carry out the complex duties of leadership both within the empire and in Portugal's relationships with other European nations, the court nobility—along with individuals in the top of that middle group identified above—became the seat of secular education and of sophisticated evaluation of aspects of the national and international order. The primary educators in the late-fifteenth and early-sixteenth centuries were the Humanists, an international group of teachers of the Greek and Latin languages and of the substance and value of Classical culture, as they interpreted it. Humanists were most often brought into Portugal by the king or the richest of the nobles; sometimes colleges were founded around a prominent Humanist.

Based loosely on an amalgam of Humanist paradigms, Christian values, and implicit economic prognostications, an optimistic evaluation of Portugal, its expansion, and its future was current in the upper class in the late 1400's and early 1500's. As I have indicated in the Introduction to this study, however, for reasons that are both complex and not entirely clear, that period of optimism reached an abrupt end —in the decade of the 1530's.

A prime example of that radical change in outlook is to be seen in the life of the king, John III, who ruled from 1521 to 1570. In the first decade of his reign, he continued the optimistic policies of his immediate predecessors, placing emphasis on Humanistic education at home, on diplomatic and commercial contacts in Europe, and on continued conquest of commercially valuable territories in the East. In that expansionistic optimism, the implicit contradictions between those various actions were—as in previous reigns—either not seen, or ignored. Nevertheless, there was great incompatability between upper-class hegemony and its supporting nobiliary ideology on the one hand, and, on the other hand, the various other social and intellectual forces at work in expansionist Portugal, such as mercantile capitalism, increased social mobility, Humanist views of human nature and of education. In the 1530's and the decades thereafter, as the period of acute frustration and pessimism began, as reasons were sought for what was seen as the national decline, and as the various social groups struggled for an ever-larger portion of the wealth produced by an economic system that was not living up to expectations, those contradictions were laid bare. And the same king who had previously supported a diversified expansion and founded Humanist colleges, now established the Inquisition in Portugal and institutionalized the Jesuit Order, thus loosing in his country the primary forces of the Counter Reformation, a movement that had evidenced as its implicit goal the elimination of social and intellectual forces that threatened the hegemony of the traditional upper class. To be sure, the life of John III was not one of complete reversal. Indeed, it manifests to its very end the confusion of the era of frustration; even in the 1540's and 1550's he would import famous Humanists from abroad and found Humanist colleges—a few years after having given the Jesuits control of large areas of the educational establishment. In his personal life, he seems to have evolved from an urbane, worldly monarch in the 1520's to something of a religious fanatic in the 1550's and thereafter.

In summary, the state of affairs in the Portugal of the 1530's and immediately thereafter was one of open contradictoriness. Social values and notions about the future directions of the socio-economic system had entered into a state of flux. The several antagonistic paradigms of intellectual and personal validity in circulation now conflicted openly. A sense of recent loss of social and intellectual stability was part and parcel of the situation.

Luís Vaz de Camões, born in all likelihood in the mid-1520's, reached maturity in that era of contradiction. Born into a marginalized lower-noble family, he apparently remained all his life on the fringes of upper-class society—both in the capital city and in the empire, for he spent the years from 1553 to 1569 as a soldier in Portuguese Asia. Recipient of a Humanistic education and, equally, of the newly reinforced anti-Humanistic intellectual and artistic currents, he produced a large quantity of lyric poetry, a number of plays, other minor works, and the single literary piece that has earned him that diversely interpreted label, "The National Poet." That work is *Os Lusíadas*, an epic poem about Portugal; it was published in 1572, after his return from the East. The poem is dedicated to John III's successor, the current king, Sebastian (about whom see the Introduction, as well as the second section of the next chapter, "Vieira: The Prophet"). In his text, Camões asks Sebastian for recompense for his services both as a soldier and as the poet of *Os Lusíadas*. A yearly stipend was granted, and the poet lived on it until his death in Lisbon in either 1579 or 1580.

Os Lusíadas is a divided poem. In terms of sheer bulk, the history of Portugal, especially of its era of expansion, dominates the work's ten cantos. The narrative centers on Vasco da Gama's epoch-making voyage to India and includes a long historical flashback (the whole of Cantos III, IV, and V) in which, in an overt recollection of Odysseus' similar act at the court of King Alcinous in *The Odyssey*, Gama catalogs for the king of Melinde first the national history from Roman times and then the story of his own voyage up to the moment in which he is presented to the king. A similar flashback of smaller proportions occurs in Cantos VII and VIII, where Vasco's brother, Paulo da Gama, relates more of Portuguese history to an official in India. A third flashback is to be found in the long, prophetic catalog of Canto X, in which first a Nymph and then a Nereid tell Vasco and his men of the glorious future that awaits Portugal in the areas that they have just opened up to national navigation and commerce (Gama's historical purpose, the obtaining of a trade agreement in India, is mentioned openly in the poem). The "foretold" events, while future happenings from the point of view of the fictionalized Gama and his crew, are, of course, historical for Camões and his audience of the 1570's. The "history" of Portugal is brought up to date through sporadic references to the current state of the empire as well.

Another element, quantitatively minor, provides a second focus in the text. That element is constituted by the poet himself, or, more precisely, the narrative voice of the poem. Repeatedly but very subtly it is suggested to the reader that the voice that speaks the words of the poem is not some neutral, technical voice, but rather the voice of the poet, a poetized speaker-figure who lurks about in the foreground of the text, occasionally suggesting textually his corporal or intellectual presence as the teller of his tale; elements of Camões's biography are linked to that speaker-figure to make the connection unmistakable (see, for example, Canto VII, stanzas 78–82). Indeed, the dominion of that speaker-figure over the poem is made universal; in Canto III, before Vasco da Gama begins to speak to the king of Melinde, the speaker's voice, in the act of invoking the Classical Muses to stand as providers of his poetic ability, makes it clear that the words that we read are in fact his words and his words alone, put into Gama's mouth in the dramatic setting of the situation at hand. That mechanism may be supposed to apply thoughout the poem; thus the only voice that we hear is in fact the voice of the speaker-figure. For that reason, I shall henceforth in this study use the term "Camões" to refer to the nexus of speaker-figure and biographical entity that is defined by the terms of the poem. That textual mechanism—by no means unique in Renaissance poetics, but to my knowledge nowhere else developed in

Camões's manner—has a number of technical ramifications. Primary among them is that it provides a platform from which the speaking voice can editorialize at will. And editorialize he does: in the stereotyped introduction (I.1–18) and conclusion (X.145–156) to the poem; in passages of a similar nature placed at the outset and close of some of the cantos; in passages set in other traditional locations (for example, invocations preceding the major historical catalogs, such as the invocation mentioned above); and in other places where thematic set-pieces and sententiae are touched on or where explanations of the action of the poem are advanced. In such places "Camões" makes an argument for Portuguese Catholic missionarism in the world, meditates on the nature of man and of salvation, discourses on the relationship between art and human experience, and so on. It is not as important, for the moment, to delve into what he chooses to say in such passages as it is to see how the position that he assumes in speaking fits within the dynamics of the total poem. Through such passages—in the main abstract, clearly non-"historical" expressions of judgment—"Camões" claims for himself a judgmental position with regard to the history, past and present, that he is narrating; to some degree, he takes a similar position with regard to the upper-class society that in fact was the audience to which in 1572 his text was presented.

That claiming of a judgmental position clearly operates at the level of meaning-making within the entire text: the editorializing passages—what I elsewhere have called the micro-poem[1]—suggest how we are to envision in general terms, and read in detail, the historical, "macro"-poem. Thus Os Lusíadas embodies a dialogue between historical material and the nature and implications of an obvious individual confrontation with, and artistic rendering of, that material. The history presented in the text therefore exists in an anomalous state: it is clearly labeled as representing the result of the poet's action upon the material given by history, and, at the same time, as recapitulating the true content of that material before it was acted upon. The following passage, from the introductory dedication to King Sebastian (whom the verses address), implicitly advances that two-fold argument:

> Ouvi, que não vereis com vãs façanhas,
> Fantásticas, fingidas, mentirosas,
> Louvar os vossos, como nas estranhas
> Musas, de engrandecer-se desejosas;
> As verdadeiras vossas são tamanhas
> Que excedem as sonhadas, fabulosas,
> Que excedem Rodamonte e o vão Rugeiro,
> E Orlando, inda que fora verdadeiro.

> Por estes vos darei um Nuno fero,
> Que fez ao rei e ao Reino tal serviço;
> Um Egas e um Dom Fuas, que de Homero
> A cítara pera eles só cobiço;
> Pois pelos Doze Pares dar-vos quero
> Os Doze de Inglaterra e o seu Magriço;
> Dou-vos também aquele ilustre Gama,
> Que pera si de Eneias toma a fama.[2]
>
> (Canto I. stanzas 11–12)

> [Hark! Thou shalt never see, for empty deed
> Fantastical and feigned and full of lies,
> Thy people praised, as with the foreign breed
> Of muses that still vaunt them to the skies.
> So great and true those acts that they exceed
> Utterly all such fabulous fantasies,
> And Rodomont and the vain Roger too,
> And Roland's tale, even if that were true.
>
> Instead I give you Nuno grim and dire,
> Whose prowess well for King and Realm was shown,
> With Egas and with Fuas. Homer's lyre
> I covet, for the like of them alone.
> For the Twelve Peers, Magriço I desire
> Among the Twelve of England shall be known,
> And offer likewise Gama's noble name,
> Who for himself snatched all Aeneas' fame.][3]

In the passage Camões first introduces the notion of earlier epic poets' creating of fictional histories; then, all the while claiming similar creative stature (in the notion of his "giving" of a history to the king as well as in his linking of himself to Homer), he arrogates a contrasting historical accuracy to himself. This is not the forum for a questioning of the nature of that claim. Suffice it here to say that in those words Camões resolves, apparently to his satisfaction, the possible contradiction about the status of history in his poem, by suggesting that his admittedly artistic medium is capable of bearing a "true" rendition of history. And, in fact, in other passages of the micro-poem he substantiates that idea in greater detail, specifying a view of his value as a poet and advancing the traditional Classical and Renaissance idealist argument that only through art is the essence of history captured.[4] That fragmented meditation on the relationship between art and history is hardly the only one carried out in the complex system constituted of the micro-poem and its implicit relations to the macro-poem. However, it is indicative of how that system works: through periodic return within the micro-poem to previously introduced questions that are in some way linked directly to an aspect of the macro-poem—in this case, to the implicit questioning of its very status as historical presentation.

Indeed, the dialogic interaction between "Camões" and his poetized "history," between micro-poem and macro-poem, is the mechanism by which central elements of the language of the poem define their own meaning. It is in that dramatic interaction that key semantic problem-areas in the poem's discourse are dealt with, these being not coincidentally key problem-areas for the biographical Camões's strife-ridden society: questions concerning the nature of human experience, of social structure, of history, of art. There are undoubtedly a number of reasons for the mechanism's dramatic character. Primary among them is that, in seeking the gift of privileged status (i.e., financial consideration as well as personal recognition) from the upper-class society of his time, Camões clearly found it useful to demonstrate the intellectual value of his poem and to emphasize his own role as its central intellectual force, thus thematizing in blunt terms his "deed" in writing *Os Lusíadas*. In fact in the passage reproduced above, his direct and implicit comparison of himself with Homer, Vergil and other established literary classics, and his suggestion that in ability to combine art and history he surpasses many—if not all—of them, represent a part of that thematization. So too does the declaration that he seeks to rival Homer not for the sake of personal renown or gain (the fact that he simultaneously seeks them does not, as we shall see, to his mind contradict that declaration) but rather because of the value of his subject matter and the role that he can play in its eternization. That declaration sets the "deed" of writing (and, as foreground figure, speaking) *Os Lusíadas* on a high idealistic-patriotic plane. He returns to and amplifies upon those matters throughout the poem, with the same implications and others as well.

Its dramatic character aside, however, the functioning of the thematized poet-figure, the functioning, then, of the micro-poem within the total poem, is really only one instance of a process characteristic of language: the effort toward contextual creation of at least apparent consistency in the meaning of terms—toward, that is, the creation of a minimally consistent discursive code so that communication can in fact be carried out.

Many of the elements that figure in that dialogic meaning-making within *Os Lusíadas* derive from the various value systems in both flux and conflict at the upper level of the Portuguese society of Camões's day. Examination of the general lines of several of those value systems therefore constitutes a necessary preliminary to further analysis of the poem.

Three major outlooks upon experience conflicted in Camões's Portugal, each with its implicit view of man and understanding of social structure. The three are not coordinate in every respect; however, since the points in which comparison between them is problematical lie, for the most part, outside the scope of present interests, the following discussion—which of course involves a great deal of simplification—will touch upon that problem only in specific applications rather than in general terms.

The first of the three systems is Thomism. As will be the case with my treatment of the other two systems as well, the ensuing paragraphs do not pretend to treat the body of Thomist doctrine on any front, much less to deal with the complex currents in its evolution, but rather merely to characterize some of its major features, as they enter Camões's discourse. Moreover, Thomism so viewed will be examined in specific conjunction with the nobiliary ideology that was, to a considerable degree, its reflex at the level of social structure in the Portugal of Camões's day.

Thomism formed the base of philosophical, theological, educational, and social thought in the late Middle Ages—and furnished the body of doctrine that would be restructured as the receptacle, on these same fronts, for justification of the Southern-European Counter Reformation. As the first pages of this chapter indicate, that process of restructuring was at work in Camões's Portugal; such was the case elsewhere in Europe as well.

Thomist thought implicitly invokes a concept of fixity in such diverse areas as astronomy, epistemology, ethics, and social order. The world, given by God, is essentially the Ptolemaic world of fixed spheres, adjusted to the exigencies of Christian doctrine. Man is a being constituted of an inextricably linked body and soul; he thus unites the physical and ideal realms. Possessed of both reason and will, he has at his disposal a hierarchy of senses from the lowest and most mundane, namely, touch, to the highest and most ideal, namely, abstracting intellect. The latter is in fact co-activated by God. By the proper exercise of his reason upon sense data, man will behave, cognitively and ethically, in a way consonant with revealed Christian doctrine. Further, he is naturally compelled to act that way: to establish correct ethical lines with his reason, and, through union of reason, the willful aspect of his being, and the capacity of his intellect, to seek clear vision of the non-material aspects of life as the basis of his understanding of the cosmos and the goal of his ethics, for those non-material aspects are considered to constitute the most important dimension of existence. Through such action, man intuits the presence of God and earns the non-material afterlife.

In terms of its conceptualization, the Thomist system involves a fixed universal paradigm given by God in a series of abstract labels that are supposed to correspond to discrete aspects of the cosmic system and, for present purposes, especially of man's being. Learning presumes memorization and discussion of previous thinkers' formulations, in syllogistic structures, about the working of the various capacities and tendencies of the system. The very fixity of the Thomistic model—i.e., its intricate system of labels—militates against any conception of radically different modes of inquiry. And of course such inquiry would be conceived as a violation of the right exercise of reason. Ascription of significant value to action concentrated in the material world alone would have similar negative implications. Many of these features of Thomist thought were propagated on a regular basis, for the day-to-day practice of Christianity was conceived according to them.

In Portugal—and, in different ways, in other European countries as well—Thomism was to a great degree supportive of nobiliary ideology, the ideological system by which the upper class of medieval society defined itself as the "warrior class" and argued for its social ascendancy. The nobleman was supported in his position at the peak of the social pyramid through the working of a system that valued him as superior by birth, through blood inheritance from ancestors who had proved their superiority, usually in just battle against enemies of the Christian faith. By means of such success, a nobleman brought renown both to himself and to the lineage from which he purportedly had derived his merit, thereby bringing glory to his nation. While such superior characteristics were presumed to be passed on from generation to generation, it was sometimes presumed as well that they had to be demonstrated by each successive descendant. Especially in the Counter-Reformational elaboration of this ideology, ability for right reason, abstract intellection, and exalted correct exercise of the willful aspect of human faculties are ascribed specifically to the upper class, much in the same way as is valor, with which they go hand in hand; that is, nobles inherit those capacities, and their use of them in turn justifies and holds their social position.

In the era of the Portuguese expansion, this ideology took the form of nobles' evidencing of their "honor" as leaders in battle against the infidels of Africa and the East. That "dedication" on their part to their "spiritual natures" was likened to Christ's dedication to other-worldly concerns; the nobleman, guided solely by attention to "honor," was viewed as living in accordance with such an interpretation of Christ's life. Consequently, it was sometimes asserted that true "honor" came from a victory in which no mundane concern whatsoever—not even, for example, the defense of one's nation—was involved. Other models for spiritual dedication so conceived were found in such romances of chivalry as *A Demanda do Santo Graal* and *Amadis de Gaula*, then in circulation.[5]

The nobleman's wealth, which in feudal times was measured primarily in land holdings, was seen as a reflex and confirmation on the physical plane of the inherent spiritual qualities that he possessed and/or demonstrated. In Portugal, that tight-knit relationship is demonstrated lexically: *honra* 'honor' referred to the complex of inherited qualities, to their demonstration in "noble" acts, and to the wealth that the nobleman held as a result, which in most cases came in the form of land given to him or to his forebears by the king as recompense for service; the same term referred to his seigniory over those lands. Thus the adjective *honrado* 'honored' came to connote, simply, 'wealthy'. And, by the sixteenth century, when that feudal ethic had been exported to serve as the ideological underpinning for the existence of Portuguese enclaves in India and elsewhere, "honor" in battle had become virtually synonymous with "booty." Other terms, such as *virtude* 'virtue' and *valor* 'value' had similar functions; a number of other terms of like nature circulated in the ideological system.[6]

In the light furnished by the foregoing brief look at nobiliary ideology, the apparent contradiction in Camões's on the one hand propagandizing of himself as a strictly idealistic poet and, on the other hand, requesting of status and money as a result of his poetic deed is resolved. For him, it is legitimate to see the latter as a natural reflex of the former; indeed in theory, the latter can be achieved, within the upper-class sphere, only as a result of the former. By contrast, he would have argued that embarking upon the writing of poetry, or, for that matter, any action principally for the worldly reward was, in all senses of the term, "ignoble." Indeed, he makes that precise point several times in *Os Lusíadas* (see, especially, VI.98 and IX.93)

There was an aspect of nobiliary ideology, especially in its Counter-Reformational formulation, that probably transgressed boundaries described by the major exponents of Thomist doctrine. An extension both of the notion that the nobleman was the repository of high spiritual value in his being and his acts and as well of the basic Christian presumption that man's worldly existence is essentially one of preparation and thus not of great value in itself, it held that the noble's actions could in a sense reach beyond worldly existence and introduce into it a hint of spirituality, thereby both defining and redeeming mundane reality.[7] The probable rift between that nobiliary notion and theological exposition is almost surely illustrative of the battle for ideological ascendancy between the Church and the secular hierarchy that characterized the late Middle Ages.

The combination of Thomism and nobiliary ideology was, then, by no means monolithic. Nor was it a wholly suffocating force. History records examples of action counter to it, as well as hints that it was seen by some for what it was—i.e., an ideological construct rather than the normative structure that it claimed to be. Nonetheless, it held sway in late-medieval and Counter-Reformational Portugal.[8]

The expansion and discoveries fostered another attitude, one which, in many of its aspects, contradicted that dominant ideology. Born in the pragmatics of navigation and conquest, often in parts of the world unlike anything Europe had ever envisioned, that attitude involved care about practical contact with the phenomenal world. At its root was, probably, the sense that it was practical knowledge rather than an abstract, inherited tendency to guidance from the spiritual realm that led to success in the world. That attitude implicitly argued for the autonomy of the perceiver and, perhaps, of the objects of the physical world as well—thus directly contradicting key Thomistic/nobiliary tenets. It is, in fact, a rudimentary empiricism, undoubtedly all along a part of the outlook of the lower and middle groups of society. Nevertheless, the social structure was not yet such that actual empirical science in the modern sense could be formulated and institutionalized. In the era of expansion, however, some Portuguese investigators did carry out quite sophisticated protoscientific analyses—for example, of flora and fauna in areas of the Orient.

The difficulty that many intellectuals had with empiricism had to do with the problems involved in its incorporation into a wider world view. The hints of human and phenomenal autonomy were not reconcilable with the Thomistic model, nor were they, really, with key aspects of Humanism, the system yet to be examined. Nonetheless, as a mode of knowledge acquisition, empiricism had practical value. In Camões's Portugal, empiricism seems to float free, in an unformulated state, as a useful but unincorporated mode of intellection. Indeed, the sense of frustration resulting from the undertaking of conquest and missionarism referred to in the Introduction to this study bears to a great extent upon the question of empiricism: the practical problems that arose with regard to actions conceived in idealistic reference systems, especially those that included the notion of divine intent, were so great that they seemed to argue the nullity of idealism, thus producing frustration, when not confusion.

The practical aspects of this empiricist tendency, taken up by the lower and middle classes, clearly represented a material threat to the upper class. The struggle that took place was waged for control of the newly forged commercial system; the major arms that the dominant class employed in the battle were the instruments of the Counter Reformation: the Jesuit Order, the Inquisition, and the Censorial Board. And in justification of their actions the Thomistic/nobiliary model was invoked.

If the conflict between those two opposing systems were all there was to be examined in the intellectual history of Camões's time, the situation would be relatively straightforward. Such is not the case, however, for a third system was at play in the middle and upper levels of society. The system is the one promulgated by the Humanists. The first intellectual elite of modern Europe, educators and advisers of the upper class and, as well, of the wealthy among the middle group, the Humanists—not usually from the upper class themselves—set forth a series of tenets that had aspects in common with both Thomism and empiricism.

For the Humanists the world had a social and intellectual structure that could not be changed. The ruling classes were the ruling classes; that fact was necessary for political stability. And like the wealthy middle class (which in many ways they resembled, save that their wealth was counted in knowledge rather than in coin), the Humanists directed their attention to the upper class; there they sought favor—both personal and financial—while educating upper-class youths and supporting the growth of monarchical centralization and royal absolutism.

As the basis of their outlook, the Humanists imputed a cultural core to existence. For them, knowledge derived from training in Classical culture, and their view of man was one that they thought they saw mirrored in Classical writings. That basically intellecualist view sees man's nature and place in the universe as defined in a multifaceted and not always clear dialogue with cultural products (literature, philosophy, art) created according to the norms of Classical society. Steeped in those products, which, for Humanists, often seemed to attain the status of Holy Writ, man could reach the zenith of "humanity," of civilization, of his potential. The ideal man for the Humanists, the so-called "courtier"—embracer of all areas of human endeavor through embodiment of the Classical view of man—derived his general contours from the norms set down by Cicero, in various of his writings, for the *orator*, the ideal man of Senatorial Rome, educated and proficient in the entire course of the Liberal Arts.[9]

The Humanist outlook evidences many points of conflict with Thomism. First, man is seen, as regards the acquisition of knowledge, as being possessed of at least semi-autonomous character. It is that tangible, somewhat complex man, man with an agential dimension rather than a God-given nature expressed in a series of labels for abstractions, who is the locus of the act of human understanding. And, as regards education, the Humanists spoke of developing man's presumed inherent qualities rather than of his debating terms having to do with a series of pre-established categories or his seeking of the realm of God through such action. Nor did the Humanists always make explicit distinctions about what social levels man should come from to possess great inherent qualities. In the area of art, taking some Classical texts as examples, they emphasized the florid, even tactile phenomenal world. And those Humanists involved in artistic creation conceived art as an extremely valuable undertaking and the artist as someone to be prized.

In short, Humanism, at its root, opposed much of the dominant ideology of the day. Many Renaissance thinkers, however, attempted reconciliation of the two. One of the primary modes of reconciliation involved proposals to reform Church liturgy with an eye to making it less "mechanical," more "personal." The Humanists' various attempts to intellectualize the social position that they occupied—one in which they represented an intellectual service corps for the "actors" of society—demonstrate a number of modes of such reconciliation. They would take up aspects of the dominant code and formulate relationships between them and aspects of their own ideological position by various combinatory or analogical processes. For example, Camões's attempt in his poem to publicize the writing of that very poem as a noteworthy "deed" is in essence an attempt to combine the Humanist evaluation of art and the nobiliary concept of idealistically motivated accomplishment in the world; in this case, of course, the effort at reconciliation is made within one intelligence rather than between bodies of doctrine existing in the social sphere. In any such proposed reconciliation, a relation between bookish, Humanist knowledge and action in the world had to be created. By implicit understanding, this reconciliation typically involved man's (i.e., the courtier's) facing of an aspect of the world, coming to grips with its topography and the forces within it (elements defined in terms much closer to those of Thomism than to those of empiricism), formulating that process, and then incorporating it into the Humanist "culture bank" so that it could be used in future Humanist training. In the actual elaboration of items in that culture bank—especially art objects—Humanism thus in effect imposed a cultural code upon experience through its preference for rhetorical figures and structures, in the main patently patterned after Classical models, that suggested arguments for an intellectualist view of man in various interpretations.

Despite the contradictions, it is not difficult to see how, in times of optimism and plenty, the implicit conflicts between upper-class ideology and Humanism would have been ignored in the name of a division of effort, and how they would have been brought to the fore in an era of socio-cultural retrenchment. Finally, in Camões's era, the Humanists' emphases on the phenomenal, on endeavor in the physical world, on man's autonomy, and on reform of the liturgy, were seen to feed social and intellectual forces that threatened the hegemony of the upper class. As a result, Humanists became targets of the Counter Reformation and its instruments. Perhaps the most graphic example of that process is to be found in the life of Damião de Góis, national chronicler under King John III and probably Portugal's most famous Humanist. His historical writings were drawn upon by Camões for many of the details in his "prophetic" history in Canto X of *Os Lusíadas*. After having occupied so prestigious a place in Portuguese society, Góis was denounced to the Inquisition by members of the Jesuit Order and sentenced to life imprisonment. Many other, less spectacular reversals of fortune are to be noted in the early stages of the Portuguese Counter Reformation.

Among the educated members of the upper class, the conflict of the era focused on the problems that arose between Thomism and Humanism, between two different world structurings, each of which provided justification for their status: Thomism through class standing, Humanism through emphasis on the value of the classically educated courtier. An additional complicating factor is to be found in the fact that, as we shall see, the language of the intellectual, his very means of arguing for his value, was linked to models developed and taught by the Humanists, at a time when the forces of Thomism were holding the center of the stage in society. Camões touches upon many aspects of the resulting problematic in the dialogue between artist and history in the text of *Os Lusíadas*.[10]

On first reading *Os Lusíadas*, one is above all caught up by the Humanistic ingredient. There are many passages in which Camões creates the lush, sensual world of the Humanistically trained artist. He also populates his poem with Classical deities; his language is Vergilian; Classical references and allusions abound. The Portuguese voyagers and their mission are made to recall features of Homer's *Odyssey* and, most specifically, of Vergil's *Aeneid*. It is easy to be so overwhelmed by the detail and complexity of references and allusions that the general cultural message that their presence communicated to a reader of Camões's time is overlooked entirely. Indeed, subsequent readers and commentators of *Os Lusíadas* have experienced various difficulties resulting from incomplete comprehension of what the mere invocation of Humanist language implied in sixteenth-century Portugal.

The presence of Humanist Classicism in the texture of a literary work signalled specific notions on several scores. For present purposes, the most important are those involving the nature of man. As has been seen, the man that Humanism prized was a "civilized," cultured man, particularly one who gave value to those qualities in the working of his society. That general orientation is imputed to various figures in the macro-poem; its primary reference, however, falls upon the author—that is, in terms of the text, the poetized speaker figure, the implicit creator and performer of every word we read in *Os Lusíadas*. Further, the structure embodied by the poem through its imitation of the Classical epic is a highly marked form in the Humanist appropriation of Classical literature. It was seen as the form in which man's tangible qualities and his adaptability were demonstrated in noble action in the physical world. Camões, in taking up that form *en bloc*, recreates many of the distinctive linguistic features of the genre as it was practiced by Homer, Vergil, and others: the epic epithet ("pious Aeneas" of the *Aeneid* becomes "wise Gama"); epic formulae ("master mariner and soldier," repeatedly applied, in slightly varying forms, to Odysseus, becomes "through never-before-sailed seas," several times applied, also in slightly varied forms, to the action of Gama and his crew); epic similes; invocations of the Classical muses; and epic catalogs (as we have seen, the past history of Portugal is told in what are in essence catalogs of principal historical figures, and the catalogs are preceded by traditionally structured invocations). To be sure, those characteristics of the Classical epic are often used by Camões in ways very different from Homer's or Vergil's use of them, but they serve first the function of marking a literary form and as well of putting before the reader and imputing to the author specific notions of man and culture automatically allied to that form.

Another device taken from the Classical epic, this one of a substantive nature, is to be found in the depiction of contention between two camps of Classical gods, each camp supporting and aiding one side in the struggle between men. In *Os Lusíadas* Bacchus is the divine enemy of the Portuguese maritime venture, rallying gods and men—namely the Arabs and the Indians—to his cause, while Venus is the protectress of the Portuguese, interceding on their behalf with her father, Jove, and as well attempting to control the elements, to the goal of Portuguese success. By making Venus the proponent of the Portuguese cause, Camões establishes a direct link to his primary model in Classical literature, Vergil's *Aeneid,* a work in which Venus supports in a similar manner the cause of the proto-Romans. In fact Camões does not hesitate to point out that link, at the outset of his poem:

> Sustentava contra ele [Baco] Vénus bela,
> Afeiçoada à gente lusitana
> Por quantas qualidades via nela
> Da antiga, tão amada sua, romana:
> Nos fortes corações, na grande estrela,
> Que mostraram na terra tingitana,
> E na língua, na qual quando imagina,
> Com pouca corrupção crê que é a latina.
>
> (I.33)

> [Against him [Bacchus] Venus bright the cause sustained
> Of Lusitania's race, whom she held dear
> For virtues which she saw in them ingrained,
> Like her loved Romans of a bygone year,
> The noble star, the courage never stained.
> That was well proved in the country of Tangier,
> And the language, which, if one lets fancy range,
> One takes for Latin with but little change.
>
> (Bacon, 11)]

Various other similar references keep that connection before the reader's consciousness throughout the rest of the poem.

Far from being an isolated parallel, that connection is elaborated upon to several ends. Aeneas' purpose in the *Aeneid* is the founding of a new state, the future Rome, and a subsequent world-civilizing empire; such, in fact, is the fate to which he is inextricably destined. Camões, in choosing to "continue" the *Aeneid,* continues the notion of destiny and of civilizing empire as well—to the point of saying that Portugal's goal is to unite the world in Christianity.[11] And, in a series of passages that echo back and forth upon each other throughout the micro-poem, he meditates on the basic insignificance of man's earthly existence. I term that series his development of the motif of the "bicho da terra tão pequeno" the 'so small animal of earth', after a line (I.106.8) in the first major passage of the series. In that meditation Camões suggests that taking part in the Christian expansionist effort provides a vehicle for man's achieving of honor and fame, for his worldly overcoming of the limits of mere "animal," mere "earthly" mortality, for his earning of Christian afterlife. To be sure, there is a radical distinction between the world-missionarism of the *Aeneid* and that of *Os Lusíadas*. Vergil depicts an empire-creating that has the immense drawback of a necessary dehumanizing of the imperialists; his Aeneas at times struggles against his destiny in the name of humanity. There is no such irony in *Os Lusíadas*; the value of Christian empire is not questioned, and the importance of participation for individual realization is in fact insisted upon. Such realization is conceived in terms of contribution to the creation of the civilizational empire that Humanist detail and rhetoric in the poem define. To be sure, it is conceived as well in terms both of aspects of the Thomist model and also of the notion, within nobiliary ideology, of man's reaching beyond mortal status through noble acts in the world. Indeed, the achieving of "fame," a term conceived in the same mixed ideological terms, is a primary theme of Camões's epic poem. At the same time, the sense of a "continuation" between the *Aeneid* and *Os Lusíadas* provides a vehicle through which Camões can continually propose himself as the Portuguese Vergil, and by extension, the Portuguese Homer as well, respectively the supreme literary exponents of Roman and Greek culture. Thus the "Camões" poetized within his own text emerges as, in essence, the artist capable of correct conception and expression of Portugal's Christian continuation of the Classical civilization and empire viewed by most educated men of the day—trained, as they were, according to Humanist precepts—as the highest form of civilization and empire thus far achieved by man.

The overwhelming textual invocation of Humanistic culture in *Os Lusíadas* serves other, allied functions as well. The "populating" of the fictional world through which Vasco da Gama and his crew voyage with creatures drawn from Classical culture has implications beyond that of mere accumulation of references. Most criticism since the work's publication has seen the plethora of allusions—to Classical deities as forces in the world, aiding or disrupting the efforts of the Portuguese mariners; to figures in Classical mythology as the animate alternative or adjunct to, for example, geographical naming (e.g., reference to the Cape Verde Islands as "the daughters of old Hesperus" in V.8), and other similar practices—as a system in and of itself. The "content" of the poem has implicitly been viewed as almost completely separate from that system, the only overlap deriving from the fact that the battle between the aiding and opposing gods provides a central dramatic focus unifying an otherwise diffuse narrative line. Thus the Classical references are accorded a functionality that is primarily if not solely aesthetic.

That view is made all the more acceptable by the remarks of the Censor who, in 1572, attempting to reconcile the Humanist texture of *Os Lusíadas* with the Thomist orthodoxy he was charged with upholding, argued:

> Vi por mandado da santa & geral inquisição estes dez Cantos dos Lusiadas de Luis de Camões, dos valerosos feitos em armas que os Portugueses fizerão em Asia & Europa, e não achey nelles cousa algũa escandalosa, nem contraria â fe & bõs custumes, somente me pareceo que era necessario aduertir os Lectores que o Autor pera encarecer a difficuldade da nauegação & entrada dos Portugueses na India, vsa de hũa fição dos Deoses dos Gentios.... Toda via como isto he Poesia & fingimento, & o Autor como poeta, não pretenda mais que ornar o estilo Poetico não tiuemos por inconueniente yr esta fabula dos Deoses na obra, conhecendo a por tal, & ficando sempre salua a verdade de nossa sancta fe, que todos os Deoses dos Gẽtios sam Demonios. E por isso me pareceo o liuro digno de se imprimir, & o Autor mostra nelle muito engenho & muita erudição nas sciencias humanas....
>
> [I have examined, by order of the Holy Inquisition, these ten Cantos, of the *Lusíadas* of Luís de Camões, about the brave deeds in arms performed by the Portuguese in Asia and Europe, finding in them nothing whatsoever either scandalous or contrary to faith or to morality. It has occurred to me, however, that it may be necessary to clarify for Readers that, in order to emphasize the difficulty of the Portuguese navigation to India, and entry therein, the Author makes use of a fiction involving the Pagan Gods... Still, since this is poetry and pretense, and the Author, being a poet, intends nothing save the adornment of poetic style, I have seen no objection to the retention in the work of the fiction of those Gods, recognizing that it is such and, in preservation of the truth of our holy faith, that all the Pagan Gods are Demons. I have therefore deemed the work worthy of print, the Author showing in it great genius and much erudition in the human sciences....][12]

Nevertheless, Camões's creation of a "populated" world does have more than merely aesthetic significance on some fronts. Aside from participating in the general invocation of a Humanistic value system, it suggests a structured universe—one filled with forces that exceed human controlling power. As I have noted above, Humanism, involved in an intellectual undertaking centered in a view of mankind and a body of writing and artistic products produced in antiquity, does not speak directly to human action that falls outside its boundaries—which, indeed, is most of human action. At best, it locates such action in relation to its own, primarily intellectual paradigms. Among those paradigms is a sense of a structure to the world, akin to Thomist notions on the same question but possessed of different implications and expressed through a large stock of images, as in Classical literature. In *Os Lusíadas,* such structure is suggested in Camões's use of the Humanist referential system.

For example, as Gama and his voyagers begin their journey, many of the landmarks they pass are identified through reference to the world of the Classical geographers—Ptolemy, Strabo, Pomponius Mela, and, especially, the elder Pliny. And when locations are not identified by direct recourse to such sources, they are linked to Classical culture through historical-mythological references that produce a texture that recalls Ovid. The fact that Classical geographers were at times either incorrect or incomplete in reference to given areas of the world does not seem to constitute a major stumbling block for the poet. Indeed, he seems not to have delved into the question to any great depth, despite the fact that he had himself been present in some of the areas in question. In fact, his implicit acceptance of the structuring value of the Classical authorities is so strong and so forcefully modifies the unrooted "empirical" ingredient provided by his own experience that he even represents the Portuguese discovery and geographical description of new areas as a continuation of the knowledge provided by the Classical authorities rather than, as we in our empirical age might expect, an obliteration of the Classical referent because of its lack of validity. Thus, the often-repeated tags "mares nunca d'antes navegados" 'never-before-sailed seas', and "lugares desconhecidos aos antigos" 'places unknown to the ancients'—intended, in Camões's re-creation of the Classical epic, to reproduce the characteristic epic formulae originally created in Homer's oral-poetic tradition—do not bespeak any sense of an act of Promethean accomplishment on the part of the Portuguese. Quite the contrary, they bespeak an act of continuation of a culturally ordered structure that was part and parcel of Camões's Humanism and of his concept of the Portuguese continuation of Classical civilization. The sense of a pre-established Humanist cultural frame in relation to which experience is to be judged is probably best revealed in a passage from Canto V in which Vasco da Gama, after speaking of seeing the Southern Cross, Saint Elmo's fire, and a waterspout—all, to his mind, new experiences—ends up declaring:

> Se os antigos filósofos, que andaram
> Tantas terras por ver segredos delas,
> As maravilhas que eu passei, passaram,
> A tão diversos ventos dando as velas,
> Que grandes escrituras que deixaram!
> (V.23.1–5)

> [If old philosophers, who went to find
> The secrets of so many lands afar,
> Had witnessed, spreading sail to every wind,
> As I have seen, the miracles that are,
> What noble works they would have left behind!
> (Bacon, 180)]

The most telling instance of Humanist structuring in *Os Lusíadas* comes, however, where the very question of the nature and value of human action in the world is to be defined. Portuguese action is epitomized by the rounding of the South African cape, an act that, by virtue of its mention's being strategically located near the center of the poem (V.37–61) and toward the end of the long historical flashback (Cantos III, IV, and V), is thereby defined as the result of Portuguese history, the culminating achievement of an entire culture rather than merely the achievement of Vasco da Gama and his group of mariners. Nevertheless, even that act, so conceived, is not characterized as an act of man-as-a-free-agent in contact with empirically verifiable reality, but rather as an act of what amounts to mortal hubris, akin to that defined in Classical drama. The Portuguese, in fact, transgress the boundaries of the sphere to which mortal man is limited, and they must pay the price for it in the ensuing loss of life. That such is the case is twice prophesied in the poem, once in general terms by the fatidic Old Man of Restelo when the Portuguese first set out on their voyage (IV.94–104), and again later more specifically by the Cape itself (personified by the Giant, Adamastor), with details that are prophetic in context but are past history to Camões's audience (V.42–48). The implicit point is, however, that the Portuguese choose to pay in order to achieve.[13] Man is not seen here as an autonomous being in a world structured only by mechanistic physical laws; he is, rather, a being bounded by structures, among them both the view of his nature authorized by Humanist precept and also the Classical culture bank, along with the cultural tradition that Camões imputes to it, onto which he grafts Portuguese imperializing as he interprets it.

To be sure, Humanist thought does not diverge greatly from Thomistic/nobiliary thought in this area, and the "cultural geography" through which Camões has his literary creations pass can be viewed as a metaphor for the structure of Thomist epistemology. In fact, critics have attempted to see the Classical deities used in *Os Lusíadas* as metaphors for human capacities or as aids to the Thomistically defined intellect in its effort to achieve greater understanding at the abstract levels of human cognition.[14] While I doubt that any specific correspondences can be consistently maintained, I think the notion of a general metaphorical relationship between a Humanist surface and a Thomistic intellectual substructure is an essentially correct one, my primary objection being that I should have it understood that the "Humanistic surface" invokes concepts of man, of art, and of tradition that are in fact anti-Thomistic—that, in fine, the metaphor is problematic.

Also, in the same vein, despite the Humanist trappings in which it is set, the sense of mortal superation of the normal limitations of mortality suggested in Camões's rendition of the Portuguese maritime ethic is most directly ascribable to elements of the nobiliary current examined above (p. 20). Indeed, as these last two examples indicate, while the Humanistic input dominates the surface of the poem, suggesting one view of man and of the cosmos, much of the poem's thematics is dominated by the Thomistic/nobiliary code. It is the social dimension of that code that is most obvious, though many other aspects —including the Ptolemaic universal model invoked by the Nymph in Canto X (74-90)—also appear.

With very few exceptions, the history of Portugal and of Gama's voyage promulgated by the poem is grounded within the central agency of the hereditary upper class. (Vasco da Gama is a nobleman, of course—and, it seems, a relative of Camões's!) When other social groups are referred to, the poet's tone changes. References to the common people are paternalistic, as Camões makes clear in this micropoetic listing of those of whom he will not sing:

> Nenhum que use de seu poder bastante
> Pera servir o seu desejo feio,
> E que, por comprazer ao vulgo errante,
> Se muda em mais figuras que Proteio;
> Nem, Camenas, também cuideis que cante
> Quem, com hábito honesto e grave, veio,
> Por contentar o rei no ofício novo,
> A despir e roubar o pobre povo;
>
> Nem quem acha que é justo e que é dereito
> Guardar-se a lei do rei severamente,

E não acha que é justo e bom respeito
Que se pague o suor da servil gente;
Nem quem sempre, com pouco experto peito,
Razões aprende—e cuida que é prudente—
Pera taxar, com mão rapace e escassa,
Os trabalhos alheios que não passa.
(VII.85–86)

[Nor who, having authority so great,
Employs it but to serve his passion base,
And, the foolish vulgar to propitiate,
More than did ever Proteus, changes face.
Nor, Muses, think that I will celebrate
One I have seen though he seem full of grace
To please the King, who once in the new job
The unhappy people still will strip and rob;

Nor one who finds that it is right and fair
The King's law harshly to enforce alway,
But never sees a just cause anywhere
The wretched people for their sweat to pay;
Nor one who, though his thought be thin and bare,
Seeks reasons, thinking the wise man to play,
And mulcts, with hands to meanness well inured,
The toils of others, which he ne'er endured.
(Bacon, 270)]

Non-noble members of the upper social levels are treated, in the main, as interlopers who have lowered the quality of the Portuguese leadership by their presence:

Outros também há grandes e abastados,
Sem nenhum tronco ilustre donde venham:
Culpa de reis, que às vezes a privados
Dão mais que a mil que esforço e saber tenham.
(VIII.41.1–4)

[And there are others high and arrogant,
Although they spring from no great-hearted strain,
For oft to favorites kings in error grant
More than a thousand wits or heroes gain.
(Bacon, 291)]

The latter passage in effect draws a crystal-clear line through the Portuguese social structure: anyone who does not belong to the hereditary nobility is suspect, if not rejected outright.

The rationale for this division is made clear, especially in the epic similes that, in imitation of Homer and Vergil, Camões creates in his poem. Of the developed similes, more are devoted to indirect characterization of the warlike "instinct" of the Portuguese than to any other single purpose. Exemplary in this regard are a pair of similes in the history of Portugal related by Vasco da Gama to the king of Melinde; in describing the action of the famous battle of Aljubarrota (1385), Gama says:

> Rompem-se aqui dos nossos os primeiros,
> Tantos dos inimigos a eles vão!
> Está ali Nuno, qual pelos outeiros
> De Ceita está o fortíssimo leão,
> Que cercado se vê dos cavaleiros
> Que os campos vão correr de Tutuão:
> Perseguem-no co'as lanças, e ele, iroso,
> Torvado um pouco está, mas não medroso;
>
> Com torva vista os vê, mas a natura
> Ferina e a ira não lhe compadecem
> Que as costas dê, mas antes na espessura
> Das lanças se arremessa, que recrecem.
> Tal está o cavaleiro, que a verdura
> Tinge co'o sangue alheio; ali perecem
> Alguns dos seus, que o ânimo valente
> Perde a virtude contra tanta gente.
>
> Sentiu Joane a afronta que passava
> Nuno, que, como sábio capitão,
> Tudo corria e via e a todos dava,
> Com presença e palavras, coração.
> Qual parida leoa, fera e brava,
> Que os filhos, que no ninho sós estão,
> Sentiu que, enquanto pasto lhe buscara,
> O pastor de Massília lhos furtara,
>
> Corre raivosa e freme, e com bramidos
> Os montes Sete Irmãos atroa e abala:
> Tal Joane, com outros escolhidos
> Dos seus, correndo acode à primeira ala.
> (IV.34–37.4)

[Our vanward men are there hurled back in flight,
So thick upon them do the foemen throng.
But there stands Nuno, as on Ceuta's height
There stands a lion terrible and strong,
Watching the horsemen gird him left and right,
Who toward the Tetuan country ride along,
And they make shift to plague him with the spear;
He rages, troubled somewhat, not in fear;

Heavily he eyes them, but wild instinct keen
And anger suffer not the beast to fly,
Who hurls where thickest set the spears are seen,
And all around him lances multiply;
So stands that champion, staining all the green
With strangers' blood. Some of his men must die,
For spirits with all gallantry endued
Lose their force, fighting such a multitude.

When John beheld that the attack was grave
Where Nuno fought, like a captain wise and ware,
Thither he raced, saw all, and fresh heart gave
By his presence and his voice to all men there.
As a lioness that has whelped, savage and brave,
Who knows her cubs, left lonely in the lair,
While she went forth their provender to find,
Are stolen by Massylia's shepherd hind,

And mad she runs, roaring, and every roar
With thunder shakes the Seven Brothers height;
So John with many a chosen warrior
Rushed to bear up the forefront of the fight.
                              (Bacon, 143–144)]

The equation joining aspects of Portuguese instinct in war with animal savagery and sense of self- or species-preservation is all too obvious. Similar characterizations of instinctual Portuguese valor, in similes, are to be found elsewhere in Gama's history (for example, III.47 and III.111), in description of action undertaken by Gama and his crew (I.88), and in the catalog of future events in India (X.34).

In many cases, the simile refers directly to the "instinct" of a nobleman; in other instances, the reference seems to be to warlike qualities that are generally "Portuguese." In the latter cases, however, it would have been understood by both Camões and his audience that the warriors were captained by nobles and thus did little more than second the quality of their leadership (he deals directly with the question of noble leadership; see esp. VI.95–99).

In any case, it is clear, through such language as that examined above and other features of the text as well, that the history and social structure of Portugal are, for Camões, unquestionably centered in the nobility. Other social groups are brought up infrequently, and then only to be placed very pointedly in a subordinate role. It is easy to forget that the word *barões* 'men' or 'barons', introduced by Camões in the first line of the poem to refer to the Portuguese and reused in that same sense many times throughout the poem, had a class implication in Camões's age: it referred only to hereditary nobles.

The ascendant nobiliary ideology is linked to—and to some extent justified by—Thomism. Within a poetic cosmos delineated according to the Thomistic model, the nobleman's value is expressly linked to his faith in God and God's working in the world and to his understanding of God's relationship to man and desire that the basis of Portugal's expansion involve Christian missionarism, to the end that the world be Christianized. (The myth of Portugal's founding by Christ is explored in III.45–54; status as a nation chosen by God is repeatedly suggested in the subsequent recounting of Portuguese history; Portugal's Christian dedication is declared in VII.1–15.) Moreover, it is repeatedly implied that the nobleman's Christian valor and capacity for high-level understanding and conceptualizing single him out as chosen to lead a life of special value in relation to God. The response to the questions raised in the "so small animal of earth" motif is, as we have seen, totally Christian. In short, while the Humanistic surface of the poem may lead to doubts about Camões's Catholicism, the sense of a metaphorical relationship between that surface Humanism and deeper Thomistic structures pervades the poem and affirms an essentially noble/Catholic stance on the part of the poet. (That interpretation is not shared by all students of *Os Lusíadas;* nor was it by the Censorial Board that, in 1584, widely expurgated the second edition of the work, making it a more overtly Catholic, less superficially "pagan" poem.)

In fact, a series of references in the "fatidic" historical catalog of Canto X clearly establishes the ascendancy of noble/Thomistic thought. First, the following interpretation is given:

> Ocultos os juízos de Deus são;
> As gentes vãs, que não nos entenderam,
> Chamam-lhe fado mau, fortuna escura,
> Sendo só providência de Deus pura.
> (X.38.5–8)

> [Judgments of God are hidden from our sight,
> And those men understand not, who miscall
> That which they term mischance and fate malign,
> Which is pure Providence of the Divine.
> (Bacon, 358)]

Then, two stanzas later, in reference to a specific historical event, we get the explanation:

> ...—que Deus peleja
> Por quem estende a fé da Madre Igreja.
> (X.40.7–8)
>
> [...God fights upon his side,
> Who faith of Mother Church spreads far and wide.
> (Bacon, 359)]

Two stanzas further along, we read:

> ...esforço e arte
> Vencerão a fortuna e o próprio Marte.
> (X.42.7–8)
>
> [...Art and heroic will
> Compel the Fates and Mars incarnate still.
> (Bacon, 359)]

Combination of the first and second passages defines Fortune as the Will of God, rather than the chaotic element within the cosmos that it might first appear to be, and also, inversely, defines God's Will as a silent structuring element favoring the Portuguese as they battle to extend Christendom. The first passage also suggests that some men can see the truth of such structuring. The content of the third passage links the stereotypical noble qualities of physical strength (in the poem the words *esforço, forças, ousadia* are usually used in this application) and conceptualizing power (terms commonly used for this characteristic are *manha, engenho, saber,* and *arte*) with an overcoming of Fortune as incorrectly conceived, as, in fact, cooperation with Fortune-as-God's-Plan. It is therefore probably the case that understanding of God's hidden structuring is being claimed for the nobility. The binary combination of "strength" and "intelligence" in reference to the Portuguese nobility—in many variations, extensions, and combinations—recurs throughout the poem. And in those instances too it should, in my view, be read with the Thomistic connection, here exemplified, in mind: God gives the nobleman "strength" and "intelligence" so that the nobleman can understand the cosmos and God's place in it and have the practical strength and reason to conceive issues correctly and fight for the good.

Finally, it must be again recalled that the poem was used by Camões to attempt to gain both position and reward in the system of 1570's Portugal. In its final form, then, with the invocation of King Sebastian, and dedication and valediction to him, it has about it the tone of a literary piece written for a special situation—that of one nobleman speaking to others about the class status they hold in common.

Such, then, is the physiognomy of each of the code systems that figure in the meaning-making dialogue between poet and history in *Os Lusíadas*. It should be emphasized, however, that the three code systems—or, really, two, since for most practical purposes Camões's primitive empiricism is an unsystematized tendency and nothing more—do not merely coexist in the poem, each going its own way in one passage while clashing with another in others. We have seen systematic reconciliation attempted: some language seems to refer to more than one code system—for example, a standing, though not unproblematic, metaphorical relationship between structuring elements from Humanism and similar elements from Thomism has been suggested in which the latter is primary. Clearly, more than merely that reconciliation must be at work in the poem; one could not have ended with summary advice to the king—and an argument for one's own value—based on the contours of the poem that the king is presumed to have just read, if that poem embodied a radically fragmented communication. In short, in the dialogue between poet and history, Camões has to resolve, at least for appearance' sake, the major code clashes in his language system, and those resolutions have to be shown in one way or another to be universal within the text.

Camões's primary mode of accomplishing such resolution is the gnomic explanation, usually in editorial tone. The following lines, put into the mouth of Vasco da Gama, constitute one such passage:

> Os casos vi, que os rudos marinheiros,
> Que têm por mestra a longa experiência,
> Contam por certos sempre e verdadeiros,
> Julgando as cousas só pela aparência,

> E que os que têm juízos mais inteiros,
> Que só por puro engenho e por ciência
> Vêm do mundo os segredos escondidos,
> Julgam por falsos ou mal entendidos.
>
> (V.17)

> [But I beheld those things, which sailors rude,
> Who long experience for their mistress own,
> Count ever truth and perfect certitude,
> Judging things by appearances alone.
> But they with more intelligence endued,
> Who see world mysteries, only to be known
> By science or pure genius, reason still
> Such things are false or else conceived of ill.
>
> (Bacon, 179)]

The passage, first and foremost, seeks to deal with the relationship between empiricism, ("Julgando as cousas só pela aparência") and other modes of perception that are referred to as *engenho* and *ciência*. The latter term refers to acquired knowledge and therefore, probably, to Humanist "culture," while the former, as we have seen, is a key word in the binary nobiliary combination, teamed with some reference to strength. Indeed, *engenho*, in the form either of the Latin *ingenium* or of its various derivations in the several modern languages, was regularly defended by the upper classes as a term implying the superior mental power that only they possessed, by blood heritage. To be sure, the attempt to appropriate that power, and the lexical item linked to it, sometimes met resistance from other classes, and the term therefore is problematic. Given Camões's frequent use of it in reference to nobility, however, there can be little doubt that within its primary denotation for him is included the connection with upper-class status. The reproduced passage seems to draw a line between direct "empirical" apprehension of the world and apprehension that involves as a necessary precondition either noble intelligence or acquisition of culture. The problems with the passage are several. First, those who use only "experience" are called *rudos*, a term that implies coarseness and non-nobility and is used throughout the poem in a negative or even pejorative manner; indeed, it is often imputed to the infidels. Second, Gama goes on in the ensuing stanzas (V.18–22) to speak of how "true" those phenomena are that are taken as they appear. Then, in stanza 23, he remarks on the matter again, in a passage part of which we have seen already:

Se os antigos filósofos, que andaram
Tantas terras por ver segredos delas,
As maravilhas que eu passei, passaram,
A tão diversos ventos dando as velas,
Que grandes escrituras que deixaram!
Que influição de sinos e de estrelas,
Que estranhezas, que grandes qualidades!
E tudo sem mentir, puras verdades.
(V.23)

[If old philosophers, who went to find
The secrets of so many lands afar,
Had witnessed, spreading sail to every wind,
As I have seen, the miracles that are,
What noble works they would have left behind!
What influences sweet of sign and star!
What qualities and what strange things uncouth!
All in good faith and everything pure truth!
(Bacon, 180)]

After expressing what seems to be a sense of the autonomy of phenomena, he abruptly collapses them back into the Humanist and/or Thomistic interpretative modes: in line 5 he makes them fodder for the abstract Humanist culture bank and in line 6 he apparently invokes the Thomistic universe and the deterministic line that runs through it. In short, he does not declare the falsity of direct experience; but he suggests that it can be reconciled with the other modes, without actually showing how. That suggestion serves to define the value imputed to pragmatic action throughout the poem.

In fact, there is a specific mechanism by which that sense of the non-primacy of pure experience is propagated throughout the text. When we come to the phrase, "só pela aparência" 'by appearances alone', in the above context, we are already prepared for it, for a similar phrase, "Co'um saber só de experiências feito" 'With wisdom only to experience due', has passed before us only twenty-seven stanzas before: in the stanza (IV.94) preliminary to the speech of the Old Man of Restelo. That phrase constitutes narrative definition of the Old Man's source of knowledge, and we have seen that the Portuguese do not accept his analyses but rather go ahead to achievement that is in fact both positive and foreordained. Thus is it confirmed by reference to history that direct experience is an incomplete basis for intellection.

A major problem arises in interpreting the use of the word "experience" in relation to the Old Man's words, however: his vocabulary and outlook are not pragmatic but rather Humanistic, the result of learned, Classical culture. Indeed, he seems to represent the conservative, Europocentric stance to be seen in many of the Humanist thinkers of Camões's time; this posture was partially touched on earlier in discussion of Humanist notions of man's limitations. The description of the Old Man as one possessed of "wisdom only to experience due" is therefore puzzling. Does Camões, by recognizing the importance that both Humanism and empiricism give to the phenomenal world (despite the fact that their respective manners and degrees of so doing are radically different), see a clear division between them and Thomism/nobiliarism, which emphasizes abstract human qualities and the presence of God in the cosmos? Probably so, though it seems strange since in the passages from Canto V reproduced above he clearly emphasizes Humanism's non-"empirical" features. The fact is that in the passage from Canto V he has in mind Humanism's nature as abstract knowledge, while in the episode involving the Old Man of Restelo he has in mind Humanism's other major aspect: its emphasizing of a semi-autonomous man and of the phenomenal world. Be all this as it may, in this series of interrelated passages in which the problem of code clash is being dealt with, empiricism and Humanism are both subordinated to Thomism/nobiliarism.

The conditions of that subordination should be noted, however. First, no cogent—or even consistent—argument is made in support of such subordination. It must be recalled, however, that *Os Lusíadas* is literature, not philosophy. That fact imposes upon Camões only that he seek to resolve code problems for the purposes of poetic discourse/communication, not that he resolve argumentative problems in order to create a consistent philosophy. He achieves the former goal; indeed, in concert with the Christian-salvation thematics of the on-going "so small animal of earth" motif and the subtle but insistent presence of nobiliary vocabulary, especially as regards social class structure, the upper-class code appears as clearly dominant. A second condition in the subordination of the other two codes is, as we have seen, that they are literally only "subordinated"; their value is not destroyed. Indeed, their presence is prized, as long as it is clearly conceived as in some way subordinate to the dominant code, which expresses the true metaphysics. The result is a work of art in which a lush texture and an evocation of almost documentary historical action placed in its vividly portrayed setting are subordinated to a dominant value system whose textual realization is in the main quite abstract.

The salient features of Camões's treatment of the relationship between the Classical deities and the Christian God—the example of code-clash that has drawn most critical attention—are exemplary of the process of subordination analyzed above. Camões begins to subordinate the Classical deities to the Christian God in IX.18; continues that undertaking in IX.90–92, with a euhemeristic explanation of the origin of the Classical deities; and completes it in X.82–83, where Tethys proclaims herself and her kind (i.e., Classical deities) to be mere human creations, valuable for the making of art but essentially untrue in any wider sense, and then proclaims the truth of the Christian God. Clearly, that last explanation is not even consistent with the euhemeristic explanation advanced before. Again, consistency is not the purpose; Camões's intent is merely to subordinate the Classical deities to the Christian God.

The situation in which the deity proclaims her own limitation is, of course, ironic, but the nature of the irony is unclear. Some critics would have Camões a pagan and the irony of the situation indicative of an implicit negation upon his part of what the goddess says. Moreover, it is often suggested that this and other passages were added to please the Censor.[15] That proposition is very doubtful. As we have seen, nobiliary/Thomist vocabulary, suggesting an outlook essentially consonant with the outlook indicated in the Tethys passage, pervades the detail of the book. Any thought of addition to please the Censor must therefore envision wholesale revamping of the entire poem. Any notion that the irony of the passage completely undercuts and reverses its surface development falls victim to the same argument when tested with recourse to the context of the entire poem. Further, such irony would not seem a part of Camões's literary baggage. Nowhere else does he attempt anything akin to such a procedure; indeed, his poem is noteworthy for its lack of irony on any major score. It is my judgment that the irony resides in the implications of the obvious; that a literary figure remarks that she and her kind are just and only that: literary figures. She thus, in condemning them to nonexistence in absolute terms, holds out for them existence as appurtenances of acquired culture, the value of which is maintained on several fronts, though clearly subordinated.[16]

The final result of Camões's implicit deliberation of code-clash problems seems, then, to be as follows. There is a standing communication that the Thomist/nobiliary code is ascendant and, simultaneously, that the other two systems have value but, in different ways and in different degrees, are to be seen as subordinate. In some areas the conditions of subordination are treated directly, though only for the purposes of communication. In other areas the subordination is simply assured by logical extension from the treated areas, and thus indicated only in general terms. One implication of the latter factor is that in areas where the issue is not vital, the subordinate code can figure strongly, even become primary, since subordination at a general level is assured. Many areas involving art and culture are so treated.

An intellectual profile of Camões emerges from this analysis. He is exclusively upper-class oriented, essentially orthodox in social and religious matters. In contrast, he does not participate in the Counter-Reformational enforcement of orthodoxy, for he allows heterodox intellectual currents (Humanism and empiricism) a place in the cosmos with a relatively autonomous existence of their own, as long as it is clear that they are finally subordinate in all concerns to the domination of Thomism. In this respect, he seems to participate in the optimistic mentality of the 1530's and before, rather than in the defensive outlook of subsequent decades.

There is, however, a thematic area of the micro-poem that modifies that profile. A few lines from the passage in which Camões commends himself to King Sebastian illustrate the thematics:

> Pera servir-vos, braço às armas feito;
> Pera cantar-vos, mente às Musas dada;
> Só me falece ser a vós aceito,
> De quem virtude deve ser prezada.
> (X.155.1–4)

> [To serve you, here's an arm for battle wrought,
> To sing you, here's a mind, the Muses' own.
> Only I need to have your kindly thought,
> To whom true virtue's value should be known.
> (Bacon, 387)]

Camões makes his case for himself first as a man of experience in battle, second as a man schooled in the Classics and capable of artistic creation on his own part, and third as a nobleman (in the word *virtude*). Indeed, he seems to imply that the first two complement the third—or, perhaps, are part of it. The situation is the same in several other passages as well: Camões recommends himself as a nobleman and seeks to exercise the noble's right to audience and to proffering of advice to the king; but his nobility includes Humanistic literary capabilities and is enhanced by wide experience in the world. It is standard critical practice to say that Camões invokes as his Muses the three categories of *experiência, engenho,* and *arte.* The first and third clearly refer to the aforementioned categories of world-wisdom and literary ability. The second, however, provides the ultimate key, for it is at times clearly an artistic conceptual power (see, for example I.2. 8.), and at others, as we have seen, it is used in the binary combinations that refer to the conceptual capabilities of the nobleman, with probable reference to inheritance through lineage. The resulting reference is one to high conceptual powers in general and to their artistic application. Camões gives that reference implications of outright visionary status both by use of marked vocabulary—in his initial invocation (I.5.1.) as well as in the invocation of poetic power before undertaking the historical catalog of Canto VII-VIII (VII.87.6.), where he uses the word *fúria*, clearly his version of Latin *furor*, 'poetic vision'—and also through the claims he implicitly makes in his literary interpreting of history. In short, he argues that literary abilities can be a part of noble *engenho*, that worldly experience can, at very least, complement that quality, and that he himself represents such abilities.

Such, in fact, is the poet who dialogues with history. And the paradigms of judgment that he uses with respect to history are intended to correspond to the confluence of the same qualities. He praises instinctual valor, Christian faith and dedication, noble leadership, experience in the world, and cultural expertise. And, inversely, taking advantage of the notion that the history of his nation depends on his poetic ability for proper interpretation and immortalization, he at one point (VII. 79–87) says that he will not mention figures who do not have such qualities, thus omitting them from history. His "history," then, will have an ethical core parallel to, and in a dialectical relationship with, the idealistic core in his personal position.

And, as was explained before, "history" includes Portugal present as well as past. It is in the light of that fact that Camões's regenerationism becomes clear. The present decline is suggested in such passages as:

> Por meio destes hórridos perigos,
> Destes trabalhos graves e temores,
> Alcançam os que são de fama amigos
> As honras imortais e graus maiores;
> —Não encostados sempre nos antigos
> Troncos nobres de seus antecessores;
> Não nos leitos dourados, entre os finos
> Animais de Moscóvia zebelinos;
>
> Não co'os manjares novos e exquisitos;
> Não co'os passeios moles e ouciosos;
> Não co'os vários deleites e infinitos,

Que afeminam os peitos generosos;
Não co'os nunca vencidos apetitos,
Que a fortuna tem sempre tão mimosos,
Que não sofre a nenhum que o passo mude
Pera algũa obra heróica de virtude;

Mas com buscar, co'o seu forçoso braço,
As honras que ele chame próprias suas;
Vigiando e vestindo o forjado aço;
Sofrendo tempestades e ondas cruas;
Vencendo os torpes frios no regaço
Do Sul, e regiões de abrigo nuas;
Engolindo o corrupto mantimento,
Temperado co'um árduo sofrimento;

E com forçar o rosto, que se enfia,
A parecer seguro, ledo, inteiro,
Pera o pelouro ardente que assovia
E leva a perna ou braço ao companheiro.
Dest'arte o peito um calo honroso cria,
Desprezador das honras e dinheiro,
Das honras e dinheiro que a ventura
Forjou, não virtude justa e dura.
                              (VI.95–98)

[Such men as are Fate's favorites, by grace
Of hateful danger, fear, and labor dire,
Often attain to greatest pride of place
And everlasting dignities acquire,
But never by relying on the race
And lineage of some great ancestral sire.
Nor upon golden couches may they lie,
Lapped in fine ermine furs of Muscovy;

Nor eat strange dishes exquisitely dight,
Nor junket soft abroad in laziest state,
Nor dally with such infinite delight
As makes a noble heart effeminate,
Nor yield to the unconquered appetite,
Which fortune ever keeps so delicate,
It suffers not a man his way to change
And find out action of heroic range;

> He with strong arm must go to seek his share
> Of honor, and thereto his just claim press.
> On watch, the forged steel on his back he'll bear,
> Enduring storm and the rough waves' distress.
> In the South's lap, vile chills he must outwear,
> Sailing in desperate regions harborless,
> And of corrupted food must eat his fill,
> Whose only spice is hard enduring ill;
>
> He forces his blanched face so to appear,
> As he were gay, resolved, and safe from harm,
> Amid the burning bolts which whistle near
> And shear away some comrade's leg or arm.
> Thus the heart hardens into honor clear,
> For which gold and promotion have no charm,
> Promotion, gold, which Fortune may bestow,
> Though just and rigid Virtue does not so.
> (Bacon, 238–239)]

In that same passage, the route to regeneration is made clear: the idealistic poet envisions return to the lost ethic of the Portuguese past. And, while the battleground in this passage is the dominant, nobiliary dimension of that ethic, other passages make it clear that experience and literary ability are also to be encouraged, if not demanded. Camões—aware of so doing or not—in fact proposes a return to the attitude that prevailed in the ruling class in his own youth, an attitude that, at least in its expression in *Os Lusíadas,* presupposes the dominance of the older, nobiliary/Thomistic values, sees no basic threat to them in limited incorporation of either primitive empiricism or Humanism, and posits that revivification of that ethic—in the (upperclass) individual, through state stimulation—will produce national regeneration. In the final stanzas of the poem, Camões gives King Sebastian precisely that advice, while at the same time pointing out that he, at least, has not fallen away from those values and is therefore deserving of recognition. At that point he has the complex communication of his entire poem as justification and exemplification of his message, an exemplification that relies upon a code-conflation, commented on above, in which Camões's act of poetizing, as defined and publicized in the poem, constitutes a "noble" deed in and of itself.

Engraving of Padre Vieira, done in 1745, reflecting the "metaphysical" plane on which the Jesuit was supposed to have concentrated. Of the several engravings of Vieira, all have precisely the same face. (Reproduced from the original in the Biblioteca Nacional de Lisboa.)

Vieira: The Prophet

An epilogue should be added to the foregoing consideration of *Os Lusíadas*. As we have seen, its regenerationism invokes a view that by the time of its publication was not favored by the forces that dominated upper-class Portugal. Exposition, however clearly subordinate, of autonomist notions about man and about physical reality and, above all else, systematic incorporation of the "pagan culture" of Humanism were, by then, conceived by the Counter Reformation as heterodox acts. The second (or third; matters are not wholly clear) edition of Camões's epic, printed in 1584, was widely altered and expurgated; many subsequent editions incorporated all or part of the 1584 changes.

That act of expurgation is to be seen as consonant with the major cultural forces of the late-sixteenth and seventeenth centuries in Portugal and, for that matter, in much of Southern Europe. The traditional ruling groups were mounting strong social action to retain and strengthen their traditional social position, which was grounded, as we have seen, in traditional Catholicism and the nobiliary code historically related to it. That ideological system was enforced in Counter-Reformational Portugal by the social force of the Inquisition and the Censorial Board. The aim of those two agencies is clear: to control both information and thought—by censoring information in circulation, reviewing any new information proposed for circulation, and attacking sources of heterodox information (acts, words, even thoughts). The attack fell heavily upon the small middle class, composed, the Inquisition seemed to believe, of Jews recently converted—the so-called New Christians, or Converts, who were, as a group, suspected of heterodox practices. The Inquisition constituted a legal and bureaucratic system in and of itself and was the largest bureaucracy in the nation (or, in fact, the empire, since one of its four regional tribunals was located in Goa, the capital city of the Portuguese territories in India and the East). It employed a large corps of informers, called *familiares*, whose task it was to report on heterodox words and deeds and who received personal privilege and gain through so doing. The implications of the situation are revealed by the fact that status as a *familiar* was a requisite for holding state office—and for mere acceptance at the upper levels of society. Of the many sentences that could be meted out to those convicted by the Inquisition, the gravest was death by burning (though the most revealing from a socio-historical point of view is to be seen in the confiscations of worldly goods that were regularly prescribed). The most conservative statistics suggest that in the era between 1543 and 1684 approximately 20,000 people, the bulk of them from the middle groups of society, were convicted by the Inquisition, with 1,379 of that number put to death by burning.[1]

A third social force of interest was active in Counter-Reformational Portugal: the Jesuit Order. Founded in 1540 by Ignacio Loyola, a Spanish nobleman, and more-or-less officially accorded special status by the Council of Trent in 1563,[2] the new order was officially called "The Company of Jesus" (in Portuguese, "A Companhia de Jesus"). The English version of that title, "The Society of Jesus," fails to do justice to the sense of the original Spanish/Portuguese formulation, which draws specifically and intentionally on military terminology. Loyola, a former soldier, drew upon and metaphorized the martial imagery that was an integral part of his conception of both his identity as a nobleman and that of the class he represented. He intended the new order to be a corps of "soldiers of Christ" within the Militant Church; the head of the order, the "Black Pope," was officially termed its "General." Theoretically, members of the order were bound to a prescribed code of conduct; an authoritarian hierarchy maintained strict discipline and allowed only prescribed ideas to be enunciated or taught. Spanish/Portuguese in conception and, to a great degree, in memberhsip as well, the order attracted adherents primarily from the sectors of society involved in traditional beliefs; it in essence set out to promulgate those beliefs, as formalized in its own theory and practice. Its chief means to that end were missionary work throughout the Spanish and Portuguese empires and control of the educational systems of both empires. In the latter activity, the Jesuits' goal was to replace both old-fashioned Scholasticism and also Humanism with their own melding of the two, a melding that retained Classical Latin and some of the educational techniques of the Humanists but returned to traditional epistemology, grounded in the Ptolemaic universe and the abstract Thomism of the Scholastics, as primary subject matter. However, that subject matter was taught not as neutral information, as it might have been two centuries before, but rather as a body of faith to be believed through training and discipline on the part of the student. Jesuit education was therefore an overtly combative response to an era of implicit materialist attack on premises founded on the spirituality of traditional Catholicism. It reflected as well the rise of Protestantism in

Northern Europe, with its rejection of many basic tenets of the traditional faith. In short, seen as a corpus of doctrine and practices, early Jesuitism,[3] as one commentator states in a felicitous phrase, is essentially a "Catholicism of the Will,"[4] rather than a faith assured of its acceptance.

A primary orientation in Jesuit thought and teaching is a kind of practicality that finds outlet in several different areas. The Order was established, after all, as a sort of combat unit in an era of conflicting claims on several scores; it expected to produce results for the outlook that it espoused. Rather than mystic or monastic retreat, the Jesuit was supposed to emphasize effective action in the world, always with an eye to winning souls—i.e., with an eye to the next world. Consequently, Jesuits could be found as political advisers, ambassadors, and economic theoreticians, as well as theologians, spiritual advisers, and writers on aspects of the role of faith in the state. In short, in its Catholic militancy, the Company sought to deal with the growing materialism of its time, seeking as well, implicitly, modes of reconciling basic Catholic idealism with various aspects of material history. Those salient aspects of its orientation will be dealt with implicitly in the ensuing pages.

It should be noted that the aforementioned expurgation of *Os Lusíadas* in 1584 apparently occurred in part because of the power of the Jesuits in the Portuguese society of that time and because of the new sort of priesthood that they introduced. Stanza 119 of Canto X provided one of the targets for such action; it reads:

> E vós outros, que os nomes usurpais
> De mandados de Deus, como Tomé
> Dizei: se sois mandados, como estais
> Sem irdes a pregar a santa Fé?
> Olhai que, se sois sal e vos danais
> Na Pátria, onde profeta ninguém é,
> Com que se salgarão em nossos dias
> (Infiéis deixo) tantas heresias?
> (X.119)

> [And for you others who usurp the name,
> Envoy of God, which Thomas was, now say
> If you are called, how can you make such claim,
> Who go not forth to preach the Faith straightway?
> For if you be the salt and fall to shame
> At home, where not one prophet stands today,
> Wherewithal shall we salt in times like these
> (Forget the heathen!) swarms of heresies?
> (Bacon, 378)]

The St. Thomas referred to is the Apostle; legend has it that he was martyred in India. Camões, through the words of the Nereid, has just dedicated eleven stanzas to him. The "others" then referred to in implicit contrast to Thomas are called "mandados de Deus" '[those] sent forth by God' (i.e., the Apostles), a clear reference to the terms of the Jesuits' publicity about themselves as, in some way, reincarnations of Christ's disciples. Camões seems to take up that notion in especially the second half of the stanza, through incorporation of detailed references to language of the New Testament—in lines that represent one of the few instances in *Os Lusíadas* of the wit that he demonstrates in other works. If, he says in lines 5 through 8, the "new disciples" are "the salt of the earth," like the disciples so defined by Christ (Matthew 5.13; Mark 9.5; Luke 14.34–35)—that is, if their purpose too is to give life the quality born of God that the metaphor of the "salt" betokens—then they cannot lose their quality, their "saltiness," and continue to be so. His language makes it clear that their "staying home" after being "sent forth" is the cause of their debasement. Read in conjunction with the passages in VIII.55 and X.150, the language seems to condemn, in general terms, any and all clerics who involve themselves in affairs of state—sometimes, according to Camões, for personal gain rather than because of calling to an idealistically definable leadership role, reserved, after all, for nobles. By contrast, he mentions in laudatory terms the Jesuit Gonçalo da Silveira, martyred in Africa (X.93). In short, he does not seem to attack Jesuitism in general, though its effort to unite the material and the spiritual, or more likely what appear to him abuses of that tendency, does seem to constitute an intended target. In some passages, he almost surely refers to the central role of clerics in Sebastian's court—with specific individuals in mind. Seen in the total context of *Os Lusíadas*, the passages I refer to seem to insist upon the exclusive right of the nobility to provide royal advisers and other leaders; and inversely, they seem to seek to relegate the clergy to spiritual and missionary endeavor only. At the time, the Jesuits quite likely were the primary culprits in transgression of those boundaries. It should also be noted that Camões was aware that he was entering a dangerous area in X.119: he begins the next stanza with the words "Mas passo esta matéria perigosa" 'But I leave so perilous a subject behind'. He was correct in his concern: conceived as a general attack on Jesuitism,[5] X.119 was completely omitted from the 1584 edition of his poem.

The second literary "regenerator" of Portugal to be examined in this study, Padre (Father) António Vieira (1608–1697), epitomizes many aspects of that new concept of religiosity. After having been educated in a Jesuit school in colonial Bahia, Brazil—the only education there available—he joined the Order in 1623 and spent the rest of his life as a priest of the Order, indeed, one of the most famous in its history. The son of a serving-family in a noble house, Vieira was apparently in the habit of suggesting that he was noble by birth. Be that as it may, he was later to frequent the circles of the nobility both in Portugal and throughout Europe and to be considered by nobles one of the most astute political and economic thinkers of his day, as well as a powerful theologian and masterful sermonizer. Such activities alternated in Vieira's life with long periods spent in a mission in the interior of the Northeast Brazilian Captaincy of Maranhão, where he put into practice among Indians the missionarism preached by the Order. It is reported that he could write seven Indian languages.

Aspects of Padre Vieira's variegated life—during his lifetime, he was both offered a Bishopric and condemned by the Inquisition—will be examined in future pages, in connection with an analysis of his regenerationist writing. To provide background against which to set that examination, however, I shall make a brief excursus into aspects of Portuguese political and cultural history in the seventeenth century.

As we have seen in the Introduction to this study, the Portuguese defeat at Alcácer-Kebir in 1578, and King Sebastian's death in that battle, paved the way for Spanish succession to the Portuguese crown. Sebastian was succeeded by his great-uncle, Cardinal Henry, the Inquisitor General of the Realm; octogenarian Henry's death in 1580 left Philip II of Spain the last clear heir to the throne. He took the crown in that year. Thus a nation consciously proud of its place as the initiator of the age of maritime exploration, consciously proud of its foreign conquests, was itself dominated by a foreign power. The Spanish domination over Portugal, officially in the form of a dual monarchy held by the Spanish King in which Portugal and its territories were to have political autonomy, lasted sixty years, until 1640. In that year a group of nobles, counting on popular support—scattered popular uprisings against Spanish rule had begun in 1637—took the Royal Palace in Lisbon and proclaimed the Duke of Bragança to be King John IV of Portugal, the first king of a new Royal House, that of Bragança. John's claim came, legally speaking, from the fact that he was a descendant, through a female line, of Manuel, the king who nearly 150 years before had sent Vasco da Gama on his epoch-making voyage. It was, of course, one thing to proclaim independence, and another to make the proclamation stand up, and only in 1668, after years of bloody fighting, did Madrid finally accept the fact.

Beneath those bare political facts lies a series of cultural events of importance for our examination of António Vieira's regenerationism. As we have seen, after the initial expansion, there set in a society-wide reaction against concentration on the material world, a reaction with different implications for different social groups. I have labelled it, in the chapter on Camões, a period of frustration and pessimism. In fact, its underlying anxiety and tendency to hark back to what was perceived as a stable past age are glimpsed, partially developed, in *Os Lusíadas*; there however, they mingle with strong Renaissance worldliness. The Counter Reformation, fueled by this reaction, in turn exacerbated it, as did the adverse political situation. By the outset of the seventeenth century, a true Age of Anxiety had dawned in Portugal. The culture of the age, for its part, reflected those preoccupations in various sorts of idealistic speculation directed both toward society and its structures and toward man and his place in the cosmos. Occultism and prophecy flourished, especially at the popular level of society.

Portugal was not alone in such experience; utopianism was Europe-wide. Before 1600, the occult brotherhood Militia Crucifera Evangelica (the title translates as 'The Cross-Bearing Evangelical Army'; obviously some elements of the Protestant cultures too were endeavoring to appropriate traditional martial imagery and its cultural resonances) was formed in Germany, wedded to the basic doctrines of spiritual alchemy and of what we today would call astrology. Its leader, one Simon Studion, reading portents, predicted the crucifixion of the last Pope in 1612 and the Second Advent of Christ—and a consequent renovation of earthly life—in 1620.[6] Elsewhere, following the lead of Thomas More's *Utopia* (1516), the Italian Tomasso Campanella wrote *La Città del Sole* (written in Italian in 1602, published in Latin in 1623). Perhaps the most striking indication of the search for a solution to the anxieties of the time was the Emperor Charles V's express hope that the unity of Papacy and Empire could be recaptured. With all its political implications, that formulation nonetheless does in effect envision recapture of the lost sense of union of spiritual and physical realms. In short, Vieira's *História do Futuro* was neither an isolated, nor a purely Portuguese, phenomenon.[7]

In Portugal, great pride in the national achievement had led some intellectuals of the sixteenth century to intuit that their nation was the chosen instrument of a divine plan to unify the entire world under the single banner of the True Faith. The scholar Raymond Cantel sees that Messianic intuition (whose immediate fulfillment, as far as its adherents were concerned, was only agonizingly postponed by the events of 1578–1580) as one of the spiritual forces of the liberating revolution of 1640; of Vieira's *História*; and of Sebastianism, that Portuguese state of mind and sometimes political movement intimately linked to the loss of political independence and as well to the anxieties of the age (*Prophétisme*, 25–26).

Historians suggest four sources for Sebastianism, all of which antedate Sebastian himself. They are: popular Arthurian legendry, Arabic messianism, Judeo-Christian Messianic prophecies in Portugal, and the antecedents of the latter—earlier prophecies of a similar nature in Spain.[8]

The Messianic prophecies of greatest currency in the sixteenth century were those attributed—with no justice whatsoever—to St. Isidore of Seville (560?–636). Those prophecies told of the coming of the Messiah; the word they employed was, however, not Messiah but *Encoberto* 'Concealed One', a formula, perhaps translated from Arabic, later to be applied to Sebastian. One of the the pseudo-Isidorian prophecies reads as follows:

> Sazon se hallegara que el Encubierto verna en Espanna caulgado [*sic*] en cauallo de madera, y aun estara aca, y de muchos no sera crido.
>
> (Azevedo, 18–19)

> [A time will come when the Concealed One will come to Hispania mounted on a wooden horse, and even though he is here he will not be believed by many.][9]

In sixteenth-century Portugal any number of Messiahs appeared and disappeared, and prophets flourished. One of the most celebrated was Gonçalo Anes (or Eanes) Bandarra, a cobbler of Trancoso (b. ca. 1500; fl. 1541). Bandarra interpreted the Bible for all those who would listen, and a great many did. He appropriated imagery from the Old Testament for use in his own prophetic poems, in which, almost needless to say, he predicted the coming of a Messiah to rid the world of its current evils. Thanks to two lines of his poetry, he was accepted by the later Sebastianist cult as a true prophet, and his name became inextricably linked with Sebastianism. The lines are "Antes que cerrem quarenta/Erguer-se-á grã tormenta [Before forty are closed, a great storm will arise]."[10]

In 1554, into that atmosphere of what may be called pre-Sebastianistic fervor, the future king was born. By that time the optimism and pride of the early Portuguese conquerors was beginning to give way to guarded fear of the future. And more immediately, the royal line was in serious trouble. All nine sons of John III had died, the last being Prince John, dead of diabetes at age sixteen. At his death he left his young wife, Joana, pregnant with the only possible salvation of Portuguese independence; the yet-unborn child had to be a male to inherit the throne and to continue the Portuguese royal line. If the child were female or died, the next in succession was a Spanish prince. Prince John died on January 2, 1554. Because of the absolute necessity of the safe birth of a prince, however, Joana was not informed of her husband's death. No one attending her was allowed to wear mourning, to speak a word of what had occurred, even to look ill at ease. Prayers were said on a national scale. The birth of Sebastian on January 20 sent the nation into jubilation. No child could have been more fervently desired by a greater number of people. Hence the cognomen *O Desejado* 'The Desired One'.

In an age given to such considerations, Sebastian's birth was considered a marvel; surely the hand of God was involved. Sebastian was the object of cult worship virtually from his birth. Even Camões, surely no doctrinaire Sebastianist, in a passage that, despite what might first be thought, is more historical than hyperbolic, could address the young king as:

> Maravilha fatal da nossa idade,
> Dada ao mundo por Deus, que todo o mande,
> Pera do mundo a Deus dar parte grande.
> (I.6.6–8)

> [Our Century's miracle decreed by Fate,
> Vouchsafed the world by God, Who all commands,
> To give its [i.e., the world's] better portion
>   in God's hands.
> (Bacon, 4)]

The miracle of the birth was seen as a sign of rebirth—rebirth of Portuguese vigor, of conquest, of power. Perhaps Sebastian was, in fact, the *Encoberto* foretold in the prophecies. Perhaps with him Portugal could conquer and rule a Christian world in Christian peace (see Azevedo, 29–31). Any such hopes were possible; all were dashed by the disaster at Alcácer-Kebir (1578). Sebastian was presumed dead, but no one knew for sure that he was. The young ruler who had been in life *O Desejado* and perhaps *O Encoberto*, and who had been the repository of a great hope, was, on his mysterious and disastrous disappearance, definitely identified with *O Encoberto*, thus becoming a focus for the hopes and fears, the prophecies and fantasies of a nation. In 1580 Portugal fell under Spanish rule. But perhaps Sebastian would return from his captivity, from the island where he lived with King Arthur (ibid., 95-97). Perhaps he would be reincarnated in a new Portuguese sovereign. Perhaps he was only the symbol of the pride and power of a nation, pride and power that could be reclaimed and again lead to glory. All those interpretations were made, and always with reference to the same concept: Sebastian, *O Encoberto, O Desejado*.

Various Sebastians were found, and discovered to be spurious. The Sebastianist sect came into being, its central tenet being that Sebastian would return to rule the world. The popular mind was filled with the hope that Sebastian offered; the Portuguese Jesuits, eager for independence, continuously encouraged that hope (ibid., 61-64). Bandarra's lines were recalled. Writings of the years immediately prior to 1640 simply advised Philip III to leave peacefully and return to Spain, since God's will was that Portugal should be freed in that year. The year 1640 arrived already fated in the popular mind; the revolution had advance billing.

And surely, it was thought, the miraculous revolution had some ultimate end other than simply the liberation of the nation. Surely Portugal was again to be God's standard-bearer in the mortal world. Great achievements and a new rise to prominence in the world as God's chosen nation were looked forward to. The new Portuguese monarch, John IV, was seen as *O Encoberto*, as Sebastian returned, even as Christ finally come to establish his kingdom on earth (Cantel, *Prophétisme*, 93-103).

Antónia Vieira, on his return to Portugal, in 1641, for the first time since his family's departure for Bahia when he was six years old, was at first skeptical of Sebastianist thinking. Nevertheless, his own thinking on the question of the problematics of the relationship between material reality and spiritual eternals virtually ensures that Sebastianism would have held some fascination for him. Soon he was using elements of Sebastianist lore, seen in his own way, in his thought and in his sermons.

To be sure, Vieira's Sebastianism, at least in the 1640's, had a pragmatic orientation: he fell loosely into the camp of the "political Sebastianists," for whom King John IV was the completion of the prophecy. Further, as government adviser on Brazil and favorite of John's court, Vieira manifested a pragmatic, patriotic "Sebastianism"; he worked to have measures adopted that would strengthen the economy of the empire, arguing that Portuguese mercantilism had to be fostered and the middle classes (as long as no heretics were involved) had to be encouraged for the nation to be able to stand on its feet again in fulfillment of the prophecies. He even succeeded in convincing the court to establish a trading company for commerce with Brazil, much like British companies of similar sorts. In short, it is difficult to know how much Vieira's 1640's Sebastianism exceeds the status of a metaphor for Portuguese patriotism in general—even for very pragmatic patriotic measures. With the death of the king, in 1656, after Vieira had returned to Brazil, any thought of simple conflation of the achievements of that monarch and the promised glories of *O Encoberto* was no longer possible. At that point Vieira's reading of the prophecies about Sebastian becomes both less specific and less pragmatic.

Another result of the death of John IV was diminution in Vieira's prestige. In fact, the enemies that he had created in his eleven years (1641–1652) in Portugal, and those he created in Brazil because of his anti-slavery stance; the anti-Jesuit feeling of elements within the Inquisition (and elsewhere within the Church); and the views of the Inquisition, first that prophecy was in and of itself a heterodox act, and second that proposing giving power to the "Converts" was nearly as bad—all contributed to Vieira's being expelled from Maranhão in 1661 and processed by the Holy Tribunal (1665-1667, a period which he spent essentially incarcerated). He was convicted, but was given amnesty when the kingship changed hands in 1667. After some years in Rome, where he sermonized in Italian, Vieira in 1681 returned to Brazil. He died there in 1697.

The express reason for Vieira's conviction by the Inquisition was his setting forth of "heretical opinions" in his *História do Futuro* [*The History of the Future*], the work that will be examined in this study. That title comprises a sprawling set of fragmentary writings that also seem to have been known by the title *Esperanças de Portugal* [*The Hopes of Portugal*]. The work was never finished. What was written of it was apparently a long "Prolegomenon," parts of Books I and II of the projected ten-book body of the "History," and an outline of Books I through VIII. Also available of Vieira's prophetic/regenerationist writings is a résumé, in Latin, of his treatise *Clavis Prophetarum* [*The Key to the Prophets*]; the résumé was done by the famous Jesuit Casnedi, to be presented as a document at Vieira's hearing before the Inquisition. It is done in Casnedi's voice—i.e., he gives summaries of, and opinions about, the original; we therefore do not see Vieira's hand at work in that document. Some of Vieira's sermons also contain material related to his prophecy/regenerationism. The ensuing analysis takes all those writings as its text, though *História do Futuro* is its focus.

To understand Vieira's conception of the Portuguese future, it is first necessary to examine the view of history embodied in the above documents. To begin, for Vieira divine creation was a firm article of faith; and from that first divine impulse world history emanated. It would run from Creation to the Last Judgment, all the while directed in some detail by God. That schematic formulation is straightforward traditional Christian doctrine; it is from Vieira's view of the nature of that historical progress and of God's role in it that his personal prophetic line of thought comes. As did many churchmen, Vieira saw the Church as the central factor upon which the mechanism of historical action centered, rather than the secular world of, say, economic endeavor and politics. For him, the Church was not only an institution in the physical world but also a body of doctrine, an edifice made up of the Scriptures and related documents, and the writings of the *Doutores* 'Doctors', a term implying those theologians accepted by the Church as accurate and trustworthy in their thought about Scripture and its relationship to human life—as, then, informed by the Holy Ghost. History, for Vieira, involved the accumulation of such writings to the end of full understanding of God's patterning of events in the world and of His eventual plan for mankind.

Within that conception, such events as political changes, geographical discoveries, technological innovations, etc., represent steps forward on the part of mankind along the historical path ordained for it. They also lead to new historical stages—replete with new phenomena more varied than in earlier stages—upon which to lay the interpretive yardstick of the Scriptures and Church writings. As Vieira explains:

> vai crescendo a inteligência, a ciência e a sabedoria pelos mesmos graus do tempo com que vão passando os anos, os séculos e a idade; e isto não só na Igreja universal e em comum, senão nos homens e doutores particulares.... Donde se deve reparar e advertir... que os Doutores antigos e mais velhos, própria e rigorosamente falando, não são os passados, senão os presentes....[11]

> [intelligence, knowledge, and wisdom continue growing through the same stages of time in which the years, the centuries, and the age pass; and this [takes place] not only in the Universal Church and in the world generally, but as well in individual people and in the *Doutores*.... Whence one should observe and note... that the ancient and oldest *Doutores*, properly and rigorously speaking, are not those of the past but rather those of the present....]

A barely latent visual image descriptive of the nature of history recurs throughout *História do Futuro*. It involves a perceptual situation in which Man—we can presume that Vieira sees himself in that role—is looking back into history to its beginning, where there is a source of light that is the Logos. Projecting from that source, along the area lateral to the aim of the vision of the observing Man, are events and accomplishments in history up to and beyond the place (i.e., place in time) where Man stands, all the way to history's end. The events are not placed randomly but rather have a precise, God-ordained structure all the way from the nuclear source where the Logos sets them in motion, to the end of the world. The Church, itself passing through various historical stages, from natural to Judaic to Christian, in concert with the overall development, provides repeated interpretations of those events. The interpretations, being themselves demi-Logoi, informed by the Holy Ghost, increase the illuminating power of the source so that more of the structure of history is revealed and less is left shadowy. Each such new interpretation/revelation then, in its turn, allows the Church to see more events in history, to understand the structure of history more nearly completely, and therefore to produce new demi-Logoi. They do not change the basics of their earlier counterparts but rather, citing them as authority, much as one does a legal precedent, reapply their essence to the newly revealed historical phenomena. Such is the view that underlies the rhetoric of the passage reproduced above.

In the system suggested by that imagery, a dialectic is created between the physical world and its spiritual core, the Church as defined above. (A second dialectic, between God's will and man's action, is suggested as well, but it is clearly left up to the resolving power of the mysterious tenet of Christian paradox, which simply affirms that there is no contradiction between those two elements.) The Church is clearly the dominant element in the dialectic, because the finality of history is spiritual and because the Church is the interpreter of history. Needless to say, Padre Vieira sees himself as a participant in that spiritual dimension, for his very exposition of the system, along with the reading of world history that he bases upon it, place him in the position of a *Doutor*.

The dialectical interchange between secular achievement and the creation of spiritually ordered knowledge is, in fact, one instance of the Jesuit attempt to give value to the material world while maintaining the primacy of the spirit. Seen in broad cultural terms, that attempt constitutes one of several different measures on the part of Counter Reformation thinkers to take into account the prominence in society of organized, complex materialist undertakings, as well as the value imputed to them in competing thought systems. Vieira's formulation has the distinct advantage of attributing value and a kind of autonomy to human achievement in the physical world. That autonomy is limited, however, for while such achievement does indeed involve man's effort to conquer obstacles, it also represents at the same time his reaching of another step in the historical fabric foreordained by God at the outset of the world's creation. Its final import is therefore spiritual.

The historical fabric that Vieira defines is structured such that similar occurrences or events recur through time, as if the initial Logos contained a number of categories, each of which then repeats itself sporadically throughout history, taking each time a form consonant with current circumstances and then carrying out another step in God-planned historical progress. Perhaps the prime example of such a category with repeated occurrences is the notion of the scattering of the Chosen People. Vieira cites as examples the Old Testament Israelites, Christ's sending forth of his disciples, and the missionarism (presumably Jesuit) in the world of his day, a world much greater than that of previous instances of "scattering," partly through the discoveries of the Portuguese.[12] He sees this pattern as one through whose repetitions God intended to have His faith spread, the ultimate goal of that act being the prophesied Christian Millenium (Revelation 20) preceding the Last Judgment. Other patterns have similar significance.

In the creation of that notion of the movement of history, Vieira clearly enthrones a mode of thought characteristic of Christian theology: typological reasoning. With origins in Old Testament expressions of the concept of a special relationship between Jewish tribal history and God's plan for history as promised to the Jews, His chosen people, the typological view of history (and of individual and collective human existence as it relates to history) came to underlie as well early Christian concepts of the same issues, albeit in somewhat different ways. These same basic notions continued to play a prominent role in Christian thought and expression well into late Medieval times, and thus in Counter-Reformational thought as well. Typological reasoning, seen in a formal perspective, is a kind of analogical process in which two events are compared in terms of the correspondence of their various features; the first one to occur is said to prefigure the second, the second to fulfill the first. There can be more than two elements within a type, all the preceding then seen to prefigure the latest, it fulfilling them. It is easy to see how one of the prime uses to which Christian theologians set this mode of conception and expression was the relating of the language of the Old Testament to the quite different language of the New Testament. For example, the Ark of the Covenant and the Cross are instances of the same type—each referring to God's giving of a sign, the faith involved, the faithful, etc.—with the former prefiguring the latter, and the latter fulfilling the former. Thus is a unified, historical Divine Plan for adherents to the faith set forth, while, at the same time, the great differences between Old and New Testament outlook and expression are minimized. Moses and Christ are linked in a similar fashion.

This process is like allegory in many formal ways, but is unlike the normal use of allegory in one key regard. Allegory normally moves from abstract to concrete: the protagonist of Bunyan's *The Pilgrim's Progress* is Christian, the human soul, and he meets in his journey other equally allegorized characters such as the "Giant Despair." Or, in the instances where allegory does not involve a movement from abstract to concrete, there still is to be found one set of items to be allegorized, one its allegory—the former, then, fundamental; the latter, primarily vehicular. Typology, by contrast, links two concrete occurrences, abstraction coming into play in the justifications for that linking, which involve both similarity of characteristics and also the notion that there is some general purpose to the similarities.[13]

Vieira's view of that purposefulness involves, as we have seen, an elaborate notion of the mechanism of the movement of history. He thus diverges from most of the Patristic writings to which he was heir, which saw typological recurrences—many of them having to do with subsequent fulfillments of the basic characteristics of Jesus' life—as historical reaffirmations of what was primarily an existentially valid promise made to the individual believer. Thus the historical aspect of the typology was subordinated to its existential aspect. Vieira was himself quite aware of that distinction; he rejects much of Patristic typologizing with the superior remark that what was done therein amounted to nothing more than an attempt to "see Jesus everywhere" (*História*, I, 184–185). His interests centered instead on an abstract concept of history, and on history as fulfillment for the collectivity; hence, probably, his predilection for use of Old Testament texts, where the historical referent is patent. He was by no means alone in that orientation; as the foregoing chapter on Camões indicates, if the European Renaissance did nothing else, it problematized history and man's role in it, thus partially liberating it from the dominance of the existential orientation of preceding Christian culture. Vieira's effort, however, is anti-Renaissant. He seeks greater unification of history and Christian thought—in essence, a partial return to the pre-Renaissance conception—though in the new manner analyzed here.[14]

Vieira's use of typology leads him to several conclusions, one being that prophecy is a valuable and true undertaking. It is a very short step from the notion that history has a typological structure to the notion that the future can be foretold, both unintentionally, by *Doutores'* entering new interpretations into a typological category, and intentionally, by prophets. This second group includes both Scriptural prophets, such as Isaiah and John the Divine, and also others, for example, Gonçalo Anes Bandarra, the Portuguese pre-Sebastianist. For Vieira, status as a true prophet can be demonstrated: if one's prophecies fit within a typological reading of history or simply come undeniably true, he is, then, a true prophet and enters the body of Scripture to be used as a precedent in Vieira's reasoning—for he clearly sees very little distinction between theology and prophecy. Indeed, he maintains that one of God's mechanisms for historical motion involves his revealing of truths to men through revelation to prophets, so that man can move forward in his vision of God's finality. Vieira goes to considerable pains, in several writings as well as in his general stance, to demonstrate that Bandarra has the status of a true prophet.[15]

Finding Bandarra a prophet has one clear implication: that Vieira himself is in a position to judge, that he possesses a true vision of history and of the Scriptures, that in effect he too can be a prophet—indeed a new sort of prophet, both intentional and sophisticated. He uses the "proved" fact of Bandarra's status as a true prophet as a part of syllogistically based argumentation that looks very much like theological argument but is in fact prophecy.[16] That procedure qualifies his implicit claim to the status of *Doutor*: just as theology is not separable from prophecy, neither is the status of *Doutor* separable from that of the prophet. In fact, Vieira's claim is that from his "advanced" position in history he has been able to see enough to understand the nature and finality of history, to see the typological vectors at work, the complete pattern, and therefore to understand all of history from its beginning to its end. His reading projects from the "illuminated" sector into the shadows at his side and behind him, "seeing" their truth before they are revealed. And *História do Futuro* is indeed unlike other prophetic works: it embodies a rational discourse, refers to precedent, proceeds step-by-step in syllogistic form.

An extended passage from the Prolegomenon to *História do Futuro* (I, 126–132) provides an example of the working of Vieira's historical and argumentative systems. The first relevant passage reads:

> ... podemos dizer em uma palavra que a primeira e principal fonte e os primeiros e principais fundamentos de toda esta nossa *História* é a *Escritura Sagrada*; com que vem a ser um só livro e um só Autor o que nela principalmente seguiremos: o livro, a *Escritura*; o Autor, Deus. Sobre estes fundamentos da primeira e suma Verdade entrará o discurso como arquitecto de toda esta grande fábrica, dispondo, ordenando, ajustando, combinando,

inferindo e acrescentando tudo aquilo que por consequência e razão natural se segue e infere dos mesmos princípios, no qual modo de fábrica se não perde a primeira verdade dos fundamentos, mas vai crescendo, dilatando-se e frutificando, não em diversos, senão no mesmo corpo, como a árvore em suas raízes.
(*História*, I, 126)

[... we can say, in a word, that the first and principal source and the first and principal foundations of all our *History* are consituted by the *Holy Scriptures*. Therefore what we principally shall be following in it is revealed to be one and only one book, with one and only one Author: the book, the *Scriptures*; the Author, God. Upon those foundations of the one and highest Truth will our discourse enter like the architect of all this grand edifice, distributing, ordering, adjusting, combining, inferring and summing everything that through logic and natural reason is to be inferred from those bases. In that mode of structuring the primary truth of the foundations is not lost; rather, it continues growing, spreading, and blossoming, not in many different bodies but in the same one, just as a tree upon its roots.]

The claims in that passage are immense. Vieira, grounding his remarks in the basic convictions that the Scriptures consitute a revealed and internally consistent, though apparently disparate, truth and that it is that truth, in organic evolution, which provides the basis of world history, conceives his role to be the role of "composition" of a God-given edifice, his "discourse" to be, in its essence, God's. Such, then is his version of the prophet—a new, more rationalistic prophet than earlier ones: he "reads" God's "language" about world history.

He goes on, in his next paragraph, in the following manner:

Deste modo crescem e se aumentam todas as ciências, não só as naturais, senão as divinas, e por isso se chamam e são ciências. Assim como a filosofia, de princípios naturais evidentemente conhecidos tira conclusões certas, evidentes e científicas, assim a teologia, de princípios sobrenaturais não evidentes mas certíssimamente conhecidos, tira conclusões teológicas, também científicas e ainda mais certas, posto que não evidentes. Nem este modo de discorrer sobre as profecias e revelações proféticas, para vir em conhecimento dos mistérios, segredos, sucessos e tempos futuros, que nelas não estejam imediatamente expressados, é alheio da reverência que se deve aos oráculos divinos, nem atrevimento do entendimento e discurso humano, ou cousa nova e desusada na Igreja e escola de Cristo, antes estudo muito lícito, muito louvável e muito recomendado do mesmo Mestre Divino e seus sucessores.

(Ibid., 127)

[In this way all sciences expand and grow, not only the natural but the divine sciences as well; it is for that reason that they are termed, and are, sciences. Just as philosophy derives certain, clear, and scientific conclusions from natural bases clearly understood, so too theology, from supernatural bases not clear but nonetheless most certainly understood, derives theological conclusions, which too are scientific and even more certain, though not clear. And this mode of discoursing on prophecies and prophetic revelations in order to come to know the mysteries, secrets, happenings, and eras of the future—which are not directly expressed in those prophecies—does not constitute a lack of reverence for divine oracles, nor an overbold act of human understanding and discourse, nor a completely new thing within the Church and School of Christ, but instead a study fully legitimate, fully praiseworthy, and fully recommended by that very Divine Master and His successors.]

The passage creates a parallel between "natural sciences"—by which Vieira means to refer loosely to the sciences that have areas of the physical world as their field of inquiry—and "divine sciences." The Portuguese word *ciência* denotes systematized knowledge or wisdom as well as science in the modern, technical sense; indeed, in Vieira's time, the latter denotation was just beginning to be formed. Nonetheless, it is clear that the Jesuit is claiming for his "discourse" the rigor of the "scientific" discourse of secular philosophy. Thus does he manifest not only the dialectic between the secular and the spiritual, but also, in conjunction with the previous paragraph, the notion that methodology becomes more sophisticated in each as they evolve through time by means of their dialectic interaction. That explanation echoes back to the material from pages 187 and 188 of the Prolegomenon, reproduced above.

After several intervening paragraphs, in which he deals with the presence of prophecy in the Scriptures, he continues:

...ajuntando o lume natural do discurso ao lume sobrenatural da profecia, com o cuidado, estudo e indústria própria, lendo, disputando e meditando, [os profetas antigos] vinham a estender e adiantar muito as mesmas profecias, conhecendo delas e por elas muitas cousas que nelas imediatamente não estavam reveladas. Bem assim como o sol ou candeia (que era a nossa comparação) não só alumeia com a luz que está ao lume ou fogo que nela se sustenta, senão também, e muito mais, com a luz que dela se vai produzindo, multiplicando e difundindo por todas as partes vizinhas e ainda distantes, conforme a sua menor ou maior esfera, assim o lume natural do discurso se vai propagando, difundindo e estendendo a muitas cousas, tempos, sucessos e circunstâncias que nelas estavam ocultas e pela conferência e consequência do mesmo discurso se vão entendendo e descobrindo de novo.

(Ibid., 128–129)

[...joining the natural light of discourse to the supernatural light of prophecy with proper care, study, and industry, reading, disputing, and meditating, they [the ancient—i.e., Old Testament—prophets] succeeded in greatly extending and advancing the [earlier] prophecies, understanding in and through them many things that were not directly revealed in them. Exactly as the sun or a lamp (which was our original image) illuminates not only by virtue of the glow that is in the light or fire upon which it feeds but also, and even more so, by virtue of the glow that from it is continually produced, multiplied, and suffused through adjacent, and even distant areas, according to its power, so too does the natural light of discourse continuously propagate, suffuse, and extend itself to many things, times, events, and circumstances hidden therein, which through the presence of that discourse are extended and revealed anew.]

Thus is the word "discourse," as Vieira uses it, further defined. It implies not only written discourse, but also the thinking that underlies it, conceived, in good Thomistic terms, as the product of the presence of God's "natural light" within man's abstract intellectual capacity. He adds, for prophetic writing, the parallel element of "supernatural light," virtually a claim to a similar God-given prophetic intelligence. And there is no doubt, especially when this passage is read in conjunction with the language of the entire extended passage reproduced in fragments above, that he is claiming the latter intelligence for himself, through citation of Scriptural precedent, in good Scholastic fashion.

Indeed, in a passage that participates tangentially in the image of light and shadow referred to above, he explains the relationship of his procedure to the Scriptures:

E pois os Profetas profetizavam para nós e as cousas nossas, razão é que nós como nossas as entendamos. Mas porque as profecias por sua natural escuridade não são fáceis de entender, e assim como se há mister necessariamente a sua luz para conhecer os futuros, é também necessária outra segunda e nova luz para as entender a elas. Esta sugunda luz serão aqueles a quem Cristo chamou *luz do Mundo*: *Vos estis lux Mundi*, e, por outras palavras, *candeia acesa*: *Neque enim accendunt lucernam et ponunt eam sub modio*, que são em primeiro lugar os Apóstolos sagrados, e em segundo os Padres Doutores da Igreja e expositores das Escrituras divinas, os quais seguiremos e alegaremos em tudo o que dissermos com estas duas luzes ou candeias: uma dos Doutores sagrados, com que alumiaremos as profecias, e outra as mesmas profecias, com que alumiaremos e descobriremos os futuros; poderemos entrar neste labirinto com todo o aparato e prevenção de instrumentos com que se entrava seguramente no de Creta.

(Ibid., 131)

[And since the prophets prophesied for our sake, it is logical that we should take their prophecies as our own. But because the prophecies, in their natural obscurity, are not easily understood, and also because we necessarily need their light to see the future, there is need of another, second and new light to be able to understand them. The second light will be constituted by those to whom Christ said: "You are the light of the world" and, in different words, "No one lights a lamp and then puts it under a barrel." We shall follow and cite in everything we say first the Holy Apostles and second the *Doutores* of the Church, expositors of the Holy Scriptures. With these two lights or lamps, one the holy *Doutores*, with which we shall illuminate the prophecies, and the other the prophecies themselves, with which we shall illuminate and reveal the future, we shall enter this labyrinth with all the preparation and provision of instruments with which the Cretan labyrinth was entered.]

And he adds a coda:

E porque o Espírito Santo, depois de fechado o número dos livros e os escritores sagrados (o qual se cerrou no *Apocalipse* de S. João), não deixou de ilustrar e ornar sua esposa a Igreja com o lume e dom da profecia; e depois daqueles seus primitivos anos houve sempre novos profetas, alumiados com o mesmo espírito, que por palavra e escrito predisseram muitas cousas futuras, assim dos seus, como dos seguintes tempos, também estes darão matéria à nossa *História*. Não meteremos porém nesta conta senão aquelas profecias somente que, ou pela santidade de seus autores, aprovados e canonizados pela Igreja, ou por outros fundamentos sólidos da razão, experiência e opinião do Mundo, tenham, na forma possível, merecido no juízo dos prudentes o nome e veneração de profecias ou predições verdadeiras.

A este fim empregarei grande parte deste presente livro na qualificação do espírito profético que tiveram todos os autores do futuro que na *História* se hão-de alegar, por ser este não só o principal, mas o único fundamento de toda a sua verdade, e sem o qual vã e não merecidamente lhe devemos prometer o crédito que de todos os que a lerem esperamos.

(Ibid., 132)

[And because the Holy Ghost, after the close of the number of the holy books and writers (which was ended with the *Apocalypse* of St. John), did not cease illustrating and adorning the Church with the light and gift of prophecy; and because after those early years of the Church there were always new prophets, illuminated by the same spirit as before, who through word and writing predicted many future things, about both their own and future times, these too will provide material for our *History*. We shall not, however, take into our accounting any except those prophecies which, either through the holiness of their authors, recognized and canonized by the Church, or through other solid processes of logic, experience, or world opinion, have, in ways possible to them, earned in the judgment of prudent men the name and veneration of prophecies, or true predictions.

To this end I shall employ the bulk of the present book [The Prolegomenon] in defining the prophetic spirit that all the authors of the future herein to be cited have had, since such is not only the principal but indeed the only foundation of all the truth of our *History*, without which only baselessly and undeservedly can we promise the believability that we expect to see ratified by all who read it.]

The last lines of the first paragraph aim specifically at Bandarra. And the word "experiencia" 'experience', which was key to an understanding of *Os Lusíadas*, means something quite different for Vieira, as this passage shows. In his era of open ideological conflict, Camões could mirror three thought systems in something like their individual integrity, one of them being a system emphasizing the "experiencing" of an autonomous phenomenal world by autonomous perceivers. Vieira, by contrast, in both an era and a sector of society in which such open conflict was not allowable, includes another vector in the word "experience." The word's full meaning becomes apparent in the following passage, from another sector of his work:

> ...conhecendo com o conhecimento experimental as razões e dificuldades que se podem ler na mesma experiência e de nenhum modo se acham nos livros, esta é a causa por que...tenho para mim que a conversão do Mundo e pregação universal do Evangelho há-de ser obra especial da Omnipotência e Providência Divinas.
>
> (Ibid., x–xi)

> [...knowing with experiential understanding the reasons and difficulties which can be read in experience itself and which are by no means found in books is the principal reason why...I hold that the conversion of the World and Universal Evangelization is to be the special work of the Divine Omnipotence and Divine Providence.]

While "experience" does not in itself have any such actual denotation, the above language makes clear that it is to be read in reference to the idealistic realm of Scriptural "truth," to which, implicitly, it must conform. Those implications then reflect back on the meaning of the word. "Experience" is thus indirectly defined as a category existing in relation to dominant Scriptural paradigms.

Vieira sets out this complex edifice for several purposes: in definition of history as a typologically structured fabric that incorporates secular history into a system dominated by a paradigm centered in Scriptural "knowledge"; in justification of prophecy as, in essence, a part of Scholastic treatment of the Scriptures seen through time; in enthronement of himself as a *Doutor* within the contours of that system. The result is a part of the mental output referred to by one student of Vieira's work as the "lucubrações de uma imaginação desregrada [lucubrations of a deranged imagination]."[17] Vieira reportedly was indignant that the text of his "proved" prophecies was not accepted by the Inquisition as the truth that, to his mind, it was.

Be all this as it may, the system, seen historically, is a significant one. It represents many of the main directions of Counter-Reformational Thomism, especially on the subject of attempted reconciliation of the category "spiritual" and the category "material," as defined and given relative weight at the time. Within Portuguese society, the language of this system is indicative of upper-class assertion of traditional definitions of experience, and also of an advance to social power of the ecclesiastical element of traditional society. Indeed, leaving aside for a moment the disparity in dates (important but not crucial in this regard), one can speak of an implicit dialogue between Camões and Vieira, between, that is, abstracts for, respectively, the nobility and the clergy. In that debate, Camões proclaims the importance of action in the world, invoking both the nobiliary code and his rudimentary empiricism to define such action, while Vieira proclaims the word of God, imbedded in the Scriptures and interpretable only by such *Doutores* as himself, as the central element in history, subsuming secular history. (To be sure, his particular claim in that regard reaches heterodox proportions.) Camões proclaims a limited role for the clergy—spiritual advising, prayer, missionarism—while Vieira claims centrality as a true interpreter of the terms of human existence. The key social factor rests on Vieira's side; by the second half of the sixteenth century, his position was able to mount successful social action against Camões's: *Os Lusíadas* was expurgated, negative references to Jesuitism completely excised. That act, seen in the perspective here created, is indicative of the code that dominated thought at the upper social levels in seventeenth-century Portugal, standing as its primary ideological weapon against other sectors of society.[18] Vieira's definition of a "regeneration" for Portugal proceeds from that social and intellectual base.

A line of reasoning within Vieira's exposition of the nature of history suggests the place within the edifice of his outlook that regenerationism occupies; indeed, it suggests a special place for the nation liberated in 1640.

The Prolegomenon is a wide-ranging book in which Vieira sets forth and argues for the methodology outlined and analyzed above, drawing on various sources in the process, many of them from Classical literature. By contrast, what we have of the body of *História do Futuro* is much more the Scholastic document that the Prolegomenon promises. With few exceptions, it cites only the Scriptures and theologians, and it proceeds in a slow, legalistic manner, citing opinions in a given area and then arguing Vieira's point of view among them. It begins by treating Daniel's interpretation of Nebuchadnezzar's dream (Daniel 2), incorporating in subordinate roles Daniel's own dream (Daniel 7) and the eighth vision of Zechariah (Zechariah 6). In the primary text,

Nebuchadnezzar's dream, there appeared to the king a huge, horrible statue with a head of gold, chest and arms of silver, stomach and thighs of bronze, legs of iron, feet of iron and earth. Suddenly a huge stone fell upon the statue and demolished it, its fragments disappearing on the wind. Then the stone grew into a huge mountain that filled all the world. Daniel, interpreting the dream for the king, says that the four metals of which the statue is made represent four empires. Vieira, from his vantage point as a new prophet whose place in time enables him to see further than Daniel and thus update the implications of Daniel's reading, explains that the four are, consecutively, the Assyrian Empire, the Medo-Persian Empire, the Greek Empire, and the Roman Empire, including the Holy Roman Empire of Vieira's day as its continuer (see, for example, *História*, II, 3–4). That succession is to Vieira's mind foreordained. The stone that crushed the statue in Nebuchadnezzar's dream and then grew to fill the world, which to Daniel foretells God's eternal and indestructable kingdom, Vieira reads as a token of the millennium, a *Quinto Império* or 'Fifth Empire' (ibid., 6–22). The term *Quinto Império* comes into existence with Vieira and through him becomes a part of Sebastianist lore—indeed, one of the most recognized features of Sebastianist terminology.

After having established that link to the "truth" of the Testament prophecies as read and inserted into history according to his methodological notions, Vieira then goes on to set Portugal in relationship to that "truth." To his mind, the millennium, characterized by the world's total and blissful union under the Christian faith, will be an age defined by both temporal and spiritual referents. He goes to some lengths to prove the inevitability of that occurrence, citing as proof instances of God's guidance of the world on both planes at once; as a final justification, he adduces Christ's existence as simultaneously human and divine, citing a multitude of precedents in proof of that point (ibid., 56–159). That characteristic becomes a historical constant, a "type," that will continue to the end of time and therefore characterize the *Quinto Império*. According to Vieira, the spiritual sway of that millennial era will be held by the Pope, and the temporal, by the King of Portugal; together they will carry out the final conversion of the world and extirpation of all heresies.

Unfortunately, Vieira's argument for the inevitability of that united theocratic arrangement, and particularly for the Portuguese role in it, is not known in detail; it was to be set forth in Books IV and VI of the *História*, but they were never written. We have only Vieira's heading-outline of what each book would contain.

Still in all, there are, throughout the chapters that we do have, traces of the elements that were being prepared to advance justification for

Portugal's position. First of all, in the body of the *História* and to some degree in the Prolegomenon and in other works as well, Vieira creates an implicit standing typological relationship between Portugal and Old Testament Israel.[19] The correspondences are several. For Vieira, the outlook and acts of the Israelites represented a stage in the growth of the edifice that is the Church; so too has Portugal, as the missionary force of greatest geographical expansion in the modern world. Thus have both spread the faith and served the Church. Both nations—miraculously—survived "Babylonian" captivity, Portugal's ending in 1640, as was foreordained by God speaking through Bandarra (*História*, I, 48, 64–65, 72–73). In short, the Portuguese too are God's Chosen People (for example, ibid., 32).

Other reasons as well are cited in support of "chosen" status. According to national mythology, Christ appeared to the first Portuguese king, Afonso I, before a battle against the Moors in Ourique, and in essence founded Portugal as His nation. Hence, for Vieira, God has had plans for Portugal all along, and a kind of covenant exists (ibid., 89). (As I note briefly in the preceding chapter, p. 35, Camões too relies on that myth.) Vieira sees Portugal's status as the foremost Christianizing nation of the world as confirmation of that covenant. Moreover, Portugal, the nation that revealed much of the thitherto-unknown world, is therefore to be seen as the primary agent of the God-ordained historical progress and provider of additional dimensions in which the types that constitute history can be seen, thus for the first time (i.e., in Vieira's work) enabling man to see history's finality.

In sum, Vieira sees Portugal as having been God's supreme temporal instrument: in carrying clergy forth to win new areas for Christianity as well as in simply revealing the existence of those areas. Further, he sees Portugal's role to have been prophesied in the Scriptures—read his way—by such as David, Solomon, Daniel, and Isaiah, among others. There can be no doubt, according to his reasoning, that Portugal is therefore fated to continue in one further issue of the type: to be the seat of temporal power in the millenium, the *Quinto Império*.

Exactly what is meant, to Vieira's mind, in the notion of Portugal's holding temporal sway in that era is unclear. What we have is a curious outline for the projected Book VII of the body of *História do Futuro*:

LIVRO SÉTIMO
Pessoa que será o primeiro Imperador instrumento temporal
do dito Império

QUESTÃO 1.ª
Se a dita pessoa que seja imperador será o imperador
de Alemanha? Resp. negativ.

QUESTÃO 2.ª
Se a dita pessoa há-de ser El-Rei Cristianíssimo de
França? Resp. negativ.

QUESTÃO 3.ª
Se a dita pessoa há-de ser El-Rei Católico de
Espanha? Resp. negativ.

QUESTÃO 4.ª
Se a dita pessoa há-de ser o Sereníssimo Rei de
Portugal? Resp. afirm.

QUESTÃO 5.ª
Se o Rei de Portugal há-de ser El-Rei D. Sebastião?
Resp. negativ.

QUESTÃO 6.ª
Se o dito Rei de Portugal há-de ser El-Rei
D. João IV? Resp. problem.

QUESTÃO 7.ª
Se o dito Rei de Portugal há-de ser El-Rei
D. Afonso ou o Infante D. Pedro? Responde-se:

Vejo subir um Infante
No alto de todo o lenho.
Bandarra

Estes são os livros e questões de que consta o livro
intitulado *Clavis Prophetarum*.
(*História*, II, 169–170)

[SEVENTH BOOK
The person who will be the first Emperor, temporal instrument
of the aforedescribed Empire

FIRST QUESTION
Will that person who will be emperor be the emperor of
Germany? Answer in the negative.

SECOND QUESTION
Will that person be the Most Christian King of France?
Answer in the negative.

THIRD QUESTION
Will that person be the Catholic Sovereign of Spain?
Answer in the negative.

FOURTH QUESTION
Will that person be the Most Serene King of Portugal?
Answer in the affirmative.

FIFTH QUESTION
Will the King of Portugal be King Sebastian?
Answer in the negative.

SIXTH QUESTION
Will that King of Portugal be King John IV?
Answer problematic.

SEVENTH QUESTION
Will that King of Portugal be King Afonso or Prince
Pedro? The Answer:

> I see a Prince climb
> To the top of all the wood.
> Bandarra

These are the books and the questions of which the book entitled *Clavis Prophetarum* consists.]

What is meant by the final remark is unclear, since *Clavis Prophetarum* seems to deal with no such subject, if we are to believe Casnedi's résumé. What seems more likely is that Vieira's thought muddies in the area of the relationship between, on the one hand, his large-scale, typologically based prophesying, and on the other, specific matters involving the input of the Sebastian myth, royal succession, and the relationship between them. After all, he had originally identified John IV with Sebastian. Then, on the death of John IV, he predicted his rising from the dead.[20] He also predicted that the year 1666 (a date with obvious fascination for those inclined to numerology, as Vieira was) would be the year of the dawn of the *Quinto Império*.[21] Apparently, after 1666 had come and gone, he abandoned *História do Futuro* for work on *Clavis Prophetarum*, though we do not know the result.

In concert with currents of his day, among them Sebastionist regenerationism, Vieira saw his nation in a God-ordained historical fabric that would lead it to a glorious rebirth. Vieira's Golden Age lies in the future, but, like Camões, he measures that future against the recent past; despite the schematic and utopian nature of his argument for the *Quinto Império*, he apparently (with good Jesuit attention to the phenomenal world) meant *império* 'empire' in a strict sense: in his view Portugal would, through its place in God's millennium, regain both the political prominence and the wealth that it had begun to lose a century before.[22] All this was seen in relatively complex political terms.

Such, then, is the Portuguese future. One major facet of Vieira's exposition of it remains to be dealt with: he seemed anxious—even desperate—to publicize his "findings." (They were finally published in 1718, with all reference to non-theological prophets deleted from the text.) His proclaimed reason for wishing publication was his sense that it would have a value within the historical framework that he envisioned. Indeed, he spends a goodly number of the pages of the Prolegomenon (*História*, I, 29–122) outlining what he calls the "utilities" of his text for the Portugal of his day. In that section he explains that as they did before, in the Age of the Discoveries, the Portuguese can again advance world progress toward the millennium, this time by enduring their temporary politically disadvantaged position and by basing their national life and international relations on faith in God and on hope for the future that He reserves for them—a hope that Vieira calls *esperanças* (hence the second title by which his book was known: *Esperanças de Portugal*). The word *esperança* seems to constitute Vieira's Portuguese equivalent of the Biblical use of the Latin word *spes*, which denotes not only 'hope' but also 'belief' and 'expectation', the latter with totally optimistic implications. It is with those implications that the word is to be read in the following apostrophe to the Portuguese, in which Vieira attempts to establish it as the practical link between past Portuguese history and the "history" to come:

> Portentosas foram antigamente aquelas façanhas, ò Portugueses, com que descobristes novos mares e novas terras, e destes a conhecer o Mundo ao mesmo Mundo. Assim como líeis então aquelas vossas histórias, lede agora esta minha, que também é toda vossa. Vós descobristes ao Mundo o que ele era, e eu vos descubro a vós o que haveis de ser. Em nada é segundo e menor este meu descobrimento, senão maior em tudo. Maior cabo, maior esperança, maior império.
> Naqueles ditosos tempos (mas menos ditosos que os futuros) nenhuma cousa se lia no Mundo senão as navegações e conquistas de Portugueses. Esta história era o silêncio de todas as histórias. Os inimigos liam nela suas ruínas, os êmulos suas invejas e só Portugal suas glórias. Tal é a *História*, Portugueses, que vos

presento, e por isso na língua vossa. Se se há-de restituir o Mundo à sua primitiva inteireza e natural formosura, não se poderá consertar um corpo tão grande, sem dor nem sentimento dos membros, que estão fora de seu lugar. Alguns gemidos se hão-de ouvir entre vossos aplausos, mas também estes fazem harmonia. Se são dos inimigos, para os inimigos será a dor, para os êmulos a inveja, para os amigos e companheiros o gosto e para vós então a glória, e, entretanto, as esperanças,
(Ibid., 18–19)

[Prodigious were those deeds of old, O Portuguese, in which you discovered new seas and new lands and revealed the World to the very World. Just as you then read that history of yours, read now this one of mine, which also is wholly yours. You revealed to the World what it was, and I reveal to you what you will be. This revelation of mine is in no way secondary and lesser, but rather greater in every way. A greater cape, a greater *esperança*, a greater empire.

In those happy times (but less happy than times to come) nothing was read of in the World except the navigations and conquests of Portuguese. That history was the silence of all [other] histories. Enemies read in it their ruin, rivals their envy, and only Portugal its glory. Such is the *History*, Portuguese, that I present to you, and therefore in your own language. If the World is to be returned to its original wholeness and natural beauty, so great a body cannot be repaired without pain or reaction on the part of the members that are out of their proper place. Some groans are going to be heard amid your applause, but they too will create harmony. If they come from enemies, for enemies will be the pain, for rivals the envy, for friends and companions the pleasure, and for you then the glory, and, meanwhile, the *esperanças*.]

In those paragraphs past history is linked to future history through metaphorization of such historically significant words as *cabo* 'cape', and through projection of that metaphorization into the future. Later in this work, Vieira ties down the historical significance of those terms: he mentions both Gil Eanes's 1434 passing of Cape Bojador on the West African coast, long considered a limit beyond which man could not sail (ibid., 145–146), and also Vasco da Gama's passing of the Cape of Good Hope en route to India (ibid., 169).

The passage has further implications for the present analysis. First, it sets up the terms in which Vieira sees his status as a prophet with respect to his nation. He describes himself, in another metaphorization of a historically charged term, as a new "discoverer," a new "revealer" of knowledge to mankind. The Portuguese verb *descobrir*, upon which he plays in the above passage, denotes both discovery and revelation; in his use of it, it refers to (and draws an analogy between) Portugal's acts of discovery and his own act of revelation. The suggestion is that Portugal's key participation in past history has created a situation in which he, one Portuguese, can see the truth of all history. He is thus both a product of the Portuguese discoveries and a continuer of those discoveries—and therefore a spiritual leader of the Portugal of his era. His tone and attitude in the above passage make that self-image quite clear. From such a position of leadership he can promise the Portuguese that they will return to their proper position of political preeminence when the millennium comes to the world, and he can advise for the meantime that curious sort of active endurance called *esperanças*.

That notion of *esperanças* calls into question the relationship between divine providence and human action. As we have seen, Vieira, in accordance with Christian paradox, does not deal with the matter as a problem; instead he assumes that it is understood that, on a level beyond that of human understanding, the two are in fact one. Nevertheless, throughout his work, his rhetoric heavily emphasizes divine foreordination. As is true with the dialectical mechanism of historical movement—and with all other human action with which he deals, his own prophesying included—the spiritual alternative is ascendant. Nonetheless, human action is necessary to history's functioning; indeed, secular (particularly Portuguese) history is a necessary antecedent to creation of Vieira's position as the first prophet to see beyond the illuminated area described in his basic epistemological image and to predict the content of the shadows, unto the end of history. The same relationship between action and providence must be seen in the notion of *esperanças* as well. Often presenting it, in good Thomistic terms, as man's overcoming of his mortal will through rational exercise of his intellectual perception of God-given truth, Vieira establishes the notion of *esperanças* as what amounts to Portuguese participation in the current role as a secondary power, with an eye to guidance from God's plan so that it may hasten the realization of that plan, thereby working toward the inevitable reascent to temporal glory.

Drawing of Garrett in the "aristocratic-bourgeois" pose indicative of the times—and of the tension in the poet's own work.

Garrett: A Poet Returned, Rebirth of a Nation

If it was ever a realistic possibility, in view of the upper-class-dominant social structures in the Portugal of the fifteenth and sixteenth centuries, that the middle groups might come to power in the nation, that possibility was thwarted by the subsequent upper-class reaction. Middle-class power of a sort was, however, eventually to come to Portugal. By the first half of the eighteenth century, Portugal was viewed by enlightened Europeans, among them some Portuguese, as a barbarous, backward country in great part because of the actions of the Inquisition. By the second half of that century, the Marquis of Pombal, Prime Minister of King José I (r. 1750–1777) found in his hands sufficent power to turn the Inquisition into a Royal Tribunal instead of an independent juridical entity. Under his rule the distinction between New Christians and Old Christians was legally abolished. Censorship too was transferred to the State; the Jesuits were expelled from Portugal in 1759.[1] Very clearly, a basic change in social forces was taking place. It would be a mistake, however, to see the Pombaline measures as libertarian, or as indicative of middle-class dominance. What seems to have been the case is that the nation that had suffered greatly in economic terms during the long years of war to maintain separation from Spain found itself in an inferior economic position with respect to its European trade partners—especially since it had virtually to abandon its empire in the Orient. As a result, it undertook a series of measures to make itself economically competitive.[2] In some respects, then, Padre Vieira's analysis of the importance of new economic activity to national regeneration was shown to be viable—though not, of course, linked to history as envisioned by the Jesuit.

Nevertheless, the undertaking of measures such as those above and others—among them, the establishing of companies for trade in Brazil, like Vieira's short lived original one—did not obey any central plan;

instead it constituted a gradual process, responding to needs felt in given periods. The agency of such action was, in this era of royal absolutism, either the king or his appointed executives. That fact is demonstrated by the fate of the various elements of the Counter Reformation: they either were taken into State hands or else were modified or abolished by State power. Symptomatic of the entire undertaking was the reign of José I, during which actual power was held by Pombal, a virtual despot, charged with rebuilding a capital city demolished in the 1755 earthquake by a king who seems to have had very little interest in active rule. Pombal's actions can be seen as specific indices of general directions undertaken before him and more or less continued afterward as well; they include, in addition to those mentioned above: prohibition of the export of gold and silver, reduction of the privileges of the nobility, creation of commercial companies within Portugal in addition to those fashioned for purposes of trade with Brazil, and closing of Brazilian ports to all other nations. The aim of such measures is obvious: to try to strengthen Portugal's economic position, especially in relation to England, which by Pombal's era was *the* nation with which Portugal (and other nations as well) had the largest trade deficit. Their concentration too is obvious: Brazil, producer of agricultural products to be exported to other European nations, had become the focus of the Empire.

Thus it seems that the dominant upper class (or, more likely, some progressive elements within it) saw a need to create a society with bourgeois features in certain sectors, in order to be able to compete with other such national entities, primarily England, the bourgeois nation *par excellence* of the era. In the process, the bourgeois sector of Portuguese society was legitimized and stimulated. The details of the relationship in that era between the nobility and the bourgeoisie are difficult to recapture. Nevertheless, two facts are clear. First, there was considerable propaganda within the upper class, justifying commerce as a "noble" undertaking. Second, the ascendancy, both structural and ideological, of upper-classness remained: structurally, in that the bourgeoisie clearly did not have control of the conditions of its own existence; ideologically, in that the wealthy bourgeois regularly saw fit to purchase titles for themselves.

The mode of the bourgeoisie's actual rise to power in the nation is rooted in political events. Napoleon invaded Portugal in 1807, causing the court to flee to Rio de Janeiro. In 1811, a combined Portuguese and British army succeeded in liberating the nation; the result, however, was the establishment of a British protectorate over the country, which had been devastated by serving as a theater of war. Meanwhile, in Brazil, John VI had opened Brazilian ports to foreign trade and proclaimed Brazil an autonomous kingdom united to Portugal; thereafter, he showed little interest in returning to his homeland. It is easy to see how the middle class, and the peasants as well, could have felt betrayed by the national leadership—and why such Liberal tenets as popular sovereignty and rule of law had wide appeal.

The so-called "Liberal Revolution" against the British protectorate (under Marshal Beresford) began on August 24, 1820, among the Portuguese troops stationed in Oporto. Popular support for the Revolution was virtually immediate. By the end of the year, elections were held for an Assembly. Elected were bourgeois property-owners and businessmen, as well as bureaucrats. Their first action was to ask John VI to return, but as a constitutional, rather than absolute, monarch. A second, unspoken condition: return of Brazil to colonial status, for much of the wealth of the bourgeoisie was involved in the mercantile relationship between the nation and its former principal colony. The revolutionaries, never very united in objectives, were for a time dominated by the very liberal faction that produced the progressive Constitution of 1822; that document proclaimed representative institutions, established civil liberties, and abolished almost all of the privileges of the hereditary noble class, thus in effect rejecting almost totally the characteristics of the *ancien regime*.[3]

In September of 1822 John's son, Prince Pedro, who had remained behind in Rio de Janeiro when his father returned to Portugal, proclaimed himself Emperor of the independent nation of Brazil. With the loss of the colony that, at the end of the prior century, had provided two-thirds of the goods exported by Portugal,[4] the nation was further divided, and twelve years of civil war ensued. In that war, Absolutists, supporting Prince Miguel, battled Constitutionalists, who were themselves divided into two large, incohesive groups: moderates, supporting the king (first John VI, then, after John's death in 1826, Pedro IV, the former Brazilian Emperor, who had abdicated the throne he had created in the New World in favor of his son), and progressives, who had in mind the principles of the French and American Revolutions. By and large, the Constitutionalist victory of 1834 enthroned the moderates and their Constitutional Charter rather than the makers of the original, progressive Constitution of 1822. In any case, the rest of the nineteenth century would be marked by constitutional monarchy and the making of a bourgeois Portugal.

Almeida Garrett (1799–1854) sums up in his life many of the vectors at work in the first decades of the nineteenth century in Portugal. His father was a public functionary, and his mother came from a commercial family grown wealthy in trade with Brazil. He was an enthusiastic supporter of the 1820 Revolution and of the 1822 Constitution. He fought in the Civil War as a Constitutionalist. His political stance and related outlook on questions of Portuguese nationality are expounded in some detail in his first political publication in prose, *O Dia Vinte Quatro d'Agosto* [*The Twenty-Fourth Day of August*] (1821), upon which his name was fixed as "o Cidadão J. B. S. L. A. Garett [*sic*]" ('the Citizen J. B. S. L. A. Garett').[5] In that pamphlet he attempts to legitimize the 1820 Revolution both by invoking as self-evident the concepts of natural law and of social contract and also by extending those concepts to expound upon causes for Portugal's past ills. As was characteristic of Portuguese liberals, he does so in rhetoric borrowed from the French Revolution, arguing that Portugal is being reborn after a period of suffocation under Absolutism, and maintaining that the nation had been a true national unit only before the Absolutist era—that is, in practical terms, only before the Spanish take-over of 1580. That argument invokes the notion that the roots of nationhood are as much spiritual-ethical as they are political. His attack on Absolutism is directed not so much toward Absolutist kings as toward government ministers, the actual day-to-day administrators who, to his mind, through arbitrary actions uncontrolled by a body of law established by contract with the nation as a whole, turned a representative government into a "tyranny." His argument for that interpretation of history centers on the traditional royal practice of calling periodic *cortes*, parliamentary assemblies of a sort; he sees that practice as constituting, in essence, representative government. That conception of the historical function of the *cortes* is greatly exaggerated; they functioned primarily as instruments of internal diplomacy on the part of very powerful monarchs and were in fact called, albeit irregularly, until the end of the seventeenth century.[6] Garrett further reads his own ideals into his nation's history by implicitly attributing only to the post-1580 Absolutist period the oppressive social structures and practices that he views as causes for ills from which, to his mind, Portugal was only now beginning to recover. Recovery, in Garrett's writing, is contemplated in institutional terms: he envisions the creation of a new national order to recapitulate, in modern terms, the true "nation," the loss of which in the sixteenth century led to national decline.

Needless to say, Garrett's optimistic expectations following the events of 1820-1822 were not realized. By 1823, civil strife between progressives and moderates within the Constitutionalist faction, as well as between the Constitutionalists and the Absolutists, had become intense; Garrett himself was forced to flee, living first in England and later in France. In all, he spent the years from 1823 to 1826 and 1828 to 1832 on foreign soil as a political exile. It would seem that, despite such adversities, he never abandoned the ambitious ideals conceived for his nation in the era of his youthful optimism; for the rest of his life he quite literally took upon his own shoulders the task of creating many of those new national institutions alluded to above. As simultaneously a politician-social planner and a poet, novelist, dramatist, essayist, literary critic, and national folklorist and antiquary, he worked consistently in two areas of national regeneration: the socio-political and the intellectual-artistic. As has been noted by students of his activities, the overwhelmingly nationalistic focus of his work in either area was paralleled and reinforced by that of his work in the other.[7] The list of his innovations in both areas is long and impressive. Perhaps his most important contribution in the socio-political sphere is his co-authorship of the reforms in Portuguese law that, according to one nineteenth-century critic, marked the end, in 1832, of old Portugal and the beginning of the modern nation (Braga, *Garrett e o Romantismo*, 509). Some of his significant contributions in the area of letters are his introduction of literary Romanticism into Portugal with his *Camões* (1825); his initiation of the practice of collecting and studying the popular and traditional poetry of his nation; his overseeing of the foundation of a national theater, for which he wrote several of his most famous plays; and his ushering-in of the modern era of creative prose narration in the Portuguese language with the novel *Viagens na Minha Terra* (1846).

In taking up the creative role that immediately after the Revolution of 1820 he had attributed to a "national spirit" reascendant, Garrett clearly betrayed a vision of himself as a man who understood and could respond to the varied needs of what he saw as a nation struggling to be reborn. That view of himself was grounded in an awareness of his considerable and diverse capabilities. Indeed, one can speak of Garrett's life and intellectual-aesthetic production as having been situated about a multi-faceted relationship between his own personality and his definition of the "national spirit." Both are analyzed in terms of a creative energy. Portugueseness, for Garrett, is a constellation of forces peculiar to the nation that manifest themselves in various areas, from folk structures to national institutions—the latter, of course, liberal, as befits his own orientation. He sees himself as an incarnation of those forces and, in part because of that incarnating of the national spirit, as an exceptional individual. Very clearly, then, there are tensions within his outlook. Indeed, the Garrett that we glimpse from a modern vantage point seems dandyish and highly aristocratic. He regularly suggested that he had noble antecedents in the Irish part of his heritage. It should be noted, however, that one of the features of early Liberal thought Europe-wide was the mythification of individuality. Thus Garrett really only epitomizes, in terms suggested by Portugal's highly aristocratic social tradition, a tension, inherent to Liberalism itself, between legal equality of individuals and the all-but-inevitable elitist consequences of the mythologizing of individuality. The result is a grandiose mythic status conferred by the poet upon himself and progressively elaborated throughout his life[8]—a complex and not wholly cohesive mythification that includes patriotism defined by liberal standards and cast in terms of a manifold relationship to the "national spirit." We shall see one specific working-out of some of the details of that relationship in the ensuing pages.

The literary piece to be examined in this study is a product of Garrett's youth; it embraces features of that developing personal mythology as it existed at that time. The work is his narrative poem *Camões* (1825), written and published while its author was exiled.

One feature of the thin volume is immediately obvious: its dependence upon Camões and upon *Os Lusíadas*. Like Camões's poem, it is divided into ten cantos, though instead of Camões's royal octaves it is written in blank verse—and in a strange mixture of Classical and Romantic diction. Furthermore, Camões is the hero of Garrett's poem. It deals with the 1570's, the era of Camões's return from the East, the publication of *Os Lusíadas*, and of the disaster at Alcácer-Kebir. All three events are touched on by Garrett in a poetic fabric that, in its structure and content, propounds a specific reading of Portuguese history and relating of that history to the situation in 1825.

In a personal letter written in 1824, Garrett stated that he had been writing a long poem—*Camões*—that would be "in great part . . . *a poetic analysis* of Camões's poem" (translation and emphasis mine). He goes on to say that some facets of *Camões* would intentionally be made to parallel aspects of *Os Lusíadas* (Gomes de Amorim, I, 345–346). And indeed we find in *Camões* paraphrases from passages of *Os Lusíadas*, especially of Camões's epic formulae, use of lines or phrases taken directly from the epic poem, the appropriation of Camonian characters and scenes for Garrett's purposes, and a number of structural parallels beyond the division into ten cantos. For example, a major flashback is found in Cantos 3–5 of *Camões*; there Garrett's Camões, just returned to Lisbon, relates to a newly acquired friend the details of his life and travels in the East. Included in that flashback is a scene of the meeting between Garrett's Camões and the giant Adamastor, on the poetic pretense that an actual vision of that sort had provided the historical Camões with the idea for the Adamastor of *Os Lusíadas*. That encounter is located in a place in Garrett's Canto 4 corresponding to the episode in the *Os Lusíadas* where King Manuel has a dream of glorious Portuguese empire in the East. The correspondence is shown to constitute an ironic inversion when Garrett's Adamastor predicts to the fictionalized Camões that Portugal will fall through a loss of vigor that it will inflict upon itself. Thus, in the correspondence between the two texts, a dream prophetic of world empire is set against an equally prophetic vision of subsequent self-inflicted debasement. (Further implications of that prediction will be touched on later in this analysis.) A second major flashback in *Camões* is found in Cantos 7 and 8, wherein Garrett's Camões reads his poem to Sebastian and his court (Garrett paraphrasing the highlights of *Os Lusíadas* all the while). As we have seen in the chapter on Camões, those two locations, Cantos III-V and Cantos VII and VIII, are precisely the places in *Os Lusíadas* where the major historical catalogs are included. Thus Garrett's "reading" of *Os Lusíadas* is structural as well as merely rhetorical.

Another major structural parallel between *Camões* and *Os Lusíadas* is division into macro-poem and micro-poem dimensions.[9] It is significant that Garrett—poetizing himself, his life, his exile—is the central figure of his micro-poem, just as Camões is the central figure of the micro-poem in *Os Lusíadas*. Furthermore, Garrett suggests an identification of himself with Camões through the vehicle of relating his self-poetization in his micro-poem to the Camões presented in his macro-poem. Garrett presents both himself and his poetic hero as true patriots spiritually and physically exiled from their nation, which is depicted as corrupt and vigorless. The tendency toward identification combines with Garrett's highly emotional rhetoric to produce a semi-subjective poem that trades upon the position occupied by Camões in the minds of nineteenth-century Portuguese. For many, the poet of *Os Lusíadas* symbolized the tradition and spirit of Portugal. Thus Garrett's identification with Camões constitutes an open solicitation of the idea that, like the so-called "National Poet," he too embodies that spirit.[10] It is a part of the personal myth-making that he was to engage in throughout his life; in *Camões*, however, it also serves to further a literary presentation.

The poem comprises a series of scenes dealing with Camões's life after he returns to Portugal. Action is not as important as characterization, tone, and depiction of the general situation in Portugal at the time; the only real happenings, aside from an intrigue having to do with a love from Camões's youth, involve his audience with King Sebastian. When Camões hears of Sebastian's plan to attack North Africa, he openly expresses the wish (4.II) that someone (presumably himself) will tell the truth about the decline that he has seen and the need for reanimation before any such adventure is undertaken. Later (7–8) he has the opportunity, in essence, to say as much directly, through presentation of *Os Lusíadas* to the king. Nevertheless, his words—and his request for recognition and reward for his poetic deed—are, in Garrett's telling, ignored. Camões later hears of Sebastian's defeat and death at Alcácer-Kebir.

Garrett's reading of *Os Lusíadas* includes as well a "reading" of Camões's character; indeed, it might be said that Garrett's presentation of Camões is the single key feature of his poem, reflecting upon his self-mythification as well. For that presentation, he draws upon elements of Camões's poetization of himself in the micro-poem of *Os Lusíadas* and also upon aspects of the legendry that had sprung up around the figure of the National Poet. The accumulation of such legendry was an ongoing phenomenon in the early nineteenth century, and Garrett's *Camões* is a prime instance of it. Into that subject matter he reads a view of Portuguese history similar to the view that he embraces in *O Dia Vinte Quatro d'Agosto*.

For Garrett, Camões's primary characteristics are idealism, honesty, and patriotism; they shine through the tired, world-weary, at times cynical surface that he presents, it being a product of disillusionment with the corrupt world in which he finds himself. Those positive traits derive from the fact that he is, in essence, a free, "natural" man; that is, he has not allowed greed for wealth or social position to corrupt his essential nature. He demonstrates that natural character in his emotional dedication to the few people who have remained loyal to him and to the ideals that he cherishes, and in his continuing, seemingly irresistible desire to see Portugal again as the vigorous, just nation he had once felt it to be. That character comes to the fore especially in moments of instantaneous action, in word or deed. In fact, Garrett makes much of man's immediate reactions, depicting them as true, noble, indicative of man's real nature. That situation is best exemplified in a scene in which Camões, on his arrival in Lisbon harbor, is debarking in a small boat, only to be called to by his Javanese serving-man:

—Oh! não abandoneis o pobre escravo!

>   Do homem, que é mau do berço à sepultura,
>   Uma só coisa à natureza deixam
>   Os hábitos ruins que não pervertam:
>   Do coração é o primeiro impulso.
>   O gesto aflito do índio suplicante
>   Dos remeiros contrai as mãos calosas,
>   E involuntária a compaixão se pinta

No parecer de todos. —Mas não tarda
A sufocar a débil voz do instinto
O que chamaram *reflexão* no mundo:
Melhor dirias *reacção* dos hábitos
Que um instante vergou a natureza.
—Avante! clama o torvo mestre. Avante!
Como que envergonhado do momento
Que involuntário ao coração cedera.
"A fé que não", gritou co acento austero
Que tão bem fica aos lábios da virtude,
Quando ante a prepotência ousam de abrir-se,
"A fé que não", bradou, e em pé se erguia
O nobre, melancólico soldado [Camões],
Sem desfitar do humilde escravo a vista,
"Encontrai a tomá-lo."
(1.X–XI)[11]

["Oh! Do not abandon the poor slave."

Of man, who is evil from the cradle to the tomb, one single thing in nature is left by the depraved habits that do not pervert it: that single thing is the first impulse of the heart. The afflicted aspect of the supplicating Indian causes the calloused hands of the oarsmen to hold back, and involuntarily compassion is depicted on their countenances. But the feeble voice of instinct is not slow to be stifled by what has been called "reflection" in the world. Rather would one say "reaction" of the habits which nature had subdued for a moment.
—"Forward!" exclaims the grim boatswain. "Forward!" as if ashamed of the moment when he had yielded involuntarily to his heart.
"No, no indeed!" cried out, with that austere accent which sits so well on the lips of virtue when they dare to open to speak out to the powerful, the melancholy noble soldier [Camões] who stood up keeping his eyes fixed on the poor slave, as he repeated: "No! Go find him and bring him along."
(Knowlton, 15–16)][12]

A confrontation ensues in which Camões persists and finally triumphs; his Javanese companion is brought along. Garrett's Camões, then, is depicted as being in touch with essential human virtues—most noteworthy among them, a care for the personal freedom of others and for "liberty" in the abstract—which lesser men touch only in unguarded moments. That depiction is clearly an exaggerated version of a view of the nature of man espoused by many Romantic thinkers throughout Europe and the Americas. For example, Jacksonism in the United States, almost exactly contemporary to the time of writing of this poem, has similar features.

Garrett, as depicted in his poem both directly and through identification with his Camões, while sharing the key facets of his poetic hero's character, is much more the angry young man. The implication is that he sees the truth about man in society and that he, like his hero, incarnates "natural" values. Further, his stance with regard to Portugal is implicitly the indignant position of a man who feels that his very indignation can have an effect upon his country.

That, what we may now call "Romantic," reading of Camões is not derived with great difficulty from Camões's self-poetization in *Os Lusíadas*. As he does in the above passage, Garrett can use a term such as *virtude* 'virtue'—a word in Camões's time marked as central to the nobiliary ideology—in its modern acceptation only. Indeed, it is difficult to know if he is aware that he is re-interpreting Camões's language through that reading. Many other similar terms—"noble," for example—are similarly handled. Indeed, where Camões writes what essentially amounts to "noblemen" Garrett reads "people," endowing his Camões with democratic elements (see 1.X–XIV) such as he ascribes to himself in politically oriented autobiographical remarks in his micropoem. Garrett's view of Camões as "natural" because he is uninterested in wealth or social position—to the extent that it intends to find justification in the language of the historical Camões's work—constitutes a noteworthy misreading. As we have seen in the chapter "Camões: The Noble Poet," Camões's treatment of that question in *Os Lusíadas* follows the lines of traditional nobiliary thought, according to which such matters as monetary reward and social position are seen as mundane reflexes of the nobleman's spiritually ordered make-up and/or results of the nobleman's worldly endeavor in pursuit of, or at the behest of, his spirituality. The Camões of *Os Lusíadas* rejects the seeking of money and social position only when it comes unaccompanied by the "noble" spiritual quest — a circumstance that is pointedly unapplicable to his own case. Garrett's attitude on the subject is contradictory, for in his poem he has Camões denied the rewards that he sought in presenting *Os Lusíadas* to the Court, and then condemns that denial as indicative of Portugal's growing loss of care for true patriotism by Sebastian's era (see 9.II and 10.I–V). The area of reward for what are really less tangible actions than those contemplated in the nobiliary ideology (i.e., the intellectual-spiritual animating and advising of a nation through poetry, which Garrett attributes to both Camões and himself) appears to represent a point of ideological confluence. Garrett sees both himself and the Camões of his interpretation as unusual, "natural" men in touch with truths, and also as artistic geniuses guiding their nation. (The aristocratic implications of the stance and its implicit conflict with either democratic sentiment or the notion of care for others' "freedom" are clear, and represent a recurring problem area in Garrett's thought.) Thus both Garrett and his Camões, while to Garrett's mind not seeking "ignoble" reward and recognition for their qualities and patriotism, are nonetheless paradoxically deserving of reward and recognition and should be offered and (we may presume) accept such.

Garrett's conscious or unaware "liberalizing" of Camões's traditionalist language experiences even more open difficulties. The sense, within Garrett's poem, that man and the world are almost perfectible, if all men can reattain their true nature, runs afoul of the tribal air and cultivation of warlike qualities present in *Os Lusíadas*. Faced with the problem of having his "noble" hero also aggressive and bellicose, Garrett glosses over the problem as well as he can. For example, in the scene of the confrontation between Camões and the boatman, depicted above, as his hero draws a sword he hastens to explain:

> ... Nesses tempos,
> Que heróicos chama o entusiasta ardente,
> Bárbaros o filósofo, e que ao certo
> Foram pasmosa mescla de virtudes
> E atrocidades,—de honra e de crueza,
> Era o sangue juiz de tais pendências,
> E ao defeito da lei supria a espada.
> Bárbara usança!... porém nobre ao menos.
> Hoje que hemos sofrido de cobardes,
> Sem pejo que nos roube a prepotência
> Dos tribunais as leis, das mãos a espada...
> Degenerados netos, ousaremos
> Nossos livres avós taxar de bárbaros?
> (1.XII)

[In those times which the ardent enthusiast calls heroic and the philosopher calls barbarous, which certainly were a fearsome mixture of virtues and atrocities—of honour and of cruelty, then the judge of such disputes was blood. The sword took the

> place of the law. It was a barbarous code, but at
> least it was noble. Today, cowards, we permitted
> without shame tyranny to rob us of our courts' laws
> and to take the sword out of our hands. Shall we,
> then, as degenerate grandchildren tax our free
> grandparents as being barbarians?
>
> (Knowlton, 16-17)]

Thus, he resolves only in appearance a basic conflict—in his reading both of man and also of Portuguese history—between traditional nobiliary ideology on the one hand and his own Romantic, liberal ideology on the other.

Indeed, the ideological battleground and primary code clash of *Camões* is to be seen in Garrett's handling of that conflict. His own universal model is grounded in the individual—any individual—seen as potentially capable of personal "nobility" and creative action. That cornerstone was necessary to the Liberals as the basis of the socioeconomic model that they implicitly envisioned, a model that saw private enterprise at work in peace and under the rule of law in a market society composed of responsible, autonomous producers/consumers. In terms of national history, however, Garrett attempts to see the qualities of Liberal man in the Age of the Discoveries, arguing that only later did an increasingly corrupt social system deform them. A similar view was propounded on the political level by the liberals in power from 1820–1823; the military of 1820 proclaimed itself the "restorer" of old values, and the Constitution of 1822 repeated more or less the same notion.[13] Because of the structural and ideological power that traditional institutions still maintained, and probably even more because of the linking of the sense of a glorious past, a national identity, to the traditional society that they were in the process of overthrowing, Portuguese liberals were unwilling to see themselves as embarking upon a radically new beginning. Instead they wished to see their undertaking as a continuation of the strength of the past. The complex relationship between Garrett and Camões within the poem participates in that same complex: Garrett "liberalizes" Camões as much as he can within the bounds of historical accuracy, while his identification with the liberalized Camões provides him with an identity within the poem and, presumably, beyond that sphere. The poem itself provides him a platform from which to propound his reading of history.

Despite that unresolved conflict in his drawing of the character of Camões at the outset of the poem, Garrett goes ahead to propound the liberal view of man and of national history, succeeding in establishing it in his poem by simply implying that his view is correct and by dint of pure insistence rather than through any actual resolution. It is, then, a "Liberal" Camões who delivers a poetic message to Portugal, only to be ignored as the debased, increasingly vigorless nation leads itself to Alcácer-Kebir.

Just as Garrett's depiction of Camões derives from the Liberal model, so too do the details of his depiction of 1570's Portugal. The Portugal that ignores Camões is depicted in the poem as a nation administered by a corrupt, ignoble government. The national failure of 1578 is shown to have been in great part the product of such corruption and debasement, an implication central to the structure of the poem. The court of King Sebastian is so presented as to exemplify corruption. Sebastian himself is depicted as "noble" but both headstrong on the one hand and inexperienced and subject to influence on the other. Around him are counselors interested in personal gain and luxury rather than in the national good. Those counselors disregard, even despise the old virtues that made Portugal a vigorous nation, and they instinctively persecute anyone who speaks for or possesses such virtues (see 6.I–V, 7.VI, 9.I) — hence Camões's rejection by the court. That reading of Portuguese history ascribes the origin of stifling Absolutism (and therefore corruption and decay) to Sebastian's reign or to the period immediately preceding it, while earlier eras are implicitly characterized as eras "of law and of justice, ... of a freedom well weighed in the balance of public fortune" (6.I; Knowlton, 65). Many of those implications are, of course, grounded in Garrett's reading according to his own presumptions of such language from *Os Lusíadas* as Camões's reference to King Sebastian as "bem nascida segurança/Da lusitana antiga liberdade" (I.6.1–2) ["High-born safeguard/Of the ancient Lusitanian liberty"]; in Camões's work, the reference is one to political integrity and independence rather than, as Garrett presumes, to institutional issues. It should be noted too that the depiction of Sebastian's court has about it the air of allegory (as, for that matter, do other passages of *Camões*, though to a lesser degree). We are asked to see that court as the analogue of the government of 1825.

Garrett chooses another forceful manner of drawing upon *Os Lusíadas* to introduce the concept of growing national decay after the age of the Portuguese discoveries: the aforementioned meeting between Camões and the giant Adamastor. In *Os Lusíadas* the historical Camões stages a confrontation between Vasco da Gama's fleet and Adamastor, who is the personification of, among other forces, the earth that Portugal symbolically encircled and conquered by rounding the Cape of Good Hope. In *Camões* Garrett speculates imaginatively that the source of Camões's Adamastor was a similar vision Camões himself had on one of his voyages, a vision that, in Garrett's telling, includes a prophecy by the giant of Portugal's coming fall through internal decay. In that passage in *Camões* Adamastor proclaims:

> ...Inimigo eterno,
> Aqui em meu tremendo promontório
> Vos espero; aqui áspera vingança
> De quem me descobriu tomarei. —Morte,
> Morte é o menor dos males que vos guardo.
> Nem da beldade as lágrimas formosas,
> Nem suspiros de amor, nem ais carpidos
> De maternal ternura hão-de amolgar-me...
> E não se acabará só nisto o dano;
> Antes por vossas mãos o mor castigo
> Recebereis: do império cimentado
> Com tanto sangue e com virtudes tantas,
> (Breve as heis-de perder) medonhos crimes,
> Devassa tirania, infandos vícios,
> Supersticão cruel minarão cedo
> Os nobres fundamentos. Aluído
> Baqueará por terra o sólio altivo
> Que sobre as ruínas erguereis dos povos.
> Vis descereis pelos degraus do vício
> Do trono a que a virtude vos alçara.
>
> (4.VIII)

[Here in my fearsome promontory I shall wait for you, your eternal enemy. Here I shall take harsh vengeance upon him who discovered me. Death, death is the least of the ills I am keeping for you. Neither the charming tears of beauty nor the sighs of love nor the laments of maternal tenderness will make me relent. And your ruin will not stop here. Rather by your own hands you will suffer the greatest punishment. Fearful crimes, base tyranny, unspeakable vices, cruel superstition will soon undermine the noble foundations of your empire consolidated by much bloodshed and great virtues which you will quickly lose. The haughty throne, which you will set up over the ruins of the peoples, shaken, will tumble to the ground. Basely you will go down by the steps of vice from the throne to which virtue had raised you.

(Knowlton, 51)]

The word "tyranny" is a key one; Garrett, as we have seen in *O Dia Vinte Quatro d'Agosto*, employs that word to refer to non-representative governments. Through such passages as that above he sets forth the concept that from Sebastian's time to his own such governments have stifled a nation that later in the poem he describes as a "nation indomitable when free" (8.V; translation mine). He very clearly traces out, then, in the course of Portuguese history a decline in national vigor after the Age of the Discoveries, a decline of which the defeat at Alcácer-Kebir and the death there of Sebastian were mere external manifestations. (The monumental symbolic importance to the Portuguese consciousness of that double loss is clearly shown in the discussion of Sebastianism in the previous chapter of this study.) Consequently, in *Camões* the narrator-protagonist Garrett often refers in passing to the decline. The word *outrora*, used in the context of an almost elegiac look at past Portuguese greatness, is insistently repeated, often in such phrases as " . . . o Português Império,/ Pátria do esforço *outrora* e liberdade" (7.XX; emphasis mine) [" . . . the empire of Portugal, which was *once* the abode of power and freedom" (Knowlton, 78–79; emphasis mine)]. Such a view divides Portuguese history into a Golden Age, a fall, and an ongoing fallen state. In effect, the Christian fall myth is reworked in national terms.

Indeed, Christian belief and practice become a sounding board for Garrett's extension of his view of the individual to include a metaphysical dimension and, by implication, for his adding of such dimensions to his view of Portugal as well. The American-French critic R.A. Lawton has noted that in much of Garrett's writing there appears as an underlying motif the figure of an exile from a lost paradise, an exile endeavoring to define himself in the uncertain realm of temporality and half-truth that is the world.[14] And the Portuguese critic Jacinto do Prado Coelho connects Garrett's expression of that world view in *Camões* with the Christian Neoplatonic concept of earthly life as a fleeting mirage, the transitory vale of tears through which man passes in his mortal state (see *Dicionário*, I, 139). That state of metaphysical exile describes the case both of the poetized Garrett and also of his Camões; both raise their voices in protest against man's imperfect, fallen state, Garrett more loudly and with greater defiance. And *Camões* contains several lamentations of the mortal state, including a paraphrase of Job 10 (2.V). Such metaphysical rebellion is reminiscent of the Byronic hero, a fact worthy of note since Byron and *Childe Harold's Pilgrimage* are referred to in the poem (Prólogo: p. 293; Canto 1, Nota K: p. 425; Canto 5, Nota D: pp. 439–440), and since critics have pointed out the similarity between *Camões* and Byron's early poetry.[15] Both of the protagonists of *Camões* are to some degree Byronic, metaphysical exiles

92   THE REDISCOVERERS

and metaphysical rebels; thus are the national-political dimensions of exile given psychological depth and widened to universal and emotionally charged application. Scenes of Catholic liturgy and, as well, a number of liturgical references maintain those dimensions before the reader's eyes throughout the poem.

The theme of exile from Portugal is in fact the first chord the poem strikes. Garrett tells his reader that he is writing the poem in exile (1.I), and a later note adds that he is living near the Seine (Canto 1, Nota B: p. 423). His *saudade* 'yearning' for his country is the force within himself that he invokes in place of a Classical poetic muse; he refers to *saudade* as a goddess who has the power to transport his thoughts back to his nation. That invocation, by a poet who was the product of a thoroughly Classical education, is significant, as is the note dealing with the peculiarly Portuguese nature of *saudade* (Canto 1, Nota A: pp. 421–423); it serves as a clear indication of his intent to treat in depth the subject of his involvement with the nation he has been forced to leave. *Saudade* then transports him, as though in a dream, to a position at the mouth of the Tagus where he can look upon his longed-for nation. The excited voices of the shipload of travellers returning home to Lisbon blend with Garrett's own excitement, and soon he is describing the scene aboard the ship bringing the long-exiled Camões back to Portugal. Thus is the presence of one exiled patriot blended into that of the other; thus is the national referent to the personal sense of exile that they share brought to the fore.

In short, the world that Garrett and his poetized Camões confront is false, filled with men who have lost touch with their essential nobility. As Garrett explains, in lines previously seen:

> Do homem, que é mau do berço à sepultura,
> Uma só coisa à natureza deixam
> Os hábitos ruins que não pervertam:
> Do coração é o primeiro impulso.
> (1.XI)

> [Of man, who is evil from the cradle to the tomb,
> one single thing in nature is left by the depraved
> habits that do not pervert it: that single thing is the
> first impulse of the heart.
> (Knowlton, 15)]

Several lines later he refers to that "first impulse" as "the feeble voice of instinct" (ibid.). Garrett expands on the subject in a note:

... [Não] creio que os homens sejam maus por natureza. Maus são, e por maus os tenho: mas fruto de hábitos ruins, e depravação que os degenerou: não que das mãos do Criador saíssem as bestas ferozes, traidoras, refalsadas e vis que cobrem a superfície da Terra.

(Canto 1, Nota M: p. 426)

[... I do not believe that men are evil by nature. They are evil, and I hold them to be so; but the product of base habits and a corruption that has caused their degeneration. I do not believe that the savage, treacherous, hypocritical, debased creatures that cover the surface of the earth issued forth from the hands of the Creator.

(Translation mine)]

That degeneration is true of institutions as well—especially of Portuguese institutions. In fact, almost precisely the same syndrome that Garrett imputes to man he imputes to Portugal: it has lost touch with its essence; its degeneracy is at root a spiritual one incarnated in the social order. Indeed, there emerges in *Camões*, more clearly with regard to the nation than to man in general, a basic image of a vital, essential core hidden beneath a non-essential but stifling surface. Garrett adduces that image in explanation of many national phenomena. With respect to the history of architectural style, he laments the subsequent "profanation" of the "ancient tower" of Belém, erected by King Manuel to celebrate the discovery of India (1.VIII). The degeneration image is applied to religion as well: the frequent references, as in the Adamastor passage, to "cruel superstition" seem to constitute a liberal's somewhat negative evaluation of traditional Catholicism and, probably, his outright condemnation of the Inquisition. That stance is elaborated in the following passage describing Dom Aleixo de Menezes, Camões's supporter at court and the only one of Sebastian's advisors who is still honorable:

> ... Pura, ingénua,
> Como a do homem de bem, era de Aleixo
> A religião sincera; detestava
> A hipocrisia, o orgulho dos ministros
> De um Deus todo amor, todo humilde,
> Que, sem comentadores, lhe mostravam
> O Evangelho e a razão.
>
> (6.V)

> [Alexis had a sincere religion, pure, ingenuous, like
> that of a good man; he detested the hypocrisy and
> pride of the ministers, preaching a God who was all
> love and humility who without commentators was
> shown to him by the Gospel and by Reason.
> (Knowlton, p. 67)]

In a note (Canto 6, Nota C: p. 442), added to the second edition of the poem (1839), Garrett rejects any notion that he was in those words defending Protestantism. Nevertheless, in 1825 he clearly was speaking of a "reasonable" natural religion within men that had become covered over by the action of the theologians.

It follows from that notion of the Portuguese experience that Garrett's hope for a regeneration of his country lies in the anticipation that it may find a national organization that will give full play to those virtues characteristic of it that once made it great and whose covering-over both he and his Camões openly lament. The solution relies first on the essential good-will and libertarianism characteristic of all men but stifled in the present world. Only a government that allows all men freedom and social equality can allow the old-fashioned Portuguese virtues to come to the fore—only the Liberal, democratic government, grounded in the concept of individual liberty and popular sovereignty, that he supported. Further, he suggests (recall that he does so in exile during an era in which Absolutists controlled Portugal) a source from which such a regeneration can come by hinting that there is latent in the popular consciousness a national spirit, a libertarian yearning on a national scale, that is at minimum capable of recognizing and reacting to a threat to the nation's existence. His Camões, on his deathbed, enunciates that belief in the following words:

> Cinza, esfriada cinza é todo o alcáçar
> Da glória lusitana.... uma faísca,
> Esquecida a tiranos, lá cintila.
> (10.XX)

> [Ashes, cold ashes, that is all that remains of the
> fortress of Portuguese glory.... In those ashes
> shines a spark which escapes the eye of the tyrants.
> (Knowlton, 105)]

And the note to that passage explains:

Esta é uma profecia de poeta, cujo cumprimento pode ser explicado pelos sucessos de 1640...ou de 1820...
(Canto 10, Nota C: 456)

[This is a poetic prophecy, the fulfillment of which can be explained by the events of 1640...or of 1820....
(Translation mine)]

The dates are, of course, important landmarks in the history of the Portuguese struggle for national integrity, being dates of successful revolts against occupying foreign powers. Thus Garrett, in consonance with his democratic political ideology, sees a subsurface vigor in the Portuguese people, which recapitulates that basic image, referred to above, of an essence covered over by some sort of stifling surface: the glowing of a spark amid the ashes of past glory, a spark that tyranny over natural liberty may fan into flames. The poem's exposition, which sets forth the principal bases (and problems) of Garrett's regenerationism in 1825 and throughout the rest of his life, has an immediate goal: it calls, in indignant tones and relatively clear language, for popular revolt, in the name of the liberal outlook, against the regime that Garrett had fled.

A constituent part of that literarily expressed regenerationism is, as we have seen, the relationship between Garrett-as-author and that latent vigor that he sees in his countrymen. Indeed, Garrett's identification with Camões is, first of all, a statement that in him that vigor is active—hence the indignation of his *Lusíadas*-like poetic message to his nation. That indignation is made clear in the epilogue to his poem:

>...—A vós meu canto,
>Canto de indignação...
>..................
>A vós, ó povos do universo, o envio.
>Ergo-me a delatar tamanho crime,
>E eterna a voz me gelará nos lábios.
>Lira da minha pátria, onde hei cantado
>O lusitano—envilecido—nome,
>..................
>...este só brado

> Alevanta final e derradeiro:
> *Nem o humilde lugar onde repoisam*
> *As cinzas de Camões, conhece o Luso.*
>   (10.XXIII; emphasis original)

> [To you, O peoples of the universe, I send my song
> of indignation.... I rise up and denounce so great
> a crime and my voice will freeze eternally on my
> lips. Lyre of my fatherland, on which I have sung
> the Portuguese name, now humbled,... raise this
> single last and final shout: *The Portuguese do not even*
> *know the humble place where the ashes of Camoëns rest!*
>   (Knowlton, p. 107; emphasis original)]

The rhetoric of that passage repeats again the image remarked upon above; in this case, Camões's ashes suggest the national vigor that, according to Garrett, Camões both immortalized in *Os Lusíadas* and then came to symbolize, while the nation's lack of care about the whereabouts of that symbolic "vigor" constitutes a testimony to its self-afflicted debasement. Rising to this challenge, Garrett himself metaphorically exhumes the spiritual dimensions of the National Poet. Thus, within Garrett's indignation and self-mythification there lies also an arrogation to himself of the role of guide to, and interlocutor with, the national spirit.

The medium of that interlocution is linguistic. First, the universal scope of the indignation that Garrett projects is indicative of a sense that the language of the poem may have an effect beyond the political moment. The multiple structural parallels and linguistic borrowings from *Os Lusíadas* serve a function beyond that of merely supporting parallels between the two poets and between the eras in which they lived. They also suggest, first, that personal and national vigor can be captured in language and, what is even more important, that it is in language that such vigor can be recognized and through language that it can be communicated and transmitted. Garrett's "mapping" of *Os Lusíadas* in the language and structure of his *Camões* thus implicitly claims for itself the capturing, holding, and transmission of the national spirit. Thus, in *Camões* language has become more than a mere instrument for the expression of ideas about personal or national vigor; it is also something of an index, or embodiment, of that vigor. In the years after 1825, Garrett, in various pronouncements, built upon the notion, albeit in relationship to changes in the political fortunes of Portugal and his own personal fortunes.

The following is his definition of literary Romanticism, advanced in 1828:

> ... A poesia romântica, a poesia primitiva, a nossa própria que não herdámos de Gregos nem Romanos, nem imitámos de ninguém, mas que nós modernos criámos, a abandonada poesia nacional das nações vivas resuscitou bela e remoçada, com suas antigas galas porém melhor talhadas, com suas feições porém mais compostas....
> (*Obras*, I, 1749)

> [... Romantic poetry, primitive poetry, our own poetry, which we did not inherit from Greeks or Romans or imitate from anyone, but which we modern men created, the abandoned national poetry of living nations has revived, beautiful and rejuvenated, but with its old adornments better fashioned, its features more harmonious....
> (Translation mine)]

Later in the same document, Garrett remarks:

> No meu poemazinho do *Camões* aventurei alguns toques, alguns longes de estilo e pensamentos, anunciei, para assim dizer, a possibilidade da restauração deste gênero [a poesia romântica]...
> (Ibid., p.1750)

> [In my little poem *Camões* I ventured a few touches, a few innovations in style and thought, I announced, so to speak, the possibility of the restoration of that genre (Romantic poetry as defined above)....
> (Translation mine)]

It should be acknowledged, first of all, that Garrett is notoriously unclear on the matter of definition of literary Romanticism. The above passages, however, are not adduced for argument on that question. They come to show that, in retrospect, he regarded *Camões* as the initiator in Portugal of a modern type of peculiarly national literature, be it named as it will. In documents such as the introduction to his *Romanceiro* (1851), he identified that new literary current as a literature grounded in the popular spirit of Portugal (*Obras*, II, 679, 682), a literature which, since Camões's embodying of the national spirit in *Os*

Lusíadas (ibid., 681), had been subordinated to an aristocratic, non-national literature dominated by foreign, Classically oriented themes and vocabulary, but which had persisted in popular legends and popular poetry, including popular prophetic poetry such as that attributed to Bandarra (ibid., esp. 690). That mingling of popular orientation with linguistic concerns is foreshadowed in *O Dia Vinte Quatro d'Agosto* (*Obras*, I, 1052) when Garrett declares that, since he is writing a document directed to the nation as a whole, he will use "everyday, plain language" (translation mine) rather than abstract, academic language suited to the few.

The effect of such theorizing is to divide the history of the national literature into an age of vigor, a fall, and an ongoing falling state precisely corresponding to the pattern Garrett earlier saw in Portuguese political history and to suggest again that the true national spirit, now viewed in its intellectual-artistic function as well as in its political function, lies in the popular mind. The correspondences are not coincidental. They result from Garrett's concept of the nation as a creative, organic unity and his interpretation of Portuguese history as not only a progression of political events but also a similar progression of intellectual-artistic events interrelated with those in the political sphere. Indeed, Garrett came to conceive a national history in which eras of sociopolitical vigor correspond to eras of both vigor in language and the cultivation of a truly national—therefore popularly based—literature. One student of Garrett's thought has observed that this theory involves a near-identification of aesthetics and politics:

> Garrett's aesthetic thought . . . takes on its true meaning only in the concept, simultaneously literary and political, of the nation as "Word," as the realized expression of an ethos, which, in order to manifest itself, in its turn demands the freedom that it arrogates, irresistibly. Literature is not merely a *reflection* of society, but it *is* society itself, idealized through language.
> (Lawton, p. 345; translation mine)

Indeed Garrett carried such thinking one step further, remarking that the relationship he saw between the national literature and social vigor was a reciprocal one, that each of the two factors influenced the other.[16] Therefore, since in retrospective evaluation Garrett viewed *Camões* as the starting point for a return to the fore in Portugal of the truly national literature lost after the era of *Os Lusíadas*, he clearly regarded it also as a landmark in the developing history created by the Portuguese nation, a landmark that would have its effect in the sociopolitical sphere as well as in the intellectual-artistic sphere. Thus is his personal myth extended in the years after 1825 to include the concept that his act in writing *Camões* initiated a new era of vigor in literature, which, by his reasoning, would be accompanied by renewed vigor in other areas of national life as well. This retrospective elaboration of what is implicit in *Camões* is the final element in Garrett's Romantic regenerationism.

The "established" Eça de Queiroz of the era of the writing of *A Ilustre Casa de Ramires*. (Provided by Dª· Maria da Graça Salema de Castro, the author's granddaughter.)

Eça de Queiroz: The Social Critic and the End of Social Criticism

In 1851, three years before his death, Almeida Garrett took the title "Viscount of Garrett," an action with several implications. First, while Portugal had become a bourgeois society, the hierarchizing structure of the *ancien regime* was not abandoned; it instead was adopted as a means to indicate prestige. In some sense, then, the dominant bourgeoisie had not yet come to accept its dominion as wholly justifiable in its own terms—that is, in terms of wealth rather than in terms of inherited rank. Even this most liberal of the liberals, at least after he had grown old in service to his nation, found prestige through title to be a just reward. To be sure, Garrett's lifelong personal elitism undoubtedly came into play as well in his acceptance of the title, but that very aristocratism merely epitomizes bourgeois vacillation on the question. A second implication of Garrett's action has a primarily literary referent: in the years in which he lived, the early years of Liberal Portugal, the writer could conceive himself a part of the state, an active participant in establishing, shaping, and publicizing the new state structure.

In the course of the nineteenth century, however, the nature of that state, or at least of how it was perceived, changed. As the bourgeois mercantile undertaking increasingly became the cornerstone of the social structure, the concerns of practical economics came to rule the national decision-making process. And economic success, especially as it affected the upper strata of the bourgeoisie, was the key factor in that process. To that end, in the 1870's and thereafter, the Portuguese began to develop the territories they claimed in Africa, especially the huge territory of Angola, as an economic substitute for the lost Brazil.[1]

That practical-business orientation in effect drew a dividing line through the Liberal ideology propounded in the first decades of the century, in the name of which Portuguese from all sectors of society fought for Constitutional rule. That ideology had proclaimed formal democratic liberties and the free-enterprise, private-sector economic model that went along with such liberties. In the course of the century, however, it became clear that survival of the system did not imply economic success for all; nor did it necessarily bring with it realization in practice of the individual liberties formally proclaimed. Indeed, many aspects of the social system, such as the major political parties or the established Church, seemed to many to be serving the ends of the upper strata of the system, in effect working to deny equal opportunity to the rest of society.

As a result of that situation—one much more complex than can be expressed in a brief development such as that above—most Liberal intellectuals and artists became estranged from the state, turning their capacities and talents to criticism of it, usually citing its failure to live up to the libertarian and egalitarian ideals originally proclaimed and, to a great degree, still maintained at the level of working social ideology. Gone were the idealist intellectualist illusions. The intellectual and artistic community increasingly became an autonomous or semi-autonomous group within the bourgeoisie, directing itself primarily toward criticism of the system's failures—"failures" as interpreted by reference to the ideal Liberal model.

The first prominent group of bourgeois intellectual/artistic oppositionists in Portuguese history was the so-called "Generation of 1870." Led by political thinker Antero de Quental, political historian Oliveira Martins, and writer José Maria de Eça de Queiroz (the subject of this chapter), the group was responsible for the Democratic Lectures in Lisbon in 1871, the primary aim of which was to discuss areas of possible social reform in Portugal.[2] Eça's contribution to the series was a lecture entitled "Realism as a New Artistic Expression" (translation mine). In that lecture (which survives only in paraphrased newspaper accounts) he defines literary Realism as a means to "paint us before our own eyes—so that we may know ourselves, know if we are true or false and so that we may condemn whatever is wrong in our society."[3] He goes on to ascribe to literary Realism a search for morality, justice, and truth, calling it "moral" and "scientific" and citing as a model of such literature Flaubert's *Madame Bovary* (1857)—a reference that doubtless scandalized Lisbon polite society of 1871. He then speaks of literary Realism as necessarily incorporating the methods of the natural sciences, especially anatomy and the psychology of his day.

Eça's earliest novels, *O Crime do Padre Amaro* [*The Crime of Father Amaro*] (first edition: 1875; definitive, third edition: 1880) and *O Primo Basílio* [*Cousin Basil*] (1878) put into practice the major elements of the theory so enunciated, in essence adapting literary Realism to the cultural situation of the Portugal of his era. The first of the two titles analyzes, with heavy irony, the various ways in which the institutional Church deforms the "Liberal" individual and "Liberal" society, and all but openly suggests that corrective social action be taken.[4] The latter analyzes in similar though somewhat less direct and less combative terms the problem of the place of woman in urban bourgeois society. The two novels are usually considered to be Naturalistic; they are seen to draw upon the scientism and deterministic theories of human personality formation enunciated as models of literary and cultural practice by Hyppolite Taine and, as well, upon Flaubert's literary realization of that theory. They are also seen to parallel the work of Emile Zola.[5] Taine was as much a part of Eça's reading as Flaubert. Of bourgeois family background, educated at the University of Coimbra, Eça read and spoke French almost as well as he did his native tongue. (He was a member of the Portuguese diplomatic corps from 1872 to the end of his life, stationed primarily in England and France—thus serving the social structure that he criticized in his works—and therefore came to speak and write English fluently as well, to the point of translating literature from English into Portuguese.) The degree of influence from Zola is difficult to assess, for the two writers (who later became acquaintances) were almost exact contemporaries; it is probable, however, that Eça read Zola's early works—possibly the second edition of *Thérèse Raquin* (1869), which contained as a preface Zola's first major theoretical piece—and that Eça drew some of his ideas about the role of literary Realism from that reading.[6]

According to Naturalist concepts, the novel is a kind of laboratory in which factors determining men's character (and ultimately their actions) are analyzed, and resultant problems for society are revealed. Such a novel constitutes an elaborate experimental tool for the analysis of life, especially of the factors that determine human character and action and the social structures in which individuals find themselves. The writer of that sort of novel is therefore implicitly a physician or a scientist; he sometimes suggests, within the structure of his novel, remedies for the problems that he points out.

The two of Eça's novels mentioned above, despite their supposedly "experimental" status, nonetheless have an almost syllogistic structure. The forces within society that produce flaws in human character are demonstrated, a crisis created by those forces and the resulting flaws takes place, and, in a third step, implications of the crisis for society are reviewed by the characters and by the omniscient narrative voice as well. Eça's first novel, *O Crime do Padre Amaro*, for example, first analyzes the formation of the psychologies of Father Amaro and Amélia, the two principal characters, and demonstrates their interaction. Second, their illicit sexual relationship, the resulting pregnancy, the murder of the newborn infant, and Amélia's death as a result of childbirth are shown. Third, Amaro's continuance in an unchanged Church is demonstrated, as are both the close relationship between the Church and the political system under the Constitutional Monarchy and also the conservative attitudes of those in power in both the ecclesiastical structure and its political counterpart. The tendency of the people to unquestioning respect for the clergy and for the civil authority, as though they comprised individuals incapable of improper action, is also brought into the equation, as is the attitude on the part of those authority figures that Portugal is a happy, forward-looking nation—both by way of grim irony.

The literary Realism defined in Eça's theorizing and in his practice in those first novels has several key characteristics. First, it deals with the problems of Liberal society in Portugal in terms of the complex relationship between large-scale social forces and the "health" (i.e., psychological and moral integrity, autonomy, creativity, etc.) of the individual. As I have remarked in the previous chapter, some such notion about the desirable—or "true"—nature of individuality constitutes a necessary cornerstone of Liberal thought. Eça's novels approach that subject in a scientistic structure: through careful analysis, or illustration, of the formative power of social forces upon the individual, almost-syllogistic plot development, etc. In contrast to the practice of Flaubert and Zola, however, and in total contradiction of the scientific model, the novelistic structure so produced is also pervaded by techniques that point back to authorship, to José Maria de Eça de Queiroz. Characters, especially the secondary characters, at times seem almost Dickensian caricatures, and heavy-handed irony abounds, usually grounded in *double-entendres* put into the mouths of characters. In those instances, a second meaning of a given phrase—one which the character himself does not perceive—reveals that character's emptiness, helplessness, or ignorance in the face of the situation at hand, and at the same time reveals the true nature of that situation. Such mechanisms pile up, creating a discursive element throughout each work that stands in indirect but overwhelming criticism of the goings-on of the characters. The presence within the text of that slowly accreted critical element illuminates the next instance of such *double-entendre* and authorizes the reader to see and take into account its ambiguity; thus that element continually builds upon itself, to the end that it has been suggested that Eça's is an aesthetics grounded in irony.[7] At times the same sort of phrase is put into the mouth of the supposedly omniscient narrator. Thus, in the final analysis, the entire text is made subservient to a structuring force that emanates from the author, from Eça de Queiroz, as authorial principle who in effect continuously ridicules aspects of Portuguese society through aggression against his own literary creations.

A prime example of such an ironic mechanism and the wide implications that it is capable of generating is to be found in *O Crime do Padre Amaro*. In order to hide their relationship from the rest of the people in the town in which the action is set, Amaro and Amélia take up the ruse that they go regularly to the bedside of a child who, paralytic and stricken with some sort of convulsive disorder, is dying and therefore, according to the thinking of the townsfolk, in need of Christian education so that she can die a Christian. At the same time, Amaro proclaims that he is introducing Amélia to holy work, possibly preparing her for life in a convent. Amaro and Amélia, while pretending to expose the child to the Christian word, in fact spend most of their visiting time in another room, which has been supplied with a bed. Members of Amélia's household remark on Amaro and Amélia's assiduousness, referring to the process as "as devoções da pequena"[8] 'the little one's devotions'. *Pequena* 'little one' is ambiguous, since Amélia is also so called in the novel; it thus applies to either the child or Amélia herself. *Devoções* 'devotions' then becomes a wide metaphor that, given the hypocrisy of Amaro and Amélia's use of a Church-related undertaking as a pretext for their relationship and the socially based mechanisms by which Amélia has been conditioned into subservience to a priest-figure, finally suggests the sex act itself. That single phrase, then, uttered by people who do not see any of its ironic dimensions, cuts to the core of Eça's criticism in the novel.

The overall context created by such language embodies a condemnation of areas of society because of their failure to create the "Liberal" individual. Suggestions for action are imbedded in the works as well. In my view, the first two versions (1875 and 1876) of *O Crime do Padre Amaro* embody the conclusion that direct action is needed to remodel major aspects of the social order. As the Brazilian critic Carlos Felipe Moisés observes, however, there is a growing tendency after that time for the textually intimated "author" to allow the cleverness of his manipulation of the novel medium in criticism of society to replace consistent analysis of social problems and/or the proposal of adequate solutions to what he points out as problematic.[9] Several reasons can be adduced in explanation of that tendency. First, after 1872 and his absence from Portugal, Eça, an executor of high-quality literature rather than an abstract social thinker, suffered from loss of the intellectual reinforcement provided by his contact with the other members of the Generation of 1870 and the substantial thought about the situation of Portugal that they produced. Second, with the publication of *O Primo Basílio* (1878), he became famous as a novelist, as, in essence, Portugal's great literary Realist, peer of such figures as Balzac, Flaubert, and Dickens. Ever in debt until his marriage in 1886, Eça undoubtedly felt it unwise to alter the profitable pattern of *O Primo Basílio*, in which solutions are relegated to intellectual-ethical areas rather than being propounded in social-structural ones, in order not to challenge too directly his reading public, the urban bourgeoisie of Portugal. Third, it should be noted that throughout Europe the spectacular capitalist growth of prior decades had begun to level off by the 1870's, producing an era not as wholly optimistic as the preceding decades. Indeed, Portugal, at best a weak spot in the European economic panorama, had begun to suffer financial crises, the first major one coming in 1876. Consequently, ideas about real social remodeling—which, in the formulation of the Generation of 1870, surely presupposed systemic strength sufficient to accommodate such remodeling—may have seemed less viable by the end of the decade and in the 1880's. As a result, Eça may have found such ideas no longer intellectually justifiable, either to himself or to his reading public.[10]

Eça's next two published novels, *A Relíquia* [*The Relic*] (1887) and *Os Maias* [*The Maias*] (1888), continue and amplify that tendency, carrying to greater lengths the abstract moralizing and philosophizing begun in 1878. In them too, narrative omniscience gives way to various sorts of other, less magisterial narrative techniques. Eça nonetheless continues both his critical outlook upon society and also basically Realist/ Naturalist concepts of the role of novelist and of novel—still accompanied, to be sure, with his characteristic permeation of the novel fabric by the authorial principle.

The reader comes away from all four of the novels thus far mentioned with the conviction that while they are in great part studies of Portuguese social problems, the social mechanisms dealt with and the "correct" model implicitly appealed to in the novelistic treatment of those problems are general in nature, that in fact the same novels could be set in a different country with only minimal rewriting. To be sure, a concept of Portuguese backwardness, of economic and cultural dependency on the European powers pervades the novels. And solutions proposed for specific problems that afflict Portugal are sometimes described by contrast to past Portuguese glory; for example, at the end of *O Crime do Padre Amaro*, Amaro, another priest, and a prominent statesman, all involved in the incident just past, gather in a public square in Lisbon beneath a statue of Camões (still, implicitly, the Romantic symbol of the national spirit) and speak smugly about Portuguese vigor (*Crime*, 494–500). The contrast between past vigor and present decline suggested in that scene is then commented on by the narrator. Nevertheless, only with Eça's next novel, *A Ilustre Casa de Ramires* [*The Illustrious House of Ramires*], published in 1900, do we see major changes in his novelistic procedure—and the presence of all the elements of national regenerationism such as we have seen in the writers heretofore examined.

The novel is a product of the 1890's. We know from Eça's correspondence that it was being prepared in 1893; in 1897 a part of it appeared in serial, in a version somewhat different from the text published as a book in 1900. The book was not fully proofread by the author before his death on August 16, 1900—and for Eça, "proofreading" was often a process that involved wholesale additions. It is thus difficult to know exactly how to evaluate the novel's status. Is it a "posthumous" work—as is, undeniably, his last novel, *A Cidade e as Serras*, published, in 1901, from unrevised proofs? When in the 1890's was the bulk of it composed? Answers to those and other similar questions would be valuable, but since they are not forthcoming, the novel must be treated in comparison and contrast to the works that preceded and followed it.

A key to Eça's language is the relationship between narrator and characters. As had been the case in several prior novels, in *Ilustre Casa* Eça eschews narrative omniscience. Young Gonçalo Mendes Ramires, the novel's protagonist, is also in a technical sense its center—indeed almost exclusively, save for the last few pages. Most of what is presented to the reader up to those last few pages either comes through Gonçalo's mind or is presented by a limited omniscient narrator. What the reader receives is always related by the narrative voice, except for conversations; but a good deal of the narrative is a reporting of Gonçalo's thoughts, often no more than a transcription of his mental soliloquies. Beyond that function, the narrator limits himself to describing the actions of the characters and setting scenes in which those actions take place, frequently by entering Gonçalo's mind and reporting his view of others' actions and of the world surrounding him. Thus much of the information that the reader receives is filtered through the consciousness of the fictitious protagonist, a fact that must be kept constantly in mind as one reads the work. Rarely does the narrator enter the mind of a character other than Gonçalo to give the reader an insight into that character's thoughts and motives for action. There are a very few cases in which the narrator may be doing so, but interpretation is disputable. Rarely too does the narrator comment in his own voice, but there are passages in which he seems to do so:

> ...[Gonçalo] reconheceu que...os amores de Gracinha eram certamente tão ignorados como se se passassem nas profundidades da Tartária. Imediatamente a sua alma doce, agora sossegada, se abandonou à doçura de tecer desculpas subtis para tódós os culpados daquela queda triste....[11]

> [...[Gonçalo] realized that...Gracinha's love-affair was as little known as if it had taken place in the depths of Tartary. Immediately, his lenient soul, now that it was calm again, abandoned itself to the sweet task of inventing subtle excuses for all those to blame in the sorry affair....][12]

It is doubtful that Gonçalo himself is saying that he has a "lenient soul" or that he recognizes the defensive reaction, common to his character, of rationalizing away the problems that face him. Those explanations surely constitute narrative character-interpretation, a technique uncommon in the novel.

Gonçalo occupies the center of the novelistic stage in a physical as well as in a technical sense. The novel involves him. His presence is constant save for the twelfth and last chapter and the final four paragraphs of the eleventh chapter, which act as a bridge between the first eleven chapters and that final chapter, in which the novelistic point of view changes.

The foregoing observations are valuable for a number of reasons. One of the most important is that Gonçalo Mendes Ramires is in part a literary symbol, in several ways a symbol of the Portuguese nation. Eça emphasizes his protagonist's symbolic status in two overt ways. First, mention is frequently made of Gonçalo's heritage. He is by birth a *fidalgo* 'nobleman', the scion of the prestigious noble line of Ramires, which antedates the establishment of the Portuguese monarchy. A Ramires has been present at almost all the important events in Portuguese history: a Ramires fought against the Moors at the side of Afonso Henriques at Ourique, another fought with King John I to place the House of Aviz on the Portuguese throne, another disappeared with King Sebastian at Alcácer-Kebir, and so forth. The history of the house of Ramires is thus in many respects a concentrated version of the national history; and the timid, indolent Gonçalo is, correspondingly, representative of the Portuguese society of his historical era, the late nineteenth-century society Eça often criticizes in his writings. Gonçalo is the Ramires of the age, for which one can read "representative spirit of the age," just as each of his ancestors represents the spirit of a past age. Thus, by means of a simple transposition that nevertheless contains a great deal of truth, one might read for *A Ilustre Casa de Ramires* some such title as *The Spirit of Portugal, Past and Present*.

Gonçalo's symbolic nature is made unmistakable at the end of the novel in a remark made to two interlocutors by one of the supporting characters—a remark the narrative voice says is a *resumo* (p. 361), or 'summing up':

>—Talvez se riam. Mas eu sustento a semelhança. Aquele todo de Gonçalo, a franqueza, a doçura, a bondade.... Os fogachos e entusiasmos, que acabam logo em fumo, e juntamente muita persistência, muito aferro quando se fila à sua ideia... A generosidade, o desleixo, a constante trapalhada nos negócios, e sentimentos de muita honra, uns escrúpulos, quase pueris, não é verdade?... A imaginação que o leva sempre a exagerar até à mentira, e ao mesmo tempo um espírito prático, sempre atento à realidade útil. A viveza, a facilidade em compreender, em apanhar... A esperança constante nalgum milagre, no velho milagre de Ourique, que sanará todas as dificuldades... A vaidade, o gosto de se arrebicar, de luzir, e uma simplicidade tão grande, que dá na rua o braço a um mendigo... Um fundo de melancolia, apesar de tão palrador, tão sociável. A desconfiança terrível de si mesmo, que o acobarda, o encolhe, até que um dia se decide, e aparece um herói, que tudo arrasa... Até aquela antiguidade de raça, aqui pegada à sua velha Torre, há mil anos... Até agora aquele arranque para a África... Assim todo completo, com o bem, com o mal, sabem vocês que ele me lembra?
>
>—Quem?...
>
>—Portugal.
>
>(*A Ilustre Casa*, 361–362; Ch. 12)

["Perhaps you'll laugh. But I declare there's a resemblance. All Gonçalo's different qualities, his weaknesses, his kindness, his goodness.... His crazes and enthusiasm, which peter out almost immediately, but at the same time his persistence and tenacity when he really latches on to an idea... His generosity, his carelessness, his invariable chaos in business matters, his sentiments of honour, certain scruples, almost puerile, don't you agree?... His imagination, which leads him always to exaggerate to the point of lying, and at the same time a practical spirit, always aware of the utility of a thing. His liveliness, his facility in understanding, in picking things up... His constant expectation of some miracle occurring, the old miracle of Ourique which will prove the answer to all his difficulties... His vanity, the pleasure he takes in dressing-up, in shining, and his simplicity, which impels him to give his arm to a beggar in the street... A streak of melancholy, in spite of his talkativeness and sociability. His terrible lack of confidence in himself which intimidates and restrains him, until one day he makes a decision and turns out to be a hero, destroying everything... Even the antiquity of his family, stuck in their old Tower here for a thousand years... Even that sudden departure to Africa... Just as he is, good mixed with bad, do you know whom he reminds me of?"

"Who?"

"Portugal."

(Stevens, 309–310)]

The status of that detailed character analysis of a man and a nation is questionable when made by a personage who has heretofore shown no such analytic powers and no such perceptiveness. Nonetheless, it does set Gonçalo in a proper perspective. In fact, the obvious symbolic aspects of *A Ilustre Casa*—aspects based almost entirely on the symbolic status of its protagonist—have led several students of the novel to label it not Naturalistic, or even Realistic, but symbolic[13] or philosophical.[14]

Gonçalo Mendes Ramires has inherited lordship over the Ramires holdings, a considerable amount of land in rural Northern Portugal on which he lives and which he leases yearly to tenant overseers. He is thereby provided with an income—not huge, but sufficient—on which he can exist without having to work. The common people of the area look up to him, just as their forebears of centuries past looked up to past *fidalgos* of the House of Ramires; Gonçalo is thus provided with a lofty social standing he has not had to earn. His social position and inherited income have allowed him to attend the University at Coimbra; indeed, he is just returned from his university years to live on the Ramires estate. In sum, in all his life Gonçalo has had to earn nothing by the sweat of his own brow; life has been easy. The almost effortless attainment of at least basic comforts has created in Gonçalo a "devil," to use a term employed by the critic Edgard Marques (192–194), a "devil" that is his almost instinctive conviction that things need not be worked for. The plot of what is in essence a sort of *Bildungsroman* involves Gonçalo's realization of the adverse effects on his character of the pact with his personal "devil" and a victory over that devil by leaving his life in Portugal for a four-year stay in Africa, during which time he presumably learns to create a life for himself instead of accepting it from his society. He thus casts off the inertia that has plagued him and becomes a vigorous, creative being.

A plot so structured is divisible into three parts. The first is establishment of the problem in its detail. In *A Ilustre Casa* that part takes the form of a presentation of Gonçalo's character while the pact with his personal devil is in full effect. The bulk of the novel is occupied with establishment of the problem; Gonçalo is followed through day-to-day existence in his small corner of Portuguese society, and his thoughts are exposed to the reader's scrutiny. The second part is the protagonist's coming to grips with his problem. Gonçalo's realization begins weakly and grows gradually to a point at which he resolves to take action to rid himself of the "devil." The third part is the "after" stage: the protagonist's living of a new and presumably better life free from the "devil." In the case of a Gonçalo Mendes Ramires, a protagonist who symbolizes a nation, his resolution of his problem—a resolution that involves his recognition of the "devil" and his ridding himself of it—obviously has importance for the nation he symbolizes.

Since Gonçalo's character is presented, in psychological detail, through his interaction with the day-to-day details of his society, he is also a single, functioning member of the society he symbolizes. Such is the nature of a symbol. It is not an abstract label standing for something else; it in some sense *is* what it symbolizes. And Gonçalo *is* a living example of the Portugal of his day. The problems of Portuguese society dealt with by reference to the character of a single symbolic being are thus at the same time presented and exemplified by an examination of social dynamics. Thus some of the basic characteristics of the laboratory novel remain in force in *A Ilustre Casa*.

The Gonçalo the reader comes to know is a witty, learned man. He had been an idealist, a liberal—even a republican—in his university days. At that time he had broken off his friendship with André Cavaleiro, now the powerful political leader of the area in which Gonçalo lives, because Cavaleiro without explanation jilted Gonçalo's sister Graça just before, as Gonçalo understood it, their engagement was to be announced. At that time Cavaleiro was already not only a rising political figure but a dashing lady's man. Consequently Gonçalo was convinced that Cavaleiro had been toying with Graça's affections, and regarded that action as an insult to the Ramires name, and, implicitly, to himself as the male continuer of that name. Since that time Gonçalo has attacked Cavaleiro as often as possible both in word and in print, thus making his feud with his erstwhile friend common knowledge.

This stance is very idealistic-sounding. But in practice it has had a severely damaging effect on Gonçalo's life, for Cavaleiro's party is firmly in power in the area, and Gonçalo, at least partially because of his animosity toward Cavaleiro, has allied himself with the opposition party. The problem in that political affiliation is that its disadvantageous nature rules out the political sphere as an area in which Gonçalo may make his name. He is acutely aware of his position as scion of the noble line of Ramires and strongly desires to accomplish something that will contribute to the ongoing fame of that line and justify his position in it.

Gonçalo's identification with the Ramires line, as well as with one area—nationalistic literature—into which he has delved in an effort to make his own name, is graphically and sarcastically pointed up in the following passage. He has spent the good part of a day working on a novelette, couched in an outdated Romantic-Medieval style, about his ancestor Tructesindo Ramires, using as source "The Castle of Santa Ireneia," a poem on the same subject that had been published by a more recent forebear, a Romantic poet, in a newspaper entitled *The Bard*. He has just finished work for the day; the narrator reports:

> ... Estava esfalfado, à banca do trabalho desde as nove horas, a reviver intensamente, e em jejum, as energias magníficas dos seus fortes avós! Numerou as tiras—fechou na gaveta à chave o volume do "Bardo". Depois à janela, com o colete desabotoado, ainda lançou o brado genial num grave e rouco tom, como o lançaria Tructesindo:—"... de mal com o Reino e com o rei, mas de bem com a honra e comigo!..." E sentia nele realmente toda a alma de um Ramires, como eles eram no século XII, de sublime lealdade, mais presos à sua palavra que um santo ao seu voto, e alegremente desbaratando, para a manter, bens, contentamento e vida!
>
> (59; Ch. 3)

[He was exhausted, at his work-desk since nine o'clock, reviving [*sic; read* reliving] with intensity, and with nothing in his stomach, the mighty vigour of his forebears! He numbered the sheets, and locked *The Bard* carefully in the drawer. Then standing at the window, his waistcoat unbuttoned, he boomed forth, in the deep, grave tone that Tructesindo would have used, the fine phrase: "I shall be on bad terms with king and country, but on the right side of honour and conscience!" And he felt these words contained the very essence of the Ramires soul, as the

Ramires were in the twelfth century—sublimely loyal, bound to their promise, ready and willing to sacrifice all their goods and peace of mind and even their lives!

(Stevens, 51)]

The remark that he is reliving in his literary stint the "mighty vigour of his forebears" is, in the larger context of the novel, ironic in Eça's usual style. The suggestion is that the effort expended in his few hours of writing in some sense matches those energies. In point of fact all Gonçalo has done is to spend a few hours without eating—he has an intermittent digestive problem anyway—and in that time he has plagiarized part of a work left by an earlier Ramires, hence his care to lock up the work from which he is plagiarizing. The discrepancy between the facts of the matter and what Gonçalo does to those facts in his mind provides insights both into Gonçalo's character and into one of the comparisons upon which Eça's consistently ironical presentation of character is based. Gonçalo is a self-deceiver, a rationalizer, a weaver of fantasies. His standard mental process is justification of his weak-willed actions, even to the point of open lying, in an effort to make it seem either that those actions are more noteworthy than in fact they are or that he is prevented by forces outside himself from performing more nobly. (The latter reason has some truth to it, but Gonçalo comes to discover that these outside forces are not insuperable.) His rationalizations, then, including his idealization, for his own and others' benefit, of his political stance, are products of a psychological defense mechanism. The reader learns of that character trait through Eça's ironic presentation of the action of the novel. In the above passage, for example, Eça manipulates three factors to create irony. The first factor is the reader's recognition of the true value of Gonçalo's literary labors; Gonçalo himself is of course aware that he is a plagiarist, but he refuses to admit that fact, even to himself. Instead he idealizes his plagiarism into laborious creation. The reader thus becomes aware of the discrepancy that exists between the true value of Gonçalo's efforts and the value that Gonçalo himself attributes to those efforts; that awareness is a second ingredient in Eça's irony. The reader is also made aware, through the novelette on which Gonçalo is working, of the brutally individualistic, self-affirmative nature of the life Gonçalo's forebears led, at least according to Gonçalo's sources, which at this point in the novel he accepts without question. Gonçalo's efforts in no sense equal those of such men—except in his mind. Thus is the irony of Gonçalo's words impressed upon the reader.

There exists in other places in the novel a very important fourth element often used by Eça in his ironic character presentation: Gonçalo's misinterpretation of precisely what the essence of his forebears' life in fact was, or rather his mistranslation of it into the terms of his own life. In the passage reproduced above he clearly recognizes the independence, integrity, and self-assertiveness of Tructesindo Ramires as depicted in the poem from which he is plagiarizing. But when he contemplates contributing to the honor of the Ramires name, he thinks, because deep inside himself he feels incapable of incarnating such characteristics, of social status instead. Even those literary labors that he sometimes idealizes to himself and more often brags about to others are in fact no more than efforts to achieve a status that will prove his worth as a Ramires both to the world and, what is more important, to himself. As is typical with him, he rationalizes away that fact and, furthermore, takes no concrete action toward attainment of even the goal of social status. He instead creates fantasies about what the nature of his glorious future atop the heap will be. Tructesindo had tried to impose his will on the world, whereas Gonçalo's key trait is his passivity; he waits for things to happen to him, for opportunities to arise, feeling that somehow they will. Actual effort toward accomplishment is minimal, as this characteristic rationalizing meditation shows:

> ...Deputado—como?...Agora só lhe restava esperar. Esperar, trabalhando; ganhando em consistência social; edificando com sagacidade, sobre a base do seu imenso nome histórico, uma pequenina nomeada política; tecendo e estendendo a malha preciosa das amizades partidárias, desde Santa Ireneia até ao Terreiro do Paço... Sim! Eis a teoria esplêndida:—mas consistência, nomeada, afeições políticas, como se conquistam? "Advogue, escreva nos jornais!", fora o conselho distraído e risonho do seu chefe, o Brás Vitorino. Advogar em Oliveira, mesmo em Lisboa? Não podia, com aquele seu horror ingénito, quase psicológico, a autos e papelada forense. Fundar um jornal em Lisboa como o Ernesto Rangel, seu companheiro de Coimbra no Hotel Mondego? Era façanha fácil para o neto adorado da sr.ª D. Joaquina Rangel, que armazenava dez mil pipas de vinho nos barracões de Gaia. Batalhar num jornal de Lisboa? Nessas semanas de capital, sempre pelo Banco Hipotecário, sempre com as "primas", nem formara relações duráveis e úteis nos dois grandes diários regeneradores, "A Manhã" e "A Verdade"... De sorte que, realmente, nesse muro que o separava da fortuna só descobria um buraquinho, bem apertado mas serviçal—os "Anais de Literatura e de História", com a sua colabor-

ação de professores, de políticos, até de um ministro, até de um almirante, o Guerreiro Araújo, esse tocante maçador. Apareceria pois nos "Anais" com a sua "Torre" [a novela], revelando imaginação e um saber rico. Depois, trepando da Invenção para o terreno mais respeitável da Erudição, daria um estudo (que até lhe lembrara no comboio, ao voltar de Lisboa!) sobre as "Origens Visigóticas do Direito Público em Portugal"... Oh, nada conhecia, é certo, dessas Origens, desses Visigodos. Mas, com a bela "Historia da Administração Pública em Portugal" que lhe emprestara o Castanheiro, comporia corrediamente um resumo elegante... Depois, saltando da Erudição às Ciências Sociais e Pedagógicas—porque não amassaria uma boa "Reforma do Ensino Jurídico em Portugal" em dois artigos maçudos, de homem de Estado?...

(28–29; Ch. 2)

[...A Deputy! How could he be?...All he could do now was wait. Wait, and work as he waited, improving his social contacts, carefully building on the foundation of his exceptional historical name, a small political reputation, weaving and spreading a precious net of political friendships from Santa Ireneia to Black Horse Square...That was it! There was the splendid theory—but how were contacts and reputation and political friends to be achieved? "Work as a lawyer, write for the papers!" had been the smiling, distraught advice of his leader, Bras Vitorino. Established as a lawyer in Oliveira, or even in Lisbon? He couldn't, with the innate, almost physiological horror he had of official records and judicial documents. Start a paper in Lisbon like Ernesto Rangel, his friend from Coimbra at the Hotel Mondego? It was a simple task for the adored grandson of Sra. Dona Joaquina Rangel who had 10,000 casks of wine stored away in warehouses in Gaia. Fight his way through a Lisbon newspaper? These last weeks in the capital, always in the Mortgage Bank or with his cousins, he had not formed any solid and useful relations with the two big Regenerator Papers, *The Morning* and *The Truth*. So really in this wall which divided him from fortune he could discover only one little hole, difficult to get through but possible—*The Annals of History and Literature*, with its collaboration by Professors, Politicians, even a Minister, and even an Admiral, Guerreiro Araujo, that thundering bore. He would therefore make his debut in *The Annals* with his *Tower* [his novelette], revealing his imagination and his wealth of learning. Then moving from Fiction to the more respectable field of

Erudition, he would produce a study (which he had thought of in the train, returning to Lisbon) on *The Visigothic Origins of Public Right in Portugal*... It's true he knew nothing about such origins and such Visigoths. But with the magnificent *History of Public Administration in Portugal* which Castanheiro had lent him, he should be able to compose an elegant summary quite effortlessly... Then, jumping from Erudition to Social and Pedagogic Sciences, why not cook up a good *Reform of Juridical Education in Portugal* in two tedious articles, from a Statesman?...

(Stevens, 24–25)]

Such plans are, of course, largely pipe dreams. Gonçalo is in fact unable to complete his proposed novelette, "The Tower of Dom Ramires," until he begins to recognize his problem and to remedy it. And even in pipe-dreaming he plans to do as little actual work as will be necessary to build a reputation. Besides plagiarizing *The Bard*, he intends his fancied article on Visigothic origins of public law to be an "elegant summary" that he can throw together "quite effortlessly."

The constant writing of the novelette throughout *A Ilustre Casa* is an excellent device to keep the various ironic comparisons before the reader's eyes. As the novelette is being written, it passes through Gonçalo's mind and is duly reported, verbatim, by the narrator to the reader. Thus the reader is ever aware, as in Garrett's *Camões*, of two historical eras. In Eça's novel the eras are the present in which Gonçalo is living and writing and the Medieval past in which the bloody tale of Tructesindo Ramires's revenge as told by Gonçalo is set. While the terms in which that past era is presented must be regarded as primarily fictitious, they nonetheless have multiple effects upon Gonçalo's concept of himself. And the reader can know about Tructesindo Ramires exactly what Gonçalo knows about him and can see and analyze Gonçalo's aforementioned misuse of the information received.

The plot of the novelette involves Tructesindo's ghastly vengeance upon a young foe who has dared to consider marriage to Tructesindo's daughter over Tructesindo's objection and who has killed Tructesindo's son. In his actions throughout the novelette Tructesindo exemplifies the motto Gonçalo feelingly and therefore laughably quotes (see above, p. 112). Tructesindo, whether right or wrong, is ever decisive and forceful.

There is one very important comparison between Gonçalo's situation in his world and Tructesindo's in his that Gonçalo through most of the novel refuses to make. For the sake of his conception of his daughter's honor and his own, Tructesindo sacrifices his son, sets in motion a battle between great numbers of men, and then puts his defeated foe to death by the horrible means of tying him half-submerged in a leech pool and watching him cringe and cry out as the leeches drain him of his blood. Gonçalo, on the other hand, sacrifices his sister to his desire to be a deputy. When the representative of his area suddenly dies, he patches up his feud with André Cavaleiro—all along rationalizing away his actions—in order to get the support of Cavaleiro's party for his campaign to fill the vacant position. In so doing he knowingly puts Graça, now married, in a position to be again prey to Cavaleiro's advances, although again he tries to rationalize away that knowledge.

At this point in the novel Gonçalo is faced with a choice between his own "devil," personified in the world outside him in the figure of André Cavaleiro, and a kind of grace, the alternative to be selected if he upholds the honor of Graça. He proves his idealism to be sham by choosing the "devil." It has been noted that Eça de Queiroz, in good Dickensian style, often names his characters significantly;[15] in this case the names are almost allegorical. The "devil" figure is named André Cavaleiro. His diabolism comes not only from his representing the easy way to status, at the price of one sister and Gonçalo's soul, but also from his personifying almost exactly what Gonçalo would like to be if all his ambitions were achieved. Cavaleiro leads a life that embodies the ease, social prominence, and political power that Gonçalo wishes. Gonçalo confesses to those wishes in the following passage, which is the beginning of the mental soliloquy that later includes the passage reproduced immediately above:

> —... Não! Não se enterraria na província, imóvel sob a hera e a poeira melancólica das coisas imóveis, como a sua Torre!... Mas vida elegante em Lisboa, entre a sua parentela histórica, como a aguentaria com o conto e oitocentos mil réis de renda que lhe restava, pagas as dívidas do papá? E depois realmente vida em Lisboa só a desejava com uma posição política,—cadeira em S. Bento, influência intelectual no seu Partido, lentas e seguras avançadas para o Poder....
> (28; Ch. 2)

> [... No, he wouldn't bury himself in the provinces, motionless beneath the ivy and melancholy dust of lifeless things like the Tower!... But how could he lead an elegant life in Lisbon, among his noble relations, with the 1,800 *mil-reis* of rent which was all he had left after his father's debts had been paid? Really he would only want to live in Lisbon if he secured a good political position—a seat in São Bento, an intellectual influence in his Party, slow and secure steps towards Power....
> (Stevens, 24)]

And in a moment of braggadocio he provides to his circle of acquaintances a more realistic view of what his ambitions entail:

> ...Portugal é uma fazenda, uma bela fazenda, possuída por uma parceria. Como vocês sabem há parcerias comerciais e parcerias rurais. Esta de Lisboa é uma "parceria política", que governa a herdade chamada Portugal...Nós os Portugueses pertencemos todos a duas classes: uns cinco a seis milhões que trabalham na fazenda, ou vivem nela a olhar...e que pagam; e uns trinta sujeitos em cima, em Lisboa, que formam a "parceria", que recebem e que governam. Ora eu, por gosto, por necessidade, por hábito de família, desejo mandar na fazenda. Mas, para entrar na "parceria política", o cidadão português precisa uma habilitação—ser deputado. Exactamente como, quando pretende entrar na Magistratura, necessita uma habilitação—ser bacharel. Por isso procuro começar como deputado, para acabar como parceiro e governar....
>
> (103; Ch. 4)

> [...Portugal is an estate, a beautiful estate run by a partnership. As you know there are commercial partnerships and rural ones. The one in Lisbon is a political partnership which rules the estate called Portugal...We Portuguese belong to two classes: five or six million that work on the land or that live on it and simply sit and watch...and pay; and some thirty odd individuals on top, in Lisbon, who form a partnership—those who receive and rule. Now I, as a matter of inclination, a matter of necessity, as a matter of family habit, wish to govern my estate. But to enter this political partnership the Portuguese citizen needs a qualification—to be a deputy. Just as one needs a qualification when entering the magistrature—a degree in law. That is why I wish to begin as a deputy so that later I can become a member of the partnership and rule....
>
> (Stevens, 88–89)]

This is a very acute analysis on Gonçalo's part of why he wishes to be like André Cavaleiro, why he would like to be precisely a *cavaleiro*, a "nobleman," which he is in name but not in fact. Hence the proper name for the "devil." The timid Gonçalo would also like to have Cavaleiro's way with women; but even in the case of his strong physical attraction to the rich widow Ana Lucena—an attraction he has succeeded in denying to himself until after her husband has died—Gonçalo acts through his cousin, who is Ana's confidante, rather than acting on his own behalf. He hopes that by some miracle Ana may be in love with him so that he will not have to win her. Gonçalo will later come to see the triviality of his wish to become a *cavaleiro*, but as of now achievement of even that ambition must be given to him.

The other alternative is grace, allegorized by his sister Graça. Graça herself hardly embodies any such spiritual quality; she is shallow and more than a bit susceptible to Cavaleiro's advances—Ramires of the age, female version. It is in Gonçalo's attitude toward Graça's situation with Cavaleiro that his grace is won or lost. Instinctively Gonçalo opposes their relationship; but his future depends upon Cavaleiro's good will. He therefore tries to ignore the existence of the renewed relationship, thereby ignoring too the necessity to make a choice between grace and the "devil." When he finds Graça alone with Cavaleiro one afternoon, he flees the scene to avoid taking a stand; his choice is thus made by default. He has chosen the "devil," but will later achieve grace by casting off the behavior patterns that suffocate him and asserting himself as an independent being, thus symbolically freeing himself from the "devil."

Gonçalo's problem, then, is moral timidity, weakness of character. He needs preestablished patterns within which to structure his psychic life. He is unoriginal, uncreative, accepting, passive. Those traits are emphasized in the relationship that he sets up between himself and the material of the novelette that he is writing: rather than evaluate himself realistically in relation to the general terms in which the character of Tructesindo Ramires is drawn, Gonçalo instead accepts the ridiculous Romantic surface of the story, lives vicariously through Tructesindo, and glories in his familial link to the historical-literary hero.

It can be said that Gonçalo is no worse than the society in which he lives; or perhaps it is better said that the society is no better than he is. After all, André Cavaleiro, who is the sum of what Gonçalo wants to be, is a highly admired pillar of that society; he embodies its noblest aspirations. Gonçalo is largely a product of societal ambitions, ambitions he has accepted in lieu of peculiarly personal aspirations based on inner individual strength. And the societal ambitions demand no more of the individual than that he seek to be an André Cavaleiro. Almost all of Gonçalo's friends encourage him to glory in his name and in the past, merely to accept his inherited social standing, and, finally, to run for the deputy's seat under Cavaleiro's guidance.

And most of these friends clearly gain in self-importance by being friends of the prominent Deputy Gonçalo Mendes Ramires. They rejoice when he wins, Graça and her husband most of all. In fact, most of the people of Gonçalo's district make the same self-satisfying identification. They are unreflective beings, just like Gonçalo in his initial stage. They demand of themselves no individuality; they seek no strong sense of individual identity. As a result, they blindly follow traditional political patterns no matter what the situation. Gonçalo notices this attitude during his canvass, and it becomes one of the factors that lead to his comprehension of the paltriness of his ambition and the emptiness of its realization. It was too easy. Anyone could have been elected. He did not *win* a seat; he instead allowed himself *to be placed* in a social structure. The people are critical neither of themselves nor of their leaders. They demand high quality of neither, thereby producing mediocrity in both. That analysis represents an attack on Eça's part against the practices of Portuguese society under the Constitutional Monarchy in the name of Liberal individualism. Thus is Gonçalo's personal situation integrated into the national situation.

Gonçalo's recognition of his lack of creativity is gradual. He is introspective by nature, but in the early stages of the novel that introspection is largely a rationalizing, self-justificatory process. He eventually becomes somewhat more realistically introspective than before, thereby seeing his position more clearly. Then he undergoes such moments of painful self-appraisal as this solitary one, in which he compares himself to the Ramireses of the past:

> ... Não! nem sequer deles herdara a qualidade por todos herdada através dos tempos—a valentia fácil. Seu pai ainda fora o bom Ramires destemido—que na falada desordem da romaria da Riosa avançava com um guarda-sol contra três clavinas engatilhadas. Mas ele... Ali, no segredo do quarto apagado, bem o podia livremente gemer—ele nascera com a *falha*, a falha de pior desdouro, essa irremediável fraqueza da carne, que, irremediavelmente, diante de um perigo, uma ameaça, uma sombra, o forçava a recuar, a fugir....
>
> E a alma... Nessa calada treva do quarto bem o podia reconhecer também, gemendo. A mesma fraqueza lhe tolhia a alma! Era essa fraqueza que o abandonava a qualquer influência, logo por ela levado como folha seca por qualquer sopro. Porque a prima Maria uma tarde adoça os espertos olhos e lhe aconselha, por trás do leque, que se interesse pela D. Ana—logo ele, fumegando de esperança, ergue sobre o dinheiro e a beleza de D. Ana uma presunçosa torre de ventura e luxo. E a eleição? essa desgraçada eleição? Quem o empurrara para a eleição, e para a reconciliação indecente com o Cavaleiro, e para os desgostos daí emanados? O Gouveia, só com leves argúcias, murmuradas por cima do *cache-nez*, desde a loja do Ramos até à esquina do Correio! ... Homem de tal natureza, por mais bem dotado na

inteligência, é massa inerte a que o mundo constantemente imprime formas várias e contrárias.... Que miséria! E todavia o Homem só vale pela Vontade—só no exercício da Vontade reside o gozo da Vida. Porque se a Vontade bem exercida encontra em torno submissão—então é a delícia do domínio sereno: se encontra em torno resistência—então é a delícia maior da luta interessante. Só não sai gozo forte e viril da inércia que se deixa arrastar mudamente, num silêncio e macieza de cera... Mas ele, ele, descendendo de tantos varões famosos pelo Querer—não conservaria, escondida algures no seu ser, dormente e quente como uma brasa sob cinza, uma parcela dessa energia hereditária?... Talvez! Nunca, porém, nesse peco e encafuado viver de Santa Ireneia a fagulha despertaria, ressaltaria em chama intensa e útil. Não! pobre dele! Mesmo nos movimentos da alma onde todo o homem realiza a liberdade pura—ele sofreria sempre a opressão da sorte inimiga!
(276–277; Ch. 10)

[... No! He had not even inherited the quality possessed by all of them throughout the centuries—natural courage. His father had still been a fearless Ramires, who, in the famous pilgrimage of Riosa, had advanced with a sunshade against three cocked rifles. But he... There, in the privacy of the darkened room, he could give vent freely to this bitter thought—he had been born with a flaw, the most discreditable flaw—this irremediable weakness of his which, in the face of any danger, any threat, any shadow, forced him to retreat, to flee....

And his soul... In the silent murkiness of his room he could face the painful fact: the same weakness constrained his soul! It was this weakness that abandoned him to any influence, that whipped him up like a dry leaf, the plaything of any little breeze. Because one afternoon Cousin Maria's sharp eyes melt and she advises him from behind her fan to take an interest in Dona Ana, he, immediately, panting with expectation, builds on Dona Ana's fortune and beauty a lofty tower of happiness and luxury. And the election? This wretched election? Who had pushed him towards it and towards the indecent reconciliation with Cavaleiro, and the resulting troubles? Gouveia, with a few shrewd remarks murmured over his muffler as they walked from Ramos's shop to the corner where the Post Office was!... A man with such a character, however intelligent he might be, is an inert lump which the world is forever moulding into various and contrary forms.... How wretched! Yet it was Man's will that counted—only in the exercise of the will does enjoyment in life reside. Because, if a carefully applied will encounters submission, there is the pleasure of serene domination; if it encounters resistance, there is the greater pleasure of an interesting battle. The only state which provides no strong, virile pleasure is that inertia which lets itself be dragged mutely along in wax-like silence and passivity. But he, descended from so many men famous for their strong will, had he not buried somewhere in his Being, warm and dormant like a hot coal beneath dead ashes, some spark of this hereditary energy?... Perhaps! But never in all his stupid and thwarted life in Santa Ireneia had the spark burst into life, into an intense and useful flame. No! Poor Gonçalo! Even in the movements of his soul, where most men achieve pure liberty, he always suffered the oppression of hostile Fate!

(Stevens, 236–237)]

This meditation, applicable not only to Gonçalo but to the other individuals of his society and in that way to the society itself, is still to some degree self-justificatory. Gonçalo has not yet allowed himself to realize that even "hostile Fate" can be challenged by the strong, individualistic will he speaks of so hopefully.

He finally discovers his own will in an unusual way. Just as the dilemma between Gonçalo's integrity and his "devil" was dramatized by means of aptly named living representations of those alternatives, so his discovery of his will is dramatized by actual events of symbolic importance. In rummaging through the attic, Gonçalo's servant Bento has found a whip that obviously belonged to one of Gonçalo's ancestors. The whip indicates the self-assertive life of past generations of Ramireses and thus serves as a symbol of that self-assertiveness—that hot coal—which Gonçalo seeks in his own makeup. Its resting-place links it to his heritage. He has quite literally inherited it from his family past as though it were a trait passed down to him. If one takes the fact that the whip has lain hidden in an attic as symbolic of Gonçalo's will lying hidden in the back of his mind, then the act he performs with the whip gains significance for his psychological development. He is confronted on the road by a bully who has been his constant bête noire, always pointing up to Gonçalo his lack of courage. This time the *fidalgo* "num inconsciente arranque, como levado por uma furiosa rajada de orgulho e força, que se desencadeava do fundo do seu ser" (285; Ch. 10) ["in an instinctive impulse, as if driven by a gust of pride and force which issued wildly from the depths of his being" (Stevens, 244)] beats back the bully with the whip. In this act Gonçalo feels for the first time the potential for self-assertion he bears inside himself.

Total recognition of himself as an independent being possessed of a will of his own takes place on the night of his success at the polls. To surprise him and to celebrate his victory, Gonçalo's servants light up the old Ramires Tower, a physical landmark dating back to the start of the line. Entering the illuminated tower for the first time in many years, Gonçalo looks down upon the land below him and, putting in proper perspective the events of past years, ruminates:

> ... Ah! que peca, desinteressante vida [a de um deputado], em comparação de outras cheias e soberbas vidas, que tão magnificamente palpitavam sob o tremeluzir dessas mesmas estrelas! Enquanto ele se encolhia no seu paletó, deputado por Vila-Clara, e no triunfo dessa miséria—pensadores completavam a explicação do universo; artistas realizavam obras de beleza eterna; reformadores aperfeiçoavam a harmonia social; santos melhoravam santamente as almas; fisiologistas diminuíam o velho sofrer humano; inventores alargavam a riqueza das raças; aventureiros magníficos arrancavam mundos de sua esterilidade e mudez... Ah! esses eram os verdadeiramente homens, os que viviam deliciosas plenitudes de vida, modelando com as suas mãos incansadas formas sempre mais belas ou mais justas da humanidade. Quem fora como eles, que são os sobre-humanos! E tal acção tão suprema requeria o génio, o dom que, como a antiga chama, desce de Deus sobre um eleito? Não! Apenas o claro entendimento das realidades humanas—e depois o forte querer.
>
> (344; Ch. 11)

[... Ah! What a stupid, uninteresting life [the life of a deputy], by comparison with others full of supreme vitality, which pulsated so magnificently beneath the flickering of these same stars! As he huddled in his jacket, deputy for Vila Clara, triumphant at this miserable success—thinkers completed their explanations of the Universe; artists achieved works of eternal beauty; reformers perfected social harmony; saints improved souls in saintly fashion; physiologists lessened human suffering; inventors increased the wealth of nations; magnificent explorers wrested worlds from sterility and silence... Ah, these really were men, improving and embellishing humanity with their tireless hands! If only he were like them, the superhuman! Did such a supreme action need Genius—the gift that, like the ancient flame, descended from God upon the elect? No! Merely a clear understanding of human realities—and then a strong enough desire.

(Stevens, 294)]

The change from earlier self-analysis is significant. Gonçalo now sees in universal terms, going beyond the ambitions he has weakly accepted from society to envisioning the possibility of an individualistic, creative life. He, who earlier referred to himself as suffering from a "wax-like silence and passivity" (see above, p. 121), now contemplates the possibility of molding life himself. The difference between those two attitudes—the one passive, the other assertive—marks the difference between the Gonçalo of the first or problem stage and the Gonçalo of the stage in which he recognizes and comes to grips with his problem. He then goes off to Portuguese Africa and becomes a successful plantation developer/owner.

Thus is there a new element added to Eça's novel-based social criticism. The analysis of social problems continues, more or less as before, as does the creation of a crisis. For the first time, however, a character overcomes the stumbling blocks and moves free of victimization by social forces—a character whose symbolic dimensions have universalizing force within the Portuguese sphere. In Eça's earlier work, the most that happened was a throwing-up of hands on the part of characters in acknowledgment of the fact that they were aware of their entrapment. It is therefore important to examine the circumstances of Gonçalo's transformation.

The change is dramatic, and it seemingly takes place in a relatively short period of time. The dramatic nature of the change, magnified by the obvious symbolic aspects of its presentation to the reader, makes it seem unreal; but the language of Gonçalo's meditations indicates, however subtly, that a psychological process is in operation deep inside him in a synergistic relationship with symbolic external events. Such external events as the one in which Gonçalo uses the whip on his tormentor only corroborate in a dramatic way the process of internal change that Gonçalo is undergoing. The plot of the novel, seen only through those external events, has an almost allegorical nature. As such it is a plot in which the protagonist exorcises the "devil," to whom he has sold his soul, by taking up the whip, emblematic of the vigor of his forebears, and using it in a show of self-affirmation. The surface mathematical precision of that plot structure reproduces, in a new way, the syllogistic/scientific plot structure of earlier novels.

The reason for the change is the introduction of a radically new element into Eça's analytical model: the element of a traditional Portuguese capacity for individual creativity. It is impossible to know what ontological status Eça ascribes to that new notion—is it an actual psychic inheritance peculiar to the nation, is it a cultural heritage that may activate an already-existing human psychological feature, or is Eça in fact proposing a literary myth that he conjectures will have an activating role similar to the latter? In any case, he postulates a factor originating in Portuguese tradition that can liberate the individual from stifling social forces. Analyses of how those forces are conceived and what one must do to liberate himself from them are to be found in the soliloquy reproduced on pp. 120-2, above. There they are couched in terms that, in their concentration on individuality, are somewhat different from those of previous novels. The traditional factor adduced to that problem-solving process is seen at work in Gonçalo's psychic processes in ever-increasing proportion as the novel proceeds.[16] Indeed, while the reader accustomed to Eça's writing at first sees nothing more than irony in such passages as those reproduced above, there is in fact more. First, we see Gonçalo slowly become aware of the very elements of his life that are used to make up the irony directed at him. He comes to doubt the validity of the information received about his ancestors, to the point of seeing them as metaphors for vigor rather than as creations true in any detail. Thus, in the process of thinking about the detail of his relationship to the past and to the present that he has inherited from it he comes to take up that past as indicative of possible action and thus to use it to liberate himself from the suffocation of his heritage. Because of growing interest generated by his work on the novelette, the historical geography of his ancestral lands becomes clear and he comes virtually to live in two times at once, an occurrence that keeps the heroic-individualist paradigm, and its possible application to the present, constantly in his mind (see Chs. 10 and 11, 275–345 [Stevens, 235–295]). Even such patently ironic formulations as his parodistic bellow or his self-flagellating comparison with his ancestors, reproduced above (respectively, pp. 112-3 and 120-2) constitute early steps of character building in a world in which, for the first time in an Eça novel, ethical resolutions can have force—presumably because of the strength of the source of Gonçalo's ethical resolve. By the time Gonçalo engages in his universalizing meditation atop the Ramires Tower, that edifice has come to symbolize both his heritage and his new inner strength, and thus the symbiosis between them as well.

Several questions, however, remain. For example, how is Gonçalo "symbolic" of Portugal? Is Eça de Queiroz, the erstwhile pseudoscientific analyst of society, now willing to engage in such vague symbolism as the equating of one man's character change to a change in some such metaphysical entity as a "national character" or a "national psyche"? It would be strange were he to do so, since he ironizes that very concept in the novel, in reference to a character who gets Gonçalo to write his novelette in the first place. That character believes in just such a "national character," capable of revivification through diffusion of Romantic-Medieval literature about the Portuguese past. He comes in for heavy verbal irony as a consequence (see, for example, 9–14; Ch. 1 [Stevens, 8–13]). *A Ilustre Casa de Ramires*, by contrast, returns to a form of social analysis to provide a means of "nationalizing" Gonçalo's experience.

The final chapter is in one sense a challenge to the Portuguese to apply Gonçalo's problem-solving process to themselves. An abrupt change in authorial point of view effectively underscores that challenge: Eça now discards the limitations in viewpoint previously placed upon the narrative voice and enters the minds of other characters—especially Graça—to probe ironically into them as he probed before into Gonçalo. After the climactic scene atop the Tower of Ramires, Gonçalo is never placed on stage again. In the following, final chapter of the novel, the narrator's view remains fixed on the *fidalgo*'s relatives and acquaintances. But Gonçalo pervades that chapter without appearing in it: his name is on everyone's tongue, his accomplishments are on everyone's mind.

The last few paragraphs of the preceding chapter are a narrative résumé of Gonçalo's successes: his novelette is a success, as is his social life in Lisbon. But these are really successes only in the minds of his friends and relatives, whom the narrator shows reading about Gonçalo in the newspapers; after he has been in Lisbon only four months, they read with dismay that, as the narrator fittingly remarks, "silently and almost mysteriously" (Stevens, 296) Gonçalo has obtained a large concession of land in Zambezia and is going there to develop it. The final chapter is set four years later. In it those same friends and relatives meet in Gonçalo's house to prepare it for the return of "o nosso grande homem" (351; Ch. 12) ["the great man" (Stevens, 300)], as one of them calls him. For them he is just that; they speak of his successes with pride and of his homecoming with anticipation. As they talk, the reader comes little by little to know how they have lived the past four years. They have gone on in the same way as before; their values and behavior patterns have remained unaltered. They read, deeply impressed, a letter describing Gonçalo's arrival in Lisbon, and remark on such matters as who was there to greet him, how much money he has made, what kind of dress one of his lady greeters wore. In short, they judge

Gonçalo's accomplishments in terms of their own unchanged psychologies; and they see him as someone from whose mere friendship self-esteem can be drawn. They are still passive and accepting, as Gonçalo once was. They still demand nothing of themselves as individuals, just as Gonçalo once failed to demand anything of himself. His example has affected them not at all. The narrator several times observes that they exist "sem história" 'without history'; that is, the reality that they inherit from the past has captured and controlled them, while Gonçalo has moved from a small, inherited frame of reference to the universal frame of human endeavor, taking up that very same past and setting about again creating history.

Throughout the novel Eça has gone about illustrating one specific sort of social mechanism that, until Gonçalo's breakout, has kept all the characters in their place: the mechanism of image-creating. Indeed, that same mechanism is dealt with throughout Eça's career as a novelist; we have earlier seen its application in *O Crime do Padre Amaro* (p. 104, above). In *A Ilustre Casa de Ramires* that mechanism appears in many areas. Gonçalo is in essence a victim of socially propagated images about his position in society and the comportment consequently expected of him as a result of his lineage and his "noble" family history. His friends and acquaintances are victims of similar image-creating in the self-giving relationship that they establish with him, even though, through most of the novel, he is unworthy of the lofty position that he occupies in their minds. The holding of political office in Portugal is placed in the same light: office holders are revered as "great men" and looked up to in a manner like that in which Gonçalo is revered by his friends, while at the same time politics itself is shown in the novel to be grounded in traditional patterns of patronage and bossism—hardly designed for a creative facing of issues. In short, the mechanism perpetuates a traditionalist status quo to the detriment of the Liberal model of man and of society. And it tends to make the people psychologically subservient to that mechanism itself. Gonçalo comes to recognize the syndrome, first in relation to the ancestral "history" with which he has been afflicted, and then in his glimpses of himself as the material for an image-in-the-making: "Eis a lenda que se forma [So there's the myth forming]" (302; Ch. 10), he observes, as the news of his whipping of the attacker spreads. And we see him continue to observe the image-creating process for several pages thereafter (302–311; Ch. 10 [Stevens, 259–266]). His growing understanding of that process at work, implicit in the mental processes reported in those pages, is a key antecedent to his meditation atop the ancestral Tower and his decision to leave a society that imposes ahistoricity upon the individual, thus stifling any possibility of real achievement.

Hence the propriety of the other characters' position with relation to the narrator/authorial principle: they occupy the place that Gonçalo occupied through the bulk of the novel; they are the objects of Eça's analysis; they bear the brunt of his irony. If Eça's reasoned playing-off of one implication of his novelistic structure against another is applied to this new prominence of those formerly secondary characters, it can be assumed that, having been given the onus that Gonçalo once bore, they are being challenged, implicitly, to follow the example that Gonçalo has created in the earlier part of the novel: to seek into themselves, to be active, creative, self-critical individuals. Society, or at least the small society in which Gonçalo moved before his departure, is being challenged, on an individual-by-individual basis, to do as Gonçalo has done.

Such is Eça's mode of bridging the gap to collective application of Gonçalo's resolution. He suggests, in essence, that national tradition seen properly, internalized rather than revered as a set of images fulfilling in and of themselves, can provide the strength for multiple ethically based resolutions. That formulation has several implications. First, while abstractly logical, it seems insufficient in the light of the detail about the power of social forces over the individual that is piled up throughout the novel. One is tempted to see Gonçalo as a heroic individual case rather than potentially exemplary. Indeed, while the escape to Africa keeps the action in what was at the time more-or-less "Portuguese" cultural space, conceived, in the bourgeois ideology of the time, to be the land of economic opportunity, it is telling that Eça has to remove his hero from continental Portuguese space to find a representation of the physical world concommitant with Gonçalo's change in character, all the while having a narrative device implicitly seek application of the hero's experience to Portugal itself. One is tempted to say that the author himself is unable to find a valid mechanism for universalizing the resolution within the nation—and, consequently, that the implicit "challenge" to the characters left in Gonçalo's former world is a pessimistic, mocking one.[17] It nonetheless does represent a real challenge and a real way out, even if the possibility of its use is not seen as likely.

A second, related problem is that, while the bringing of the focus of resolution down to the individual analyzed in concert with social forces avoids "national mythologies," there is still a sort of vagueness to it when examined in social terms. For the first time in his work Eça proposes the very un-"scientific" notion that, no matter who is lord and who is subject within the complex of forces that is Portuguese society, all individual existences in the country are in one way functionally identical, bound together by a vague something called "nationality" or "tradition" and therefore open to individual ethical actions grounded in that common nationality. The effect is to subordinate close social analysis to an overarching generality. Thus, for Eça, while regeneration involves a recapturing of vigor through a detailed, tangible, individually based dialectic between past and present to the benefit of the terms of the present alone, the invocation of the symbols of regenerationism nonetheless marks the end of hard social criticism.

Fernando Pessoa in the mid-1910's—the era of both *Orpheu* and the first *Mensagem* poems. The dark tone and ultra-posed appearance may not be accidental; several *Orpheu* collaborators were wont to dress theatrically, in visual reinforcement of their anti-bourgeois *épater*.

Pessoa: the Messenger

Eça de Queiroz's last novel, the posthumously published *A Cidade e as Serras*, continues the mix of scientific and spiritualistic analysis seen in *A Ilustre Casa de Ramires*. The spiritualistic dimension deepens in that novel, however, for the work embraces in its structure the circular view of history thematically rejected in *A Ilustre Casa de Ramires*, as well as the rudiments of mythic or archetypical structuring and a corresponding view of human psychology. Seen in conjunction with our analysis of *A Ilustre Casa de Ramires*, those changes betoken a trajectory in Eça de Queiroz's novel-writing career: away from scientific social criticism in literature, toward accommodation of idealist analytical positions.

It is always difficult to postulate reasons for such changes in literary practice.[1] Nevertheless, since literature involves the artist's expression of what is for him a viable position with respect to the reality in which he finds himself, it must be presumed that by the late 1880's and the 1890's, Eça found his 1870's scientism an inadequate mode of expression. In my view, changes in the bourgeoisie's perception of the Portuguese system, in other words, of the "reality" of Eça's native country and social class, provide the cornerstone of that changed practice. The basically optimistic perception of a viable, expanding, though somewhat fragile establishment in the 1860's and 1870's gave way by the turn of the century—in the face of financial and budgetary crisis, demonstration of military inferiority on the international scene,[2] and revelation of government corruption—to a view that was decidedly pessimistic. The optimism of the 1870's supported Eça's scientism: the novelist could legitimately sense both that the bourgeois system possessed the strength and versatility to undergo such structural "purifications" as he implicitly proposed in works such as *O Crime do Padre Amaro*, and also that the bourgeoisie was sufficiently secure in its society to accept such literarily based criticism within its intellectual and artistic marketplace. By the turn of the century, however, such considerations no longer constituted viable expression.[3]

The foregoing analysis, though clearly not a totalizing explanation of the changes in Eça de Queiroz's novelistic practice, is nonetheless given greater credibility if one examines the literature of the writers ten or twenty years younger than Eça. The so-called "Generation of 1890," for example, cultivated primarily subjective literature in which there appeared imagery of Portuguese decadence and a sense that what was left of Portugal was a series of peculiarly national psychological-spiritual qualities that had cultural distinctiveness and were good for the making of literature. Those qualities were implicitly limited to that sphere of endeavor, though it must be pointed out that the resulting literary relationship between artist and text is very different from the relationships present in the literature earlier in the nineteenth century. In some senses it can be said that in Portugal Romanticism reached total fruition only at the end of the nineteenth century and the outset of the twentieth. Perhaps because of the slow rhythm of the establishment and elaboration of the bourgeois state in Portugal, the establishing of the work as the vehicle of the artist's exploration of the nature and the contours of his personality, a primary thematic and procedural vein of literary Romanticism, came to be fully explored only at that time. While Garrett sees the subjective dimensions of the individual as the core and source of life, overflowing with gigantesque emotions, they nonetheless do not constitute the peak of self-realization; nor for that matter, does he find self-realization to be the totalizing goal that it is for many of his European Romantic contemporaries. Instead, he holds that subjective resolutions are to be reflected outward to the public forum—still the primary sphere of human endeavor. To him, literature is still primarily a means of dramatizing such resolutions rather than a vehicle through which they can be derived and refined. Such was also the case with most of his Portuguese contemporaries. Eça de Queiroz's habitual drawing of individual psychology as a function of external—even public—events represents part of that continued tendency. While European post-Romantic literature, especially poetry, developed a concept of the individual self as truly labyrinthine, the Portuguese did not really begin such areas of literary exploration until the last decades of the century. The internalizing and aestheticizing of nationalistic concerns by members of the Generation of 1890 is not as trivial as it might first seem, for it was felt that in the area of aesthetically based exploration of subjectivity, a significant, if only personal, understanding of such matters might be reached.

The "Saudosista" group, of the first decade of our century, continued that orientation with a bit less defeatism, positing, in a manner akin to Garrett's, a mutual relationship between clarification through literature of the cultural roots of "Portugueseness" and revigoration in the social sphere. Linking social revigoration to an individual, subjective understanding of the nexus between personal psychology and national status was not, to be sure, a "find" of the Saudosistas. It is present, in a minor way, in the work of the poets of 1890; as we have seen, it occurs, on an ethical basis that implicitly rejects overarching idealisms, in Eça's *Ilustre Casa*. The Saudosistas, however, brought that linking to the fore—but then they had a built-in social referent to bolster the optimistic element in their outlook: they were, in the main, Republicans. In fact, Republicanism had been a major current of political thought since the 1890's, especially in the lower echelons of the bourgeoisie. Grounded primarily in that social level, Republican revolution broke out in Lisbon in 1910; the royal family was deported; the First Portuguese Republic was proclaimed.[4]

The following paragraphs have been excerpted from a semi-literary passage that reads like a diary entry; the entire passage, dated October 30, 1908 comes from the era of pre-Republican fervor, indeed, the year in which the king and his eldest son were assassinated in Lisbon. The writer of the entry was twenty-year-old Fernando Nogueira Pessoa. The paragraphs are written in English which Pessoa had learned during the nine years (1896–1905) he spent in the South African city of Durban, where his step-father was Portuguese consul. The paragraphs read as follows:

> My intense patriotic suffering, my intense desire of bettering the condition of Portugal provoke in me—how to express with what warmth, with what intensity, with what sincerity!—a thousand plans which, even if one man could realise them, he had to have one characteristic which in me is purely negative—the power of will. But I suffer—on the very limit of madness, I swear it—as if I could do all and was unable to do it, by deficiency of will. The suffering is horrible. It holds me constantly, I say, on the limit of madness.
>
> And then ununderstood. No one suspects my patriotic love, intenser than that of everyone I meet, of everyone I know. I do not betray it; how do I then know they have it not? how can I tell their care is not such as mine. Because in some cases, in most, their temperament is entirely different; because, in the other cases they speak in a way which reveals the non-existence at least of a name patriotism.
>
> ....
>
> Besides my patriotic projects—writing of "Portugal Republic"—to provoke a revolution here, writing of Portuguese pamphlets, editing of older national literary works, creation of a

magazine, of a scientific review, etc.—other plans, consuming me with the necessity of being soon carried out... combine to produce an excess of impulse that paralyses my will. The suffering that this produces I know not if it can be described as on this side of insanity.

Add to all this other reasons still for suffering, some physical, others mental, the susceptibility to every small thing that can cause pain (or even that to a normal man could not cause any pain), add this to other things still, complications, money difficulties—join this all to my fundamentally unbalanced temperament and you may be able to *suspect* what my suffering is.[5]

The "patriotic" fervor is not uncharacteristic, either in detail or in kind, for the era. It is not surprising, then, that in the years immediately after 1910, Pessoa was a member of the Saudosista group.

Another note of interest in the passage reproduced above is Pessoa's bent for dramatic, even truculent self-analysis. Indeed, it is obvious from references in his writing that he had read the psychologists and psychological theorists of his day and applied their conclusions to himself. This appears both in such directly analytical language as that above, and also in its use as a primary basis for his literature, to a great extent a mode of the time. That inward concentration would be elaborated on and continued throughout Pessoa's literary career, until his death in 1935, producing his well-known division of himself into many different "poets" with different styles and philosophies, the most famous being: the post-Symbolist "Fernando Pessoa, himself," the "Sensationist" Álvaro de Campos, the "pagan" Alberto Caeiro, and the "decadent neo-classicist" Ricardo Reis. Pessoa apparently felt that each "poet" corresponded to a discrete frame of mind through which he occasionally passed. He therefore referred to them as "heteronyms," as distinct from mere literary "pseudonyms." He gave each a physiognomy and birth date, and has them criticize each other's work. The result is one of the most complex—and highly studied—corpuses in Portuguese literary history.

Another element characteristic of Pessoa that comes to the fore in the reproduced paragraphs is his sense of separation from most of the rest of society. In that respect he is different from most of the Saudosistas, who identified with public life in the initial years of the First Republic in a way akin to Garrett's concept of his role at the outset of the Constitutional Monarchy. Pessoa, by contrast, manifested in his writing the elitist disdain for bourgeois society common to the European avant-garde artist of the first decades of this century.[6] In fact, Pessoa was both aware of and a collaborator in that general movement, especially with the long odes of Álvaro de Campos, which clearly draw upon Marinettian Futurism.

Of the "patriotic projects" to which Pessoa refers (most of which were never completed, as was the case with many of his grandiose projects), the one that will provide the basis for the present study is his book, *Mensagem*, containing forty-four short poems about Portugal.

A commercial correspondent by trade, in his lifetime he was almost totally unknown to the Portuguese literary public, remaining essentially a cult figure known only in Bohemian artistic circles. Subsequent generations of poets publicized his existence and brought attention to his work. Critical acclaim is the product of the 1950's and later. In his life, Pessoa published almost totally in a number of small literary journals, many of which he founded, the most famous being *Orpheu*; it published only two numbers, in 1915, but gathered for that purpose much of the literary talent of the Portugal of that day. Pessoa's message to a friend and fellow collaborator in that journal is perhaps more indicative than any other formulation of his avant-garde stance: he wrote to Armando Côrtes-Rodrigues, then living in the Azores, that "the edition should be sold out soon" and that the *Orpheu* writers were "the topic of the day in Lisbon," adding, happily: "the scandal is enormous."[7] The symbiotic combination of interest in sales and pleasure in scandalizing the bourgeois public with a product that did not conform to prevalent taste accurately profiles the contradictions in Pessoa's position with regard to the public at large.

In an often-reproduced remark, Pessoa, looking back and summing up his literary career at the ripe old age of twenty-two, said: "I was a poet animated by philosophy, not a philosopher with poetic faculties" (*Páginas Íntimas*, 13). Again, the original was written in English. That statement, as is obvious from its form, is combative. In reacting to the notion, suggested to Pessoa or perhaps formulated by him, that he was a "philosophical poet," it attempts to draw a rigorous line between poetry and philosophy. For all its precision, however, it does not explain away the thematics that Pessoa's poetry would embrace throughout his life, a thematics that involved much more than mere employment of philosophical material as content for something separate to be called "poetry." The fact is that from its outset Pessoa's verse explores in minute detail the contours of subjectivity, the relationship between subjective and objective, and the implications for the first of the above problems of whatever answer was reached with regard to the second. Such stylistically experimental poems as "Impressões do Crepúsculo" (1913) and "Chuva Oblíqua" (1914) explore those problems in an almost formal manner, invoking specific bundles of imagery that are all but openly labeled "objective" in one case and "subjective" in another and then showing their intersection as the voice of the poem "perceives" reality. Indeed, the second of those poems was the poem-manifesto of a kind of poetry that Pessoa dubbed "Intersectionist." In 1914, the major heteronyms were created, and much of the philosophical-stylistic experimentation was ascribed to them, especially Campos and, to a lesser extent, Caeiro.

The heteronyms are in themselves, however, another sort of step in the problem-solving process described above: they are personified compartments representing major directions in Pessoa's thought, each the repository of a series of rationalized arguments, in poetic form, in justification of his specific direction. For that reason their poetry has about it the sense that it is the product of a process that has reduced it to the abstract and the argumentative. That sense pervades especially the work of Reis and Caeiro. Campos's "Sensationism" includes a dramatic element—that is, many of his poems revolve about himself as speaker/perceiver in an immediate, dramatic circumstance—which supports a sense of human presence and a variety of tangible imagery that mitigates in him the syllogistic nature of the heteronymic work in general.

The analysis and the rigid compartmentalization of mental directions that produces the heteronyms is indicative of another characteristic of Pessoa's thought: an almost-scientific observation of a set of phenomena—in this case, his own mental phenomena—and creation of laws, representing consistencies observed in that set, that are at the same time analytical tools for the further analysis of the system. The heteronyms in effect exercise both of those functions within the totality of Pessoa's mental "system": they are both the incorporation of consistent directions and also analytical tools. Thus it does not stretch a point too far to argue that Pessoa, in his own way, still participates in the "scientific" attitude of early Eça de Queiroz.[8] Just as Padre Amaro, of *O Crime do Padre Amaro*, represents the personification of a scientifically analyzed category—the victim of forces connected with a specific social sub-system, namely the institutional Church—so too does an Alberto Caeiro exercise similar functions for Pessoa. The differences are that in Pessoa the "system" is a subjective one, the scientism is truncated by reduction to an analytical process carried out without any accompanying accumulation of previous findings from which to begin, and the expected results are personal-existential.

That curious mixture of subjective and objective, in which subjectively reached formulations about subjective matters become ingredients of rational, even para-scientific discourse, is frequently noted about Pessoa. The Portuguese critic João Gaspar Simões treats it as follows:

"Deus geometriza", disse Platão. E Fernando Pessoa, citando este aforismo do filósofo grego, comenta: "Tanto o que temos..." "como o que teremos, já nos está dado, porque tudo é lógico". Ora, se Deus "geometriza", e tudo é lógico, que fazer quando se procura uma certeza no mundo incerto? Fiar-se da inteligência, confiar na razão,...atribuindo à inteligência, à razão, ao raciocínio poderes discricionários para resolver todos os problemas que se relacionam com a aceitação do mistério que é a vida, o mundo e o homem.

Uma distinção se impõe, todavia. Fernando Pessoa é escravo da inteligência, mas não da razão. É uma natureza intelectual, porque nele a inteligência governa os sentidos: os sentidos, nele, dependem da inteligência, o *sentir* está subordinado, nele, ao inteligir.... O racionalista pode admitir, num dado momento, a ininteligibilidade de um certo aspecto do mundo, mas nem por isso duvidará da sua inteligibilização, isto é, da sua subordinação, mais tarde ou mais cedo, às leis universais da razão; o intelectualista do tipo de Fernando Pessoa, esse, não obstante a *geometrização* a que submete o mundo, como esta geometrização é independente da experiência que o racionalismo pressupõe, faz entrar na sua construção mental tudo quanto nela pode caber: o inteligível e o ininteligível, o racional e o irracional, o visível e o invisível, o claro e o misterioso, tudo explicando, a tudo dando um sentido, dentro desse sistema, lógico nas suas conclusões, embora inteiramente desprovido de comprovação objectiva.[9]

["God geometrizes," said Plato. And Fernando Pessoa, citing that aphorism by the Greek philosopher, comments: "Both what we have...and what we shall have is already given us, because everything is logical." Now, if God "geometrizes," and everything is logical, what is one to do in the search for certainty in the uncertain world? One relies on the intelligence, on reason,... attributing to the intelligence, to reason, to ratiocination discretionary powers to solve all the problems related to the acceptance of the mystery that is life, the world, and man.

Still, one distinction is imperative. Fernando Pessoa is the slave of the intelligence but not of reason. He is an intellectual being, because in him the intelligence governs the senses: the senses, in him, depend upon the intelligence, *feeling* is subordinated, in him, to intellection.... The rationalist can admit, in a given moment, the unintelligibility of a certain aspect of the world, but he will not therefore doubt that it can be made intelligible, that is, he will not doubt that it can be subordinated, sooner or later, to the universal laws of reason; an intellectualist of Fernando Pessoa's sort—the *geometrization* to which he subjects the world notwithstanding—since such geometrization is independent of the experience presupposed by rationalism, includes in his mental construct everything that will fit in: the intelligible and the unintelligible, the rational and the irrational, the visible and the invisible, the clear and the mysterious, explaining everything and within that system giving everything a meaning logical in its conclusions but wholly devoid of objective proof.]

Pessoa's logical processing of the subjective seems to constitute a somewhat inchoate following-out of the various possible lines and modes of thought that formed his intellectual and cultural heritage; its main, though by no means sole, lines involve, on the one hand, the adoption of neo-Romantic concepts both of the centrality of the individual "self" and also of the work of art as a vehicle for self exploration and, on the other hand, a scientific analysis and organization of those concepts. In connection with the exploration of the "self," it should be noted for the reader who does not speak Portuguese that "Pessoa," a not-uncommon last name, means, as a common noun, "person" or "persona" and, by extension to its well-known roots in Classical culture, "mask," denotations upon which Pessoa constantly trades in his writing. It should also be noted that Pessoa would by no means have accepted the application to his stance of the term "neo-Romantic." Perhaps because of the peculiar trajectory of literary Romanticism in Portugal, Pessoa saw that movement as characterized only by sentimentality and a Liberal humanitarianism, both of which he found abhorrent. Unaware of the deeper senses in which he was imbued with Romanticism, he conceived of his art as anti-Romantic both in a strict literary sense and in any social applications that it might have.

In that mixture of modes of thought, he had recourse to a series of formalized resolutions to the problems that he faced in the form of the various "occult sciences" that flourished at the end of the nineteenth century and in the first decades of the twentieth. Pessoa was well versed in various branches of esoterica: he had read in Theosophy, astrology, Freemasonry, and Rosicrucianism and had progressed from them to other types of occultism, including spiritualism, automatic writing, and by the time of his death, alchemy and magic. He had read works dealing with the cabala and consequently knew of numerology. On at least one occasion he claimed the possession of certain psychic powers, including clairvoyance. He often stated that he felt he was controlled by dark forces. That he wholeheartedly believed in what he was doing at any time in his progress in the occult arts is questionable, but for the present discussion the matter is not pertinent, except as a general caveat: as is the case regarding virtually everything he dealt with, Pessoa at one time or other either hinted that he was an adept at or at least defended each of the esoteric systems into which he delved, only later to deny belief in its value, either directly or implicitly. One of his own remarks may perhaps serve better than any analysis to explain the degree of his actual belief in esoteric lore (or, for that matter, on any other single front): "A possibilidade de que ali, na Teosofia, esteja *a verdade real me hante* [The possibility that there, in Theosophy, lies *the real truth haunts me*]."[10] The point to be made is that most of those systems, in one way or another, attempt to put "selfhood" on a "scientific" basis, an attempt consonant with Pessoa's own.

Pessoa's writing, then, while not "philosophical" in a strict sense, nonetheless not only treats in practical application the systematic intellectual problems of the day but also does so at a level of abstraction and in a mode of presentation that approach many of the formal properties of traditional philosophy.

By contrast, another famous remark of his:

> ... As artes que por natureza ministram ... [o] aperfeiçoamento [do homem] são ... a música e a literatura, e ainda a filosofia, que abusivamente se coloca entre as ciências, como se ela fora mais que o exercício do espírito em se figurar mundos impossiveis.[11]

> [... The arts that by their nature provide ... [the] perfection [of man] are ... music, literature, and even philosophy, which wrongly has been located in the sciences, as if it were something more than an exercise on the part of the spirit in imagining impossible worlds.]

That pronouncement serves to modify further the above considerations. The reduction of philosophy to a process having only aesthetic value represents, in effect, Pessoa's realization, and resolution, of the question raised above about the ultimate validity of the systematic investigative processes embodied in his poetry. A characteristic of all his work is his awareness of most of the implications of what he is doing and also of possible counter-arguments. (Hence both the understated Romantic irony that pervades some sectors of his work—mostly the literary criticism and philosophical speculation ascribed simply to

"Fernando Pessoa"—and also his reduction of other sectors—i.e., the heteronyms, among them "Fernando Pessoa, himself"—to a status so simple and schematic that ironic perspectives are avoided.) The above formulation answers the implicit question as to the validity of such investigations as his own, by stating that their *results*, seen as pure product rather than as knowledge in a positive sense, constitute the only ultimate value; by implication in the general scope that the formulation arrogates to itself, it also calls into question the ultimate validity of any such process. That aestheticist stance is frequently taken up by Pessoa in his writings, either directly or implicitly. One should be careful, however, not to see it as his final answer to the basic questions with which he deals. It is really only one of the more regularly taken directions in this thought, commingling with the validity implicitly claimed by the terms of many of his arguments themselves, at least at the time of their proposition, and commingling too with a third notion: that, in carrying out his poetic investigations, while perhaps not producing answers, he is in effect increasing his own insight into the nature of existence and thus creating value within himself. Indicative of that third resolution are the various elaborations of his poetic "depersonalization scale," in which he sees the poet as increasing in insight the less he directly identifies with his poetic creation and in which he proposes a series of ascending degrees of depersonalization ("de-Pessoa-ization") through which the poet can pass in that internally productive relationship to his creation.[12]

This mixture of combined subjectivist-objectivist investigation, evaluation of investigation, and aestheticism has, so far as this one student of Pessoa's work can discern, no particular hierarchy; that is, no one direction assumes definite ascendancy over the others. Instead, a series of tensions arise that enter and add to the thematics of Pessoa's work.

Mensagem, ascribable to the heteronym "Fernando Pessoa himself," incarnates those tensions, as well as many of the other basic directions within Pessoa's work outlined above. The date commonly assigned to *Mensagem* is 1934, the date of its publication. That assignation is only superficially exact, however, as it gives no idea whatsoever of the long period of gestation that the volume underwent.

The impetus for *Mensagem*, or a book very like it, is documented as early as 1913. In that year Pessoa wrote a poem entitled "Gládio" 'Sword' and outlined in notes a plan for a book with a mystical-nationalistic theme, also to be entitled *Gládio*. It is the earliest known precursor of *Mensagem*, and it contributed directly to that later-realized volume with the poem "Gládio," which, slightly altered, became the second *Quina* 'Shield' of *Mensagem*, "D. Fernando, Infante de Portugal." The makeup of Pessoa's proposed book of nationalistic poems changed often and drastically between 1913 and 1934. By 1920 it was to be called *Portugal*, a title it seems to have kept until just before its publication.[13]

Pessoa did not hesitate either to publish parts of *Mensagem* in advance of volume publication—if we assume that he in fact always conceived of eventual volume publication—or to change, rewrite, and substitute poems up to the time of publication. One of the incentives for a final creative burst in 1934 may well have been the establishment in that year by the Secretariat of National Information of the Antero de Quental Prize for the best volume of nationalistic poetry. It should be noted, however, that by that date, the First Republic had been dead for eight years; in 1926 it had fallen to military dictatorship. By that time too, the elitism fundamental to his stance with respect to the general public having come to the fore, Pessoa had become an inveterate enemy of the Republic. He had strongly supported the dictatorship, even to the point of publishing an elaborate though highly idiosyncratic pamphlet in defense of it.[14] That stance was a characteristic one. In 1910, a good many Portuguese, as the historian Oliveira Marques has observed (*História*, II, 243–244), were in effect Republicans unclear about exactly what "Republic" might imply; by the 1920's they had wearied of the weakness of the First Republic, heir to the deficits and international dependencies of the Constitutional Monarchy—and, for that matter, of the Absolutist regime that preceeded it.[15] Nevertheless, the contest was put on not by the military men of the 1926 dictatorship but by the Estado Novo government of António de Oliveira Salazar, which gradually took over from the generals in the late 1920's and early 1930's and remained until April 25, 1974, at which point it was the longest-lived authoritarian state in Europe.[16]

Two features are immediately evident on a first reading of *Mensagem*. First, it is not a simple collection of poetry; instead the book comprises forty-four individual poems organized and interrelated in such a way as to make, if not in essence a single poem, then at least a unitary though composite work of art. The implications, for meaning-making, of the complex organization of the book are given to the reader to decipher as a part of his reading of the work. *Mensagem* constitutes, then, a highly intellectualized presentation. Second, Pessoa draws upon occultist and Sebastianist sources for considerable portions of the diction and imagery of the book, a fact that he openly publicized in his critical writings about *Mensagem* (see, for example, *Páginas Íntimas*, 433–438).

Those two features collaborate in creating the overall structure of the work. It is divided into three sections. The first, entitled *"Brasão"* 'Coat of Arms', contains nineteen poems, each, after the first two general poems, concentrating on a figure from Portuguese history. Each poem is assigned to a facet of the Portuguese Royal Coat of Arms. The first two "background" poems correspond to the two heraldic *Campos* 'Fields' upon which the detailed devices of the Coat of Arms rest. The next eight poems correspond to the *Castellos* 'Castles' on the Coat of Arms. The following five correspond to the five *Quinas* 'Shields' of the Coat of Arms. The next poem refers to the *Coroa* 'Crown' and the last three to the head and two wings of the griffin that represents the *Timbre* 'Crest' of the Coat of Arms. Thus, for example, the eleventh poem of the book is called "The First Shield, Duarte, King of Portugal" and it deals with that king, the seventeenth poem is called "The Head of the Griffin, Prince Henry," and so on. The second section of the book, entitled *"Mar Portuguez"* 'Portuguese Sea', contains twelve poems dramatizing the vicissitudes of the Age of the Discoveries in terms that are primarily psychological-ethical. The third, *"O Encoberto,"* contains thirteen poems divided into three sub-sections: the first, *"Os Symbolos"* 'The Symbols'; the second *"Os Avisos"* 'The Signs'; and the third *"Os Tempos"* 'The Eras'. The poems of this third section are clearly involved in a process of giving wide symbolic dimensions to such relatively concrete language of the first two sections as references to historical figures, historical events, and processes in Portuguese history. The second of the three sub-sections invokes that process in a specific way: it includes three "Signs," the first being Bandarra, the second Padre António Vieira, and the third (though such is only implied) Fernando Pessoa. As I have argued at length elsewhere,[17] the book's tripartite structure draws upon the three-step initiatory hierarchy to be found in many of the occultist sources that Pessoa knew, from Freemasonry to ritual magic to Theosophy. Such systems, while they do not agree in detail, basically envision a first step corresponding to the ignorance of a new initiate who wishes to gain spiritual insight, the second to a struggling vicissitudinous beginning in his effort to gain such insight, and the third to his reaching of sufficient insight to proceed on his own in unending ascent into awareness of the occult secrets of the cosmos—hence, I believe, the subdivision of the third section into further levels.

Each of the three sections includes an introductory Latin epigraph that defines the nature of the contents of that section. And there are Latin formulae that precede and conclude the book. As I have shown ("The Structure of Pessoa's *Mensagem*"), they derive verbatim from a book on Rosicrucianism that Pessoa had read, constituting, within the *Mensagem* context, a salutation and valediction that can be conceived of as beginning and ending an occultist ritual. Thus the entire volume is given an air of ritual, of initiation, of inculcation of spiritual truth.

The implications of that ritual air are not immediately clear. What is the nature and purpose of the ritual, how is it accomplished, what are its lessons? The key lies in the referential system of the pronouns used in *Mensagem*.

That there is a foreground figure in some of the poems of *Mensagem* is undeniable. A number of the poems—all the "Castles"; the "Crown"; the poems of "The Crest"; "Portuguese Sea" I, V, VIII, IX; the third poem of "The Symbols"; and the first two poems of "The Signs" (nineteen poems in all)—include a foreground speaker, or *persona*, who addresses or describes the subjects of the poems, occasionally referring to the Portuguese nationality that he has in common with them. He is examining the history of his nation. It is clearly indicated in the poems that his examination takes the form of a search both for an understanding of the vigor that characterized that past and for the knowledge of how that vigor may be recaptured in the near future. The speaker is therefore a kind of epic voyager, one who journeys through the various ages of Portuguese history seeking by means of his journey to learn about the forces at work in his nation. These poems thus involve the present in confrontation with the past and invoke a constant comparison of the two eras. Most of the rest of the poems of the book—"The Fields"; "Portuguese Sea" II, IV, VI, VII, X, XI, XII; the second, fourth, and fifth poems of "The Symbols"; and "The Eras" (seventeen more poems)—are the speaker's meditations on the nature of the world and of Portugal's place in it, or his mythologizing of aspects either of that world view or of Portuguese history and Portuguese cultural dynamics. The key differences between this group of poems and the previous group are differences of subject matter and approach; the first group tends toward the concrete and the dramatic, the second toward the abstract and the meditative. The speaker's position remains the same in all thirty-six poems.

When the speaker refers to himself in those thirty-six poems (and he often does), it is always as *nós* 'we', except in the one instance of "The Final Ship," the penultimate poem of "Portuguese Sea." In that poem and in a thirty-seventh poem, the aforementioned third poem of "The Signs," the speaker is clearly singular and is almost as clearly the poetized Fernando Pessoa. In the light of that factor, *nós* might be interpreted as "I and the other present-day Portuguese." The nature of the framework in which the *Mensagem* poems are placed, however, suggests that such an interpretation is incompletely descriptive of the full meaning of *nós* in *Mensagem*. An examination of that framework indicates that the obvious speaker "I and the other present-day Portuguese" commingles in *nós* with another, more exact antecedent: "you, my present-day Portuguese reader(s) and I." The latter interpretation suggests that Pessoa, as the speaker in the poems, is leading or guiding his readers on a sort of epic voyage through the secrets of the Portuguese past and of Portuguese nationality as he, Fernando Pessoa, conceives them, and that he is inculcating upon the reader, through the language, symbolism, and structure of *Mensagem*, both the lessons that he has found in the national past and also certain conclusions that he has drawn from those lessons. Pessoa is the guru and his reader the neophyte to be initiated into the mysteries to which Pessoa holds the key. The two are thus co-voyagers, in a master-neophyte relationship to each other, through ever-more abstract formulations of the Portuguese experience, toward understanding of the nationality that they have in common and application of that understanding to the future that they hold in their hands.[18]

Here an aside should be added to Pessoa's self-poetization as a guru. In Theosophy, the terms "Messenger" and "Message" are frequently used. According to Theosophical theory the Universal Will gave one initial impulse that created the solar system. That was the Logos. Since then, the Will has sent messages to aid in the evolution of the human species, and those messages have been borne by such messengers as Christ, Lao-Tse, and so on down to Madame Blavatsky, one of the pillars of Theosophy and probably Pessoa's source for this terminology (he translated at least one of her books into Portuguese).[19] The precise manner in which a messenger becomes aware of his role and conceives of himself in that role is not totally clear, but it is clear that each message is a minor Logos, a new divine word. In entitling his book of poems *Mensagem*, Pessoa is thus playing with a multitude of possible meanings. If the book is a message, he is presumably the messenger, the bearer of a divine word—in this case, one having to do with the nature, and presumably, if he *is* such a messenger, the *future* of Portugueseness.

The voyage on which the messenger takes his initiate(s) begins, in "*Brasão*," with a canvas of the great figures of the Age of the Discoveries and before. The first two poems, in several senses "background" poems, corresponding to the heraldic background, set forth the bases of "*Brasão*" thematics. The first poem, "The Field of the Castles," suggests a fated place for Portugal in world history and hints at a "non-Romantic" Portuguese ethic. That background is added to by the second poem:

O [CAMPO] DAS QUINAS

Os Deuses vendem quando dão.
Compra-se a gloria com desgraça.

Ai dos felizes, porque são
Só o que passa!

Baste a quem baste o que lhe basta
O bastante de lhe bastar!
A vida é breve, a alma é vasta:
Ter é tardar.

Foi com desgraça e com vileza
Que Deus ao Christo definiu:
Assim o oppoz à Natureza
E Filho o ungiu.[20]

[THE FIELD OF THE SHIELDS

The Gods sell when they give.
Glory is bought with misfortune.
Pity the contented, for they are
no more than passers-by!

Let suffice to him for whom sufficient is sufficient
the sufficiency that suffices!
Life is short, the soul is vast:
to have is to lag.

It was with misfortune and with lowliness
that God defined Christ;
thus He opposed him to Nature
and anointed him His Son.]

    The poem begins with a curious statement: "The Gods sell when they give." In the second line the point of the first is driven home: what is sold is glory, and the price is misfortune (literally, 'the state of being out of grace'). The contented are transient, because, whether by choice or by fate, they achieve neither misfortune nor glory; they remain contentedly fixed between the two extremes and there effect nothing. It should be mentioned that later in *"Brasão,"* especially in the five "Shields" for which this poem is "background," Pessoa makes it clear that in his view the spirit that in the past led Portugal to preeminence in the world was a reckless, all-or-nothing spirit according to whose dictates a man's life was lived at the two extremes (which the poem suggests exist in symbiosis), never in the characterless middle ground. He hints too in the "Shields" that such a spirit is in fact characteristic of the Portuguese national genius. In the final stanza of the above poem Christ is offered as an example of the observation set forth in the first stanza. The word *vil* 'lowly', often used by Pessoa in his writings to describe Portuguese degeneracy, and appearing here in the substantive form *vileza* 'lowliness', describes Christ's earthly state.[21] Christ is "defined" as opposed to "Nature," a definition that is both a reference to the unusual depths of misfortune to which He fell before returning to Grace and a reference also to the state of Grace itself, which He was fated to achieve. "Nature," then, lies between those two extremes, approximately corresponding to the status held by "the contented," or by the persons referred to in lines 5 and 6. They are comfortable, "natural"; they will remain so, they will not attain Grace. As is suggested in the examination of such poems as "A Ultima Nau" ("The Final Ship") and "Prece" ("Prayer") of "Portuguese Sea" and the first of the "Symbols" poems, Pessoa conceives of the Portugal of his day as paying the price of the "sale," as living the lower of the two extremes. The present, he suggests in the first of the "Symbols" poems, is an interval during which the Portuguese psyche is preparing the Portuguese recapturing of preeminence. And he hints in "The Final Ship" and in "Nevoeiro" ("Fog"), the final poem of *Mensagem*, that the necessary psychic preparations will have been undergone when the Portuguese psyche becomes so undefined—becomes, indeed, a "fog" as the title of the poem suggests—that it will begin, Christ-like, to reascend to "glory." The concept underlying that notion of reascent probably derives from the theory, advanced in alchemy and in other areas of esoteric pursuit as well, that a period of benightedness is a necessary stage in the process leading to the revelation of truth.

What Pessoa offers, then, is an ethic of striving to achieve and of consequent sacrifice; all the figures of the "Shields" poems are in fact depicted as martyrs to that peculiarly national ethic. In application to King Sebastian, the fifth "Shield," that ethic is called "madness," with the addition:

> Sem a loucura que é o homem
> Mais que a besta sadia,
> Cadaver addiado que procria?
>
> [Without madness what more is man
> than a healthy animal,
> a behindhand corpse that procreates?]

The other subjects of *"Brasão"* poems are characterized as successful bearers of Portuguese fate and the Portuguese ethic so defined, in a poetic fabric that focuses on the individual, psychological, and historical—on, then, the appearances of the physical world, in concert with the focus of the first of the three steps of the generalized occultist initiatory hierarchy that gives the book its structure.

The "madness" that Sebastian above all others epitomizes is a creative ethic that emphasizes striving for achievement at all costs and is connected increasingly closely to the figure of that king in the *Mensagem* poems until "Sebastian" literally becomes a synonym for that ethic itself. In the second section of poems, "Portuguese Sea," the concentration is similar to that in the first section of the book, save that here the ethical and psychological qualities themselves provide the primary organizing element rather than the historical incarnations of those qualities. The first nine of the section's twelve poems profile either in wholly abstract terms or in broad interpretation such figures as Prince Henry and the famous navigators, Diogo Cão, Bartolomeu Dias, Magellan, and Gama. Primarily dealt with are the attitude underlying the historical achievements of such figures and the place in world history consequently earned. The eleventh and twelfth poems of the section, however, show the other extreme: the era of degeneracy, of loss.

The eleventh poem, "The Final Ship," depicts, with broad and polivalent symbolism, King Sebastian, symbol of the creative ethic, sailing off into the sea that Portugal had once "conquered," on his journey to the battle at Alcácer-Kebir:

A ULTIMA NAU

Levando a bordo El-Rei D. Sebastião,
E erguendo, como um nome, alto o pendão
Do Imperio,
Foi-se a ultima nau, ao sol aziago
Erma, e entre choros de ancia e de presago
Mysterio.

Não voltou mais. A que ilha indescoberta
Aportou? Voltará da sorte incerta
Que teve?
Deus guarda o corpo e a fórma do futuro,
Mas Sua luz projecta-o, sonho escuro
E breve.

Ah, quanto mais ao povo a alma falta,
Mais a minha alma atlantica se exalta
E entorna,

148   THE REDISCOVERERS

E em mim, num mar que não tem tempo ou spaço,
Vejo entre a cerração teu vulto baço
Que torna.

Não sei a hora, mas sei que ha a hora,
Demore-a Deus, chame-lhe a alma embora
Mysterio.
Surges ao sol em mim, e a nevoa finda:
A mesma, e trazes o pendão ainda
Do Imperio.

[THE FINAL SHIP

Carrying King Sebastian aboard
and raising high, like a name, the pennant
of the Empire,
the final ship left, alone in the ill-boding
sun, among laments of anxiousness and of prophetic
mystery.

It never returned. At what undiscovered island
did it arrive? Will it return from its uncertain
fate?
God keeps to Himself the body and the form of the future,
but His light projects it, a brief, dark
dream.

Ah, the more the people's soul fails,
the more my atlantic soul exults
and overflows.
And within me, in a sea that has neither space nor time,
I see in the fog your dim shape
returning.

I do not know the hour, but I know that there is an hour,
even though God delays it and the soul calls it
a mystery.
Within me, you appear in the sun, and the fog ends.
You look just as before, and you still bear the pennant
of [the] Empire.]

The poem embraces several thematic lines important for the overall meaning-making of *Mensagem*. First, the notion of the "dream" that is a projection produced by God's "light." Both "dream" and "God" are terms used repeatedly in *Mensagem*—and, for that matter, throughout Pessoa's writing—in restricted and idiosyncratic senses. In *Mensagem*, "God" or "Gods" imply at least in part a subjective quantity: the image that a man or a culture construes about itself that then animates its actions. Such a definition has rooting in Pessoa's speculations too complex to be developed here.[22] Suffice it to say that in the "Field of the Shields," reproduced above, as well as in the poem currently in question, that subjectivistic definition, if it is not in fact the primary denotation of the term, at very least contends with a sense of "God" as a quantity separate from man—perhaps the planner of the Portuguese destiny, much as in Padre Vieira's writings. And the establishing of an unresolved tension between those two meanings would recapitulate tenets of several occultist systems. Thus "dream," a term that at one time or another in Pessoa denotes everything from "fantasy" to "speculation," here refers to the subconscious presence in the Portuguese of a positive self-image, built upon the creative ethic and lost at the end of the Age of the Discoveries. The third stanza of the poem introduces the "I," and the poetized Pessoa, speaking to "Sebastian" (i.e., to Portuguese creativity incarnate) manifests his role as guru: he says that as he sees growth of the despair created by the negative self-image, he is conversely encouraged, for he knows that, in good occultist terms, the way down is the way up, that debasement will lead to regeneration, that the intimate linking between a life of "dis-grace" and a life of "glory" will again be realized and one will be transformed into the other. Exactly how this miraculous transformation will be achieved is dependent upon further reading.

The last poem of "Portuguese Sea" is a prayer to "God," or, perhaps—though it is less likely— to the national creative ethic itself as personified by Sebastian. The last stanza reads:

Dá o sopro, a aragem—ou desgraça ou ancia—,
Com que a chamma do esforço se remoça,
E outra vez conquistemos a Distancia—
Do mar ou outra, mas que seja nossa!

[Blow gently, give us the breeze—either "dis-grace" or aspiration—
with which the flame of effort is rejuvenated;
and let us again conquer the Distance—
the Distance of the sea or another Distance, so long as it is ours!]

The lines, suggesting that "dis-grace" itself or some sort of aspiration can provide an animating force, clearly call for both a rebirth in Portugal of the creative ethic and, as a consequence, for new conquest as well. Force to effect that rebirth is prayed for from either "God" or "Sebastian," either of which terms stands as a metaphor for aspects of the national psyche. And a new wrinkle is added: the new "distance" to be conquered may not be physical. Indeed, in elaborating upon Portugal's "Fifth Empire" to come, Pessoa often claimed that the nation's new hegemony would be not physical but cultural-intellectual. The following explanation of Portugal's future is characteristic:

> —O Quinto Império. O futuro de Portugal—que não calculo, mas *sei*—está escrito já, para quem saiba lê-lo, nas trovas do Bandarra, e também nas quadras de Nostradamus. Esse futuro é sermos tudo. Quem, que seja português, pode viver a estreiteza de uma só personalidade, de uma só nação, de uma só fé? Que português verdadeiro pode, por exemplo, viver a estreiteza estéril do catolicismo, quando fora dele há que viver todos os protestantismos, todos os credos orientais, todos os paganismos mortos e vivos fundindo-os portuguesmente no Paganismo Superior? Não queiramos que fora de nós fique um único deus! Absorvamos os deuses todos! Conquistámos já o Mar: resta que conquistemos o Céu, ficando a terra para os Outros, os eternamente Outros, os Outros de nascença, os europeus que não são europeus porque não são portugueses. Ser tudo, de todas as maneiras, porque a verdade não pode estar em faltar ainda alguma cousa! Criemos assim o Paganismo Superior, o Politeísmo Supremo! Na eterna mentira de todos os deuses, só os deuses todos são verdade.[23]

[The Fifth Empire. The future of Portugal—which I do not calculate but *know*—is already written, for whoever knows how to read it, in the lays of Bandarra and also in the quatrains of Nostradamus. That future is our being everything. What Portuguese can live the narrowness of only one personality, of only one nation, of only one faith? What true Portuguese can, for example, live the sterile narrowness of Catholicism, when beyond it there are all the protestantisms, all the Oriental creeds, all the paganisms living and dead to be lived, fusing them in Portuguese fashion into the Superior Paganism? Let us not allow a single god to remain beyond us! Let us absorb all the gods! We have conquered the Sea: it remains for us now to conquer Heaven, the earth remaining for the Others, the eternally Others, the Others by birth, the Europeans who are not Europeans because they are not Portuguese. To be everything, in all ways, because the truth cannot exist if even one thing is missing! Let us thus create the Superior Paganism, the Supreme Polytheism! In the eternal lie of all the gods, only all the gods constitute truth.]

Other instances of similar language on the subject are to be found throughout Pessoa's work.[24]

"*O Encoberto*," the third section of *Mensagem*, is both an elaboration of the Sebastian symbolism that was introduced, modified, and given historicity in the first two sections, and also an exposition of how the forces betokened by that symbolism are at work in Portugal.

In the first poem of "The Symbols," the first sub-section, the metaphorical Sebastian says to Portugal:

D. SEBASTIÃO

Sperae! Cahi no areal e na hora adversa
Que Deus concede aos seus
Para o intervallo em que esteja a alma immersa
Em sonhos que são Deus.

Que importa o areal e a morte e a desventura
Se com Deus me guardei?
É O que eu me sonhei que eterno dura,
É Esse que regressarei.

[KING SEBASTIAN

Take heart! I fell upon the sands and upon the adverse hour
that God grants to His own
as the interval in which the soul may be immersed
in dreams that are God.

What do sands and death and misfortune matter
if I have remained in the presence of God?
What lasts forever is the Person that I dreamed I was,
and as that Person I shall return.]

The implications of the poem's imagery are clear in the light of the foregoing discussion. The new notions are those involving the mechanism of Portuguese history: God has "granted" Portugal its current *vileza*, and it represents only an "interval" before a rebirth. It should be noted too that the poem sets forth a subjectivist definition of

"God": He *is constituted* by "dreams"—which presumably refer to the self-image of the dreamer, be that dreamer man or nation.

The third poem of "The Signs," the second sub-section, establishes Pessoa as a prophet of Portuguese regeneration, in a line begun by Bandarra, the figure in the first poem of the sub-section, and Vieira, the figure in the second. In that positioning, Pessoa is clearly calling upon both numerology and some of his readings in magic, wherein the number three is given special significance. In such sources too the third instance of a prophecy is said to be the final, true one and, according to an almost typological mode of thought, the one in whose terms the event prophesied will be realized. Presumably, Pessoa's third prophecy will refer to the "Quinto Império," interpreted more or less in the terms of his description of it in the prose passage above. What is interesting is that the poem itself is a prayer to "Sebastian" in which Pessoa depicts himself as degenerate, aware of the mechanism of Portuguese history, but uncertain of the timing. He depicts himself as writing a "book" in that state; it does not seem a wild presumption to see that book as *Mensagem*, the vehicle of the third prophecy.

The first poem in "The Eras," the final subsection, contains a formula that represents an important elaboration of imagery that has been analyzed in application to the last poem of "Portuguese Sea." The poem speaks of the Portuguese psyche's wish to begin to seek again, its wish to break out of its benighted "prison" and to look for who it is in what the speaking voice calls the "distancia de nós." The phrase is meaningfully ambiguous, for it may mean "distance from ourselves" or "distance of ourselves," thus defining both the historical conquest and a new, intellectual "conquest" to come.

The final poem of the book sums up a good many of the thematic lines heretofore established:

NEVOEIRO

Nem rei nem lei, nem paz nem guerra,
Define com perfil e ser
Este fulgor baço da terra
Que é Portugal a entristecer—
Brilho sem luz e sem arder,
Como o que o fogo-fatuo encerra.

Ninguem sabe que coisa quer.
Ninguem conhece que alma tem,
Nem o que é mal nem o que é bem.
(Que ancia distante perto chora?)

Tudo é incerto e derradeiro.
Tudo é disperso, nada é inteiro.
Ó Portugal, hoje és nevoeiro...

É a Hora!

[FOG

Neither king nor law, neither peace nor war
defines to perfection
this dull glow of earth
that is Portugal growing sad.
Gleam without light or fire,
like the gleam of the will-o'-the-wisp.

No one knows what he wants.
No one recognizes what soul he has,
or what is evil or what is good.
(What distant anxiousness cries so near?)
Everything is uncertain and late.
Everything is dispersed, nothing is whole.
O Portugal, today you are fog...

It is the Hour!]

The poem begins with a sociological remark that intends to characterize the Portugal of the late 20's and early 30's. It was an era of clash between supporters of the fallen Republic (alluded to in the word "law") and supporters of a return to Monarchy (alluded to in the word "king"); many people merely wanted stability at any cost and as a result looked to the military for maintenance in the nation—hence the military dictatorship of 1926 and the subsequent controlled state. Indeed, the social analysis in this poem recalls the terms of Pessoa's *Interregno*, which to a great degree advances that argument. Nevertheless, the clash of directions and interests along the social spectrum produced an era of civil strife, suggested in the first four lines of the poem. Pessoa then goes on to say that Portugal is a thoroughly split, characterless nation. He sums up that delineation in the fifth and sixth lines of the second stanza and then, in the seventh line, says that such characterlessness is "fog." *Mensagem* relies to a great degree on a patterning of images of light and darkness, both reinforced by their usage in occultist writings. Light implies revelation; darkness, basement or degeneracy. Within that patterning, "fog" takes on a special significance, for it draws upon traditional Sebastianistic lore. In Sebastianism, the king is depicted as returning on a foggy day; the fog then parts enough for a ray of sun to fall upon him, thus revealing him to his countrymen. Hence the reference to fog parting and to revelation at the end of "The Final Ship"; hence too the title of the poem currently being analyzed. In this poem, however, Pessoa redefines both Sebastianism and the nature of the imagery of light and dark that he has built up throughout the volume. "Fog" takes on now a sociologically based definition: it is a cover-term for the confused, disunified state of the Portugal of his time. The poem then goes on to say that "It is the Hour" of Sebastian's return, the implication being that complete characterlessness has been reached, complete debasement, and also that, simultaneously, glory has returned.

The occultist tenet that debasement leads to regeneration is clearly being invoked in those final lines, but its impact is merely formal. It too is being given a specific sense in application to Portuguese cultural dynamics as interpreted by Fernando Pessoa. What Pessoa is suggesting specifically can be understood only from a thorough reading of *Mensagem* and also of much of the rest of Pessoa's writing. It involves the fact, suggested in the relationship between Pessoa and the Portuguese nation hinted at in "The Final Ship," that underlying the thematics of *Mensagem* is an elaborate parallel between Pessoa and Portugal. Both are depicted as, in different ways, degenerate geniuses. The basis of the degeneracy of both is the inability to be unified. The case for Portugal's disunion is summed up in the final poem of *Mensagem*; that of Pessoa has in effect been analyzed in the first section of this chapter, for the inability to accept any one system or investigative procedure always has for Pessoa a personal, psychological referent, spoken or not. His youthful self-analysis, found in the passage with which this chapter begins, is indicative of his concept of personal degeneracy; it is expressed in many of his writings throughout the rest of his life.

The immediately obvious difference between the two "degeneracies" is that Pessoa channels the one that he sees in himself into a relativism that informs a fascinating literary corpus, one based not on the ability to affirm in any one area but rather on a process of taking up all seemingly viable directions. Pessoa was of course aware of this procedure; it constitutes a key part of his self-mythification. One of his most gnomic expressions of that ethical position is the following sentence, which is the culminating sentence of the prose description of the "Quinto Império" reproduced more extensively above: "Na eterna mentira de todos os deuses, só os deuses todos são verdade [In the eternal lie of all the gods, only all the gods constitute truth]." "God," as we have seen, can imply a personal or collective quantity. Indeed, the language of the above sentence applies equally to Pessoa and to his vision of Portugal's future. In fact, "polytheism" and, specifically, "paganism" are terms that he uses to imply his own conscious "embracing of all the gods," be those gods metaphysical, scientific, or whatever.[25]

This is not the only overt parallelism between Pessoa and Portugal. It will be recalled that he speaks of an ascending scale of "depersonalization" in authorial identification with the products of his poetic creation, that formulation in effect representing another resolution of his own problem of inability to affirm on any score. The term "denationalization" existed within the political jargon of Pessoa's day, implying Portugal's loss of "Portugueseness" and consequent stagnation. The term was usually used by monarchists, traditionalists, and other conservative elements.[26] The argument suggested in the use of the term at the time, interestingly enough, trades upon notions of national dynamics much like Garrett's; the existence of a national spirit frustrated by a non-national regime. The difference, however, is that for the conservatives of the 1920's and 1930's, Pessoa being among them, the Liberal structures defended by Garrett as being traditionally "Portuguese" are precisely the stultifying elements.

For the purposes of the present analysis of *Mensagem*, however, another implication of Pessoa's appropriation of the concept of "denationalization" is key. Much as in the poem "Fog," he at times saw the negative implications of "denationalization" as simultaneously positive as well. The following somewhat cryptic passage demonstrates as much:

> Estamos tão desnacionalizados que devemos estar renascendo. Para os outros povos, na sua totalidade eles-próprios, o desnacionalizar-se é o perder-se. Para nós, que não somos nacionais, o desnacionalizar-se é o encontrar-se. Apesar dos grandes obstáculos à nossa regeneração—todas as doutrinas de regeneração—estamos no início de tornar a começar a existir. Chegámos ao ponto em que colectivamente estamos fartos de tudo e individualmente fartos de estar fartos. Extraviámo-nos a tal ponto que devemos estar no bom caminho. Os sinais do nosso ressurgimento próximo estão patentes para os que não vêem o visível.
>
> (*Análise*, "Addenda," 6)

[We are so denationalized that we must be being reborn. For the other peoples, themselves in their totality, to be denationalized is to be lost. For us, who are not national, to be denationalized is to find oneself. Despite the great obstacles to our regeneration—all the doctrines of regeneration—we are at the beginning of starting to exist. We have arrived at the point where collectively we are fed up with everything and individually we are fed up with being fed up. We have strayed so far that we must be on the right road. The signs of our coming resurgence are patent for those who do not see the visible.]

What has happened is that "denationalization" has taken over characteristics of the parallel term, "depersonalization," and thus too of Pessoa's thought and practice about his own psychology, his artistically based investigations, and the connection between them.[27] The same seems to take place in the relationship between the personal term "paganism" and the term "Superior Paganism" (see above, p. 150)—both of the terms applicable to external reality taking on areas of positive implication in the process.

When one reads such parallels with Portugal into the *Mensagem* thematics, it becomes clear that Pessoa is saying that in his personal resolution he is merely ahead of the rest of his nation. In his view both he and his nation are parallel, essentially creative entities and the problem both have is the loss of a unified basis for creativity. He further implies that, at least in application to the nation, only that intellectual prerequisite (the creation of a unified basis for creativity) is necessary to its reassuming of creative status. His suggestion, then, is that Portugal has finally reached a sufficient disunion to take up *his* solution: a creative ethic like the one lost after the Age of the Discoveries, but one that accepts and legitimizes disunion itself as its basis, one that, as has he, takes up a negative syndrome and makes it positive. What is more, Pessoa on occasion stated that Portugal would be the bearer to the world of the creative ethic so conceived, that that status would constitute its new world leadership.[28] That notion is probably being referred to in his *Mensagem* in the idea of a new Portuguese conquest of a "distance" that is both internal and external, a conquest parallel to the conquests of "distance" in the Age of the Discoveries (see above, pp. 149–50, 152). Such are the lessons inculcated upon his reader in the ritual that is *Mensagem*.

What if any validity did Pessoa impute to this extravagant literary exposition? The question, like a similar question applied to any of his work, is not susceptible of quick answers; and, in *Mensagem*, it suffers the added complexity of the presence of a clear exterior referent to the history, past and present, of Portugal.

Gaspar Simões states that in the early 1930's, an era in which the two men corresponded, Pessoa felt that the national psyche was in a crucial stage of remodeling and that that process could be affected through injection of *Mensagem* into it (*Vida e Obra*, 636–638). That affirmation, if true—and it nowhere conflicts with *Mensagem* thematics—serves to confirm again the constancy in Pessoa's thought of an extremely idealistic approach to the Portuguese problem. In itself, however, it merely points up a need for further explanation. How, after all, does one "affect" a "national psyche"?

Pessoa himself, both in *Mensagem* and elsewhere, sets forth an argument that goes some way toward answering that question. Part of his answer to an opinion poll taken in 1934 reads as follows:

> Há só uma espécie de propaganda com que se pode levantar o moral de uma nação—a construção ou renovação e a difusão consequente e multímoda de um grande mito nacional. De instinto, a humanidade odeia a verdade, porque sabe, com o mesmo instinto, que não há verdade, ou, que a verdade é inatingível. O mundo conduz-se por mentiras; quem quiser despertá-lo ou conduzi-lo terá que mentir-lhe delirantemente, e fá-lo-á com tanto mais êxito quanto mais mentir a si mesmo e se compenetrar da verdade da mentira que criou. Temos, felizmente, o mito sebastianista, com raízes profundas no passado e na alma portuguesa. Nosso trabalho é pois mais fácil; não temos que criar um mito, senão que renová-lo. Comecemos por nos embebedar desse sonho, por o integrar em nós, por o encarnar. Feito isso, por cada um de nós independentemente e a sós consigo, o sonho se derramará sem esforço em tudo que dissermos ou escrevermos, e a atmosfera estará criada, em que todos os outros, como nós, o respirem. Então se dará na alma da nação o fenómeno imprevisível de onde nascerão as Novas Descobertas, a Criação do Mundo Novo, o Quinto Império. Terá regressado El-Rei D. Sebastião.[29]

> [There is only one kind of propaganda with which the morale of a nation can be lifted—the construction or renovation and the consequent multifaceted diffusion of a great national myth. By instinct, humanity hates the truth, because it knows, with that same instinct, that there is no truth, or that truth is unattainable. The world is run by lies; whoever wishes to awaken it or to lead it

will have to lie deliriously to it, and he will do so with the more success as he lies more to himself and more deeply imbues himself with the truth of the lie that he has created. Fortunately, we have the Sebastian myth, with deep roots in the past and in the Portuguese soul. Our task is therefore lighter; we do not have to create a myth but merely to revive one. Let us begin by saturating ourselves with that dream, by integrating it into ourselves, by incarnating it. Once that is done by each of us independently, alone with himself, the dream will pour forth effortlessly in everything that we say or write, and the atmosphere will be created in which all others, like us, may breath it in. Then there will take place in the soul of the nation the unforeseeable phenomenon from which the New Discoveries, the Creation of the New World, the Fifth Empire will be born. King Sebastian will have returned.]

Pessoa thus sets forth a view of mythology as essentially untrue but valuable as a catalyst of human action.

In fact, Pessoa has made that same argument in *Mensagem* itself. The first "Castle" of "*Brasão*," the poem immediately after the two "background" poems referred to above, reads as follows:

ULYSSES

O mytho é o nada que é tudo.
O mesmo sol que abre os céus
É um mytho brilhante e mudo—
O corpo morto de Deus,
Vivo e desnudo.

Este, que aqui aportou,
Foi por não ser existindo.
Sem existir nos bastou.
Por não ter vindo foi vindo
E nos creou.

Assim a lenda se escorre
A entrar na realidade,
E a fecundal-a decorre.
Em baixo, a vida, metade
De nada, morre.

[ULYSSES

The myth is the nothing that is all.
The very sun that opens up the skies
is a shining and silent myth—
the dead body of God,
live and naked.

This man, who landed here,
existed by not existing.
Without existing he was sufficient for us.
By not coming he came
and created us.

Thus legend seeps
into reality,
and flows along impregnating it.
Below, life, half of nothing
dies.]

Ulysses fits into Portuguese history in a tangential way. He was so well-known a mythological figure that the Portuguese, seeking an ancient origin for the city of Lisbon, hit upon the concept (based on a supposed similarity between the words Ulysses and Olisipo, the Latin name from which the name Lisbon derived) that Ulysses had founded the city. The value to the nation of the Ulysses myth is emphasized in lines 8 through 10. In a special sense, then, Ulysses arrived without arriving and created the nation, for his myth, according to the poem, was a factor in the formation of Portugal's image of itself. In the third stanza, legend is pictured as a force apart from life entering life and animating it. Legend, "the nothing that is all," as the terms from the first stanza affirm, is created by the living and then becomes "God," and then animates or impregnates life, as the verb *fecundar* suggests. The poem thus suggests that Ulysses provided Portugal with a valuable sense of unity grounded in total untruth. In touching on the question of Portugal's need of a self-image at the outset of *Mensagem*, Pessoa is in fact preparing a justification for the book's conclusion. "Ulysses," then, is in many ways a third "background" poem. It sets the epistomological limits of the rest of the book's argumentation: that *Mensagem* pretends to be a myth, a lie that is true in its functioning.

There are several problems with even that stance, however. The first is that still there is nowhere specified a social mechanism through which a myth may "affect" a national psyche. In fact, it is evident that such a notion constitutes another of the several instances in Pessoa's work of his attributing to the external world of phenomena and processes developed in application to his own psyche. It is relatively easy to see how the notion of animating self-image may be applied to an individual, especially if the goal is consistent creativity; it is all but impossible to see how that notion alone can be realistically applied to a society.

A second problem with the "myth" explanation is that, as the foregoing analysis manifests, the thematic development of *Mensagem* is extremely complex and personalistic. It involves not only the above-analyzed projection of individual resolutions outward upon the nation but also an elaborate reinterpretation of aspects of Sebastianism and of several occultist systems as well. In fact, as the foregoing analysis shows, an adequate reading of *Mensagem* depends upon exposure to aspects of Pessoa's expression that have no direct relationship whatsoever with nationalistic concerns. All those central features of what is really a very close-knit poetic texture would seem unnecessary to mere myth-making for the purpose of stimulating the national psyche.

Seen within the total scope of the Pessoa problematics, the notion of myth-making, personal or national, really represents but one more formulated solution to Pessoa's seemingly insistent questioning of the validity of his intellection. In invoking the concept of a vivifying myth-making, Pessoa is offering yet another value in function for what is really a purely aesthetic process.[30] In *Mensagem*, then, the myth-making is in part a myth-making about the power and value of myth-making.

That argument, flawed as we have seen it to be in its attempted justification of *Mensagem*, is perhaps best conceived as just another "direction" taken in Pessoa's elaborate aesthetic process. Likewise, we should retreat one step in our evaluation of *Mensagem*—as of all of Pessoa's work—and see it as a purely aesthetic formulation to which Pessoa, in his complex action of affirming and criticizing, might at one moment have given the positive status of "myth" and which at another moment he might have seen as a mere artistic pattern with no external applicability whatsoever, the result of a process in which nationalistic elements merely provide building blocks for a self-contained work of art.

The Rediscoverers:
A Retrospect

In the summer of 1934, three *Mensagem* poems appeared in the seventh issue of the new monthly journal *O Mundo Português*, published jointly by two newly formed Estado Novo agencies: The General Agency for the Colonies and the Secretariat of National Information.[1] It will be recalled that the latter agency sponsored the contest that probably provided the impetus for Pessoa's completion of *Mensagem*. The first number of *O Mundo Português*, issued in January of that same year, begins with a lead editorial stating the journal's orientation and goals. The initial paragraph of that editorial reads as follows:

> Destina-se esta Revista à gente nova—e traz grandes ambições. Vem para alentar a fé, o ideal patriótico, a esperança no grande futuro de Portugal, que as gerações de cépticos, de desanimados, de descrentes, que para trás de nós viveram, com pertinácia e inteligência tentaram apagar. Pretende trazer à larga mocidade das nossas escolas de aquém e de além-mar a certeza de que, vinda de glorioso passado, dispõe ainda dos elementos precisos para construir próspero e prestigioso destino. Quere dar-lhe a visão, o amor e o orgulho do verdadeiro Portugal—que se estende por mais de 2.100.000 quilómetros quadrados em quatro partes do mundo e abrange mais de 15 milhões de habitantes.[2]

> [This publication is directed to the youth, and it brings with it lofty ambitions. It comes to foster faith and patriotic idealism, the hope for a great future for Portugal that the generations of the skeptical, ideal-less, and unbelieving who lived before us have attempted with persistence and acumen to extinguish. It

endeavors to transmit to the many young people of our schools on both sides of the sea a sense of surety that, descended from a glorious past, they still possess the elements necessary for the construction of a prosperous and prestigious destiny. It seeks to give them a vision and love of, and pride in, the true Portugal—which extends over more than 2,100,000 square kilometres in four sectors of the world and embraces more than 15 million inhabitants.]

The rhetoric definitively categorizes the publication as an example of the Salazarist appeal to nationalistic idealism and to a specific view of national tradition; so too do the glossy photographs of generals, of government ministers (among them Colonial Minister Armindo Monteiro), and of Salazar himself that dot the pages of the 1934 issues. (The rhetoric has other implications as well and could be analyzed at length; such analysis, however, would not serve my motives in adducing it here. To keep the record straight on one major score, however, it should be pointed out that the pro-colonialist stance of the Estado Novo mirrored in the above paragraph does not in itself represent a basic change from the Republican outlook; only the traditionalist cast of the justificatory rhetoric is new.)

The presence of selected *Mensagem* poems in what is essentially an Estado Novo propaganda organ does, of course, indicate ignorance of both the interdependence of the individual poems in *Mensagem* and also the personal referent built into it—not to mention the unrealistically intellectualist nature of the "Quinto Império" that Pessoa foresees and the obvious lack of direct applicability to socio-political reality therein manifest.

Thus such use of *Mensagem* poems represents a misreading of the book. In another wider sense, though, the use is not wholly illegitimate; Pessoa's *Mensagem* trades upon the concept of a national spirit and a heroic past indicative of that spirit that can be revived in the present to inform the future. While specific notions within the overall vision may differ, Pessoa does propound a traditionalistic heroic idealism very like the idealism that provided the cornerstone for the politics-of-the-spirit characteristic of the Salazar regime. Indeed, as the preceding chapter suggests, Pessoa, in his own very idiosyncratic manner, participated in the anti-Republican reaction that took place with ever increasing insistence in various segments of Portuguese society virtually from 1910 on and led to the consequent founding of the Estado Novo. His participation in the government-sponsored contest for best book of nationalistic poetry is therefore only fitting, as is his inclusion in *O Mundo Português*.

Moreover, such state incorporation of regenerationist literature into the process of ideologizing an aspect of that state itself really only serves to highlight a feature common to the five literary pieces here examined. Each proceeds from an outlook compatible with the social position of its author to ideologization of national reality, each in a time of transition for Portugal. In the case of Pessoa's *Mensagem*, the new, entrenching state merely recognized the fact that Pessoa's ideologization came basically in its support and, for that reason, in turn incorporated his work into its own ideologizing.

In manners that vary with his specific set of circumstances, each "rediscoverer" expounds an analysis of national history, links the history so analyzed to some aspect of present social reality, sets forth a means of that present's recapturing of the past, and then suggests a means of the efficacious projection of that entire complex into the future, a means of achieving national regeneration. And each does so through manipulation of what in my Introduction I have termed the "symbols of regeneration": a set of images that the writers examined hold more or less completely in common. Moreover, with the possible exception of Eça de Queiroz, each involves himself in such regeneration as a biographical entity rather than merely as a creative principle, thus confirming one last implication of the title "The Rediscoverers": each "rediscovery" not only recapitulates past national "discoveries," but also bespeaks a means of psychological identification of self, a degree of personal rediscovery not dealt with in detail in the foregoing chapters. Thus too is drawn out a strong interrelationship between individual identity and national identity. Let us review each case from that perspective.

Camões's *Os Lusíadas* includes both a description of past Portuguese glory and as well a sense of present decline. In his treatment of both of those elements of his work, he focuses on a dedication or spirituality typical of a Portuguese—or, rather, of a Portuguese nobleman. To his mind that ethic is needed for resumption of Portuguese cultural expansion. He sees it, however, to be in decline in the nobility of his time, attested to by the presence, within the ruling circles of the nation, of non-noble people, who therefore cannot possibly possess that needed quality. Hence, in his view, the present degeneration. Camões's concept of national regeneration involves a reemphasizing of the qualities which constitute that noble ethic, as he perceives it, by means of the king's bestowing of influential positions upon those nobles who retain such qualities. He so advises King Sebastian, to whom *Os Lusíadas* is dedicated. In adopting that stance he may be seen to speak for the lesser nobility, substantially disfranchised in political terms at the time.

It is abundantly clear, however, that he himself occupies such a position and that he speaks primarily for himself. His mythologizing of himself in the process includes another dimension as well: his inclusion of artistic vision and literary merit among the qualities characteristic of a nobleman and as well a concomitant sense of his own genius. He in fact suggests that the writing of *Os Lusíadas* represents a noble deed and demonstrates his retention of the nobility of spirit that he feels is being lost in his day.

Padre António Vieira, a Jesuit priest, formulates his myth for the regeneration of Portugal in his *História do Futuro*. In that work Vieira interprets world history as a fated, structured fabric that can be read, just as a book is read, by one who knows what signs to look for. The yoking of physical events and guiding divine will to create that conception of history represents Vieira's version of the Jesuits' solution to the social and intellectual conflicts of the age. Clearly feeling that he is an insightful man who can interpret better than any other person the signs that history, so conceived, affords, he reads the foreshadowing of a great new temporal and spiritual empire in his aptly named *History of the Future*, a work which he believes will have the effect of preparing the way for the new era that he foretells. Thus he is not only the prophet of a regeneration for Portugal, but also the stimulator of progress toward that regeneration.

It should be noted that, in contrast to the three rediscoverers dealt with after them, Camões and Vieira seem to conceive of Portugal's actual regaining of its imperial impetus, albeit in very different ways. Vieira, in fact, seems to contemplate Portugal's fated return to the imperial status of the past after a fated hiatus of benightedness is ended—a return for the purpose of completing the task of world conquest that, to the minds of many sixteenth- and seventeenth-century Portuguese, the nation had undertaken. None of the later "regenerations" examined has that reactionary cast about it; even Pessoa, who in his regenerationism does draw to some extent upon Vieira's writing and upon the Sebastianistic lore that Vieira propagated, organizes those elements and the references that he makes to early Portuguese glory into a symbolic complex that has the effect of predicting the coming of a second, future glory quite different from the past possession of a physical empire. Thus the term "regeneration," when applied to Camões's and Vieira's theorizing, contains implications unlike those of the three "regenerations" to come: for Camões and Vieira, "regeneration" involves, in large part, Portugal's return to what they conceive as its proper place in the ongoing course of world affairs.

In contrast, Almeida Garrett looks forward to a true "re-generation"; he wishes his nation to recapture the spirit that had once made it powerful and then to use that spirit to create a viable modern nation. At various points in *Camões* he suggests that Portuguese degeneration since the Age of the Discoveries has resulted from the nation's failure to maintain a socio-political structure grounded in what he feels are the characteristics that animated that former era of greatness— characteristics, related to the key concept of liberty, which by and large correspond to the ideals found in his own political philosophy. He hints that those characteristics, which now lie dormant in the popular psyche, can be recovered. He presents himself as the indignant incarnation of those characteristics, and as the reincarnation of Camões's spirit, which, according to his interpretation, manifested them. He berates his nation for abandoning them, thus putting himself in the position of spiritual leader of his country. His identification with Camões has a number of ramifications. For example, just as does Camões in *Os Lusíadas*, Garrett advances what is primarily a personality myth. As is also the case with Camões, however, in his proclaiming of his "personal" qualities Garrett speaks for a specific social class: the rising middle class of his era. In later years—advancing further the basically cultural framework in which he saw Portuguese political history (hence his identification with the poet Camões, one based in part on parallels in literary structure)—Garrett also formulated socio-literary theories which suggested that this writing of *Camões* had in itself represented a step toward recapture of the lost national characteristics, and thus a step toward national regeneration.

Eça de Queiroz's regenerationism is grounded in his own person to a lesser degree than are those of the other four subjects of this study. Eça's outlook centers not on himself as a person (unlike the other rediscoverers, he does not patently set himself up as a leader of his nation or as a prophet of its regeneration), but rather on his belief in the value of reflective analysis of social problems, a belief characteristic of the social planners of the Generation of 1870. He shows that orientation in many of the literary techniques that he employs in his writing, from his first novel, *O Crime do Padre Amaro*, to the text here studied, *A Ilustre Casa de Ramires*. In the early works, however, that orientation is reflected only in the authorial principle, the structuring force behind bitterly ironic analyses of Portuguese social problems. In *Ilustre Casa*, for the first time in Eça's work, a *character* is made capable of taking up that analytical position with respect to himself, and thus is made capable too of personal response to socially based problems. Through the structure of that novel Eça also implies (with what degree of optimism it is impossible to know) that the Portuguese can resolve the problem of national degeneration by similarly analyzing, and then dealing with, themselves as individual social problems within the scope of the national problem. In so doing, he suggests, they can begin in themselves the regeneration of their nation. He also intimates that there is to be found in the psyche of individual Portuguese a long-lost capacity for creative self-assertiveness that reasoned self-analysis can discover, bring to the fore, and reestablish in the nation. For Eça, then, regeneration seems to imply a recapturing of that lost creative self-assertiveness, first by individual Portuguese and then, as a result, by the nation as a whole.

The fifth "regeneration" involves the intricate "myth" that Fernando Pessoa elaborates in *Mensagem*, where he predicts the coming of a new empire for Portugal, a cultural-intellectual empire rather than a physical one. Like Padre Vieira, Pessoa concentrates not on the social applications that figure prominently in the thinking of Camões, Garrett, and Eça de Queiroz, but instead on a visionary interpretation of the process of world history. The myth that he creates is comprehended only when seen in the light afforded by an examination of Pessoa's work as a whole. A key to the nature of that myth lies in understanding the relationship, often implied in Pessoa's writing, between his image of Portugal and his image of himself as proposer of a way to regeneration for his country: nation and writer are to a great degree identified. They are viewed as two entities possessed of similar psyches and beset by similar problems. What Pessoa proposes for his nation as a solution to the national problem is that it take up the intellectual stance that he has assumed in an effort to solve his personal problem, a stance that embraces an avant-garde, elitist valuation of individual creativity above all else. That myth for national regeneration both compares and contrasts with the course of action that Eça de Queiroz proposes. Like Eça, and to some extent Garrett as well, Pessoa builds his myth upon what he sees as an inherent creativity in the Portuguese psyche; Eça, however, proposes merely that individual Portuguese try to realize their inherent creativity in realistic terms, that through individual action, Portugal can again become *a creative nation*, while Pessoa suggests that the nation become *a creator*, a Pessoa-like "poet." In a position much like Padre Vieira's in *História do Futuro*, Pessoa seems to suggest that the adoption by Portugal of his solution to the national problem is both fated to take place because of the action of historical forces at work within the nation, and also destined to be realized through the influence of *Mensagem*. Thus he goes beyond identification of himself with Portugal to take up, like Vieira, the role of prophet, mythologizing himself as the fated bearer of a message to Portugal and, through Portugal, to all the world. However, both that personal myth and the national regenerationism to which it is allied contrast with the other four myths proposed; Pessoa concludes, in the process of his myth-making, that myths do not contain truth but rather are mere products of human creativity, "true" and able to animate human action only as long as they are believed. Thus the myth proposed by this rediscoverer may claim not truth but rather only efficacy. As a consequence, it probably does not represent an article of belief in the same sense that the other rediscoverers' myths do for them. In the final analysis, it may be no more than a creation for the sake of creation. Thus *Mensagem* may be viewed as a work in which the Portuguese problem functions as a literary motif in Fernando Pessoa's philosophical-aesthetic myth-making.

That possible dichotomy in Pessoa between nationalistic fervor and intellectual conviction suggests, in terms somewhat different from the idiosyncratic ones applicable to Pessoa's case, another analytical perspective upon Portuguese national regenerationism as it has been seen in the foregoing chapters. While it would seem at first thought that the past-oriented symbolism characteristic of regenerationism would inevitably produce a reactionary stance in socio-political terms, such is clearly not the case. While such symbols may indicate a repository immediately available for, and more readily tailored to, reactionary orientations (as their incorporation by the Estado Novo suggests), and while, as the present study has pointed up, an aristocratic pressure has long obtained in Portuguese society that may well compound matters further, a basic separability nonetheless exists between the regenerationist symbols and the ends to which they can be set. Indeed, Almeida Garrett's "rediscovery" is in the main progressive, while those of Eça de Queiroz and even António Vieira have progressive features, though in the latter only as regards the realistic economic activity that it provides for within its framework. Even Camões's "rediscovery" provides a place for modes of knowledge that are actually radically progressive within the traditionalist ambit of his work. And Fernando Pessoa, whose exposition, along with Camões's, in my (purely subjective) judgment, represents the most aesthetically complex of the five texts examined, presents a regeneration "myth" that in some respects is not directly applicable to the social scene of his day in any manner whatsoever. Thus, in Portuguese regenerationism, or at least in the five literary examples here examined, it becomes very clear that in the coming-together of the individual and social forces of the present and the symbols of the past there is no necessary subservience of the former to the latter. Indeed, the symbols seem virtually to be the variable element, contemporary reality the constant; the symbols are reworked by the individual, they do not dictate to him. And while they undeniably provide culturally validated patterns of intellection and expression, they are not indicative of a static or nearly static "language" in which national identity is molded. Thus what finally emerges from this examination of examples of Portuguese regenerationist literature is the identification of a constant reference system made up of symbols of the past, but in a continual historical interaction with the present in which the latter predominates. These remarks, to my mind, further define the notion of regenerationism as the "cultural constant" touched on in the Introduction to this study.

My stated purpose in this work has been to show the "texture" of regenerationist literature, the complexities, even intricacies that it can achieve. The reader is, of course, the ultimate judge of whether or not the foregoing has fulfilled that purpose. To my understanding, it has, and I hope it has also set out lines for further work in the literary area (from which I may well have taken the pick of the crop, but surely not the harvest itself) and other areas of national cultural expression as well. Summarizing analysis such as that above awaits further work for its refinement if not modification. However, one conclusion here stated I expect to see stand: my sense that it is the dominance of the forces of the present over the symbols of the past, at least in the literary sphere, that has led to the high degree of creativity in the various "rediscoveries" set forth—culminating in Fernando Pessoa's *Mensagem*, a work of unquestionable intricacy but uncertain referentiality.

I shall end where I began, with Américo Castro's evaluation of Portuguese cultural creativity in a formulation that is now, I hope, much more meaningful: "A great novelist does not work differently."

Notes

Introduction

1. Américo Castro, *La realidad histórica de España* (Mexico City, 1954), 649, 651. The English is quoted from the translation by Edmund L. King, *The Structure of Spanish History* (Princeton, 1954), 669, 671.

2. See Raymond Cantel, *Prophétisme et messianisme dans l'œuvre d'António Vieira* (Paris, 1960), 22; Marcel Bataillon, "Novo Mundo e Fim do Mundo," *Revista de História* (São Paulo), Ano V (1954), No. 18, 343–351. For a treatment of the subsequent continuation and intensification of these currents, see the first two sections of my chapter "Vieira: The Prophet."

3. António Henrique de Oliveira Marques, *História de Portugal*, 4th ed. (Lisboa, 1974), I, 359–360. Background material for my outline of early Portuguese history has been drawn primarily from this volume.

4. For a treatment of that aspect of Sá de Miranda's writing, see Carolina Michaëlis de Vasconcellos, *Poesias de Francisco de Sá de Miranda* (Halle, 1885), xviii–xxi. For António Ferreira, see António José Saraiva, *História da Cultura em Portugal*, II, em colaboração com Óscar Lopes e Luís de Albuquerque (Lisboa, 1955), 643–644. For Camões, see the following chapter of the present study.

5. Many examples can be adduced of the educating (or, at least, advising) of the young king in directions indicated by the spirit of the age. António Ferreira, for instance, advised Sebastian's tutor to instill in his pupil the now-lost "austere courage" (my translation) of his forebears; see Saraiva, II, 643. For a general evaluation of the king's education and resultant character, see M. Gonçalves Cerejeira, *Clenardo e a Sociedade Portuguesa*, 4th ed. ([Coimbra], 1974), 181–184. Camões too, as I note in my next chapter, "Camões: The Noble Poet," offers advice to Sebastian. And for a comment on how Sebastian was regarded by the Portuguese of his day—a factor that had much to do with how he was educated and also, surely, with how he perceived himself—see the chapter entitled "Vieira: The Prophet."

6. Another investigator interested in regenerationism is the historian Joel Serrão. His approach, somewhat different from mine, is outlined in his two articles "Decadência," in *Dicionário de História de Portugal* II (n.l., 1975), 270–274, and "Regeneração," ibid., V (n.l., 1975), 251–256.

Camões: The Noble Poet

1. For treatment in greater detail both of that term and of aspects of the micro-poem's role in the text, see both my "A Poet and His Nation: The Foreground Myth of *Os Lusíadas*," *The Texas Quarterly*, 15 (1972), No. 4, 19–31, and also my "Os Lusíadas: Voz Poética/Leitura," *Estudos Ibero-Americanos* (Porto Alegre), in press.

2. The Portuguese, here and henceforth, is reproduced from the edition by Hernâni Cidade, which comprises volumes IV and V of his Luís de Camões, *Obras Completas* (Lisboa, 1946–1947). I henceforth refer to passages by canto, stanza, and line numbers only, rather than by page numbers.

3. Here and henceforth I use the English translation by Leonard Bacon, *The Lusiads of Luiz de Camões* (New York, 1950); this particular passage is to be found on his pp. 5–6. All of Bacon's divisions into canto and stanza correspond to the divisions of the Portuguese edition referred to in n. 2. All translations and glosses not noted as Bacon's are my own.

4. On the question of the relationship between epic poetry and history in Renaissance poetics, see Bernard Weinberg, *A History of Literary Criticism in the Italian Renaissance* (Chicago, 1961), I, 13–16, 40–45.

5. The importance to the thinking of the time represented by ideals found in romances of chivalry can be exemplified by many instances. Nun'Álvares Pereira, the Constable of the realm under King John I, expressly patterned his life after Galahad's (see Saraiva, I, 318). And the mid-fifteenth-century chronicler Fernão Lopes, in the second part of his *Crónica de D. João I*, depicts a scene in which King John I and his lieutenants compare themselves, in banter, to knights of the Round Table; see Fernão Lopes, *Crónica de D. João I* (Porto, [1945]), II, 186–188.

On the score of idealism in general, in a letter of 1436 to his brother King Duarte, Prince Henry the Navigator outlined in a few words the choice to be made between idealism and practicality as a guiding ethic. Prince Henry, the very practical instigator of much of the early expansion and discovery—he would later obtain a trade monopoly over any areas that his explorers discovered—nonetheless clearly felt that he was following the idealistic, noble way of life. The relevant passage of his letter is reproduced by Saraiva, I, 578.

6. For treatment of some aspects of the semantics of nobiliary ideology, see João Lúcio de Azevedo, *Elementos Para a História Económica de Portugal (Séculos XII a XVII)* (Lisboa, 1967), 94; and Saraiva, III, 245.

I should make it clear that here and throughout this study I treat social classes and their ideological manifestations in relatively uncritical terms. That is, I implicitly invoke the notions first that there is, in a given era, a more-or-less fixed class hierarchy, and, second, that the boundaries between classes are clear. While those notions provide a useful and generally accurate working model, the reality was more fluid and far more complex than they suggest. Indeed, the actual nature of class relationships in the earlier eras of Portuguese history constitutes a problem that has long vexed historians. For basic reading that bears—not always centrally—on the question, see Vitorino Magalhães Godinho, *A Estrutura da Antiga Sociedade Portuguesa* (Lisboa, 1971), 11–137.

7. This element is documented and analyzed implicitly throughout José Antonio Maravall, *La cultura del barroco* (Esplugues de Llobregat, 1975).

8. Despite his advocacy position and his frequent intellectual vagaries, João de Scantimburgo, *Interpretação de Camões à Luz de Santo Tomás de Aquino* (São Paulo, 1979) does document many of the areas in which Camões's work is imbued in Thomist thought. And, when one takes into account Alexandre Correia's admonition, prefatory to Scantimburgo's work (p. 15), that Camões should be seen not as a student of Aquinas's thought but rather as a normal receiver of cultural assumptions about man and his existence that can be traced to Thomist formulations, the nature, pervasiveness, and detail of Thomist influence become clear.

9. For a discussion of the terms "orator" and "courtier," as well as for a treatment of central aspects of Humanist thought, see William Harrison Woodward, *Desiderius Erasmus Concerning the Aim and Method of Education* (1904; rpt. New York, 1964).

10. Indeed, Saraiva, in the chapters "As Contradições de Camões, ou o Humanismo Impossível" and "A Epopeia" (III, 497–684), structures his analysis of Camões's work around the poet's attempt to resolve that conflict. I am indebted to Saraiva for many aspects of my analysis of Camões's embodiment both of nobiliary ideology and of Humanist thought.

11. The best treatment of the entire matter of the textual parallels and their implications for the respective views of empire is still to be found in the chapters on Vergil and on Camões in C.M. Bowra, *From Virgil to Milton* (London, 1945).

12. The Portuguese is reproduced from volume IV, p. lv, of the Cidade edition of Camoes's *Obras Completas;* the translation is mine.

13. The only treatment of the matter of which I am aware is my "Philosophical Implications of Camões' Use of the Classical Mythological Tradition in the Adamastor Episode of *Os Lusíadas*," *Garcia de Orta*, Número Especial, 1972, 535–546. Unfortunately, however, I no longer judge adequate the terms of that analysis.

14. For a thorough digest of sources within the critical tradition on *Os Lusíadas*, in which this question is treated, see the apparatus of the school edition of *Os Lusíadas*, ed. Emanuel Paulo Ramos (Porto). There are many reprintings and re-editions; those before 1974 are not up to date.

15. For one detailed, though eclectic, analysis, see the relevant passages scattered through Reis Brasil, *Os Lusíadas; Comentários e Estudo Crítico*, 6 vols. in 7 (Lisboa, 1960–1967). For sources, see again the Ramos edition; see too Cidade's note to the passage in question, in vol. V, p. 226, of his edition.

16. For details about the arguments that were adduced in the Renaissance in support of this procedure in specific application to the Classical deities, see Jorge de Sena, *A Estrutura de* Os Lusíadas *e Outros Estudos Camonianos e de Poesia Peninsular do Século XVI* (Lisboa, 1970), pp. 73–74, n. 7. Some of Sena's methodological suppositions are different from those of this study, and thus the information that he adduces will have to be separated from them to be inserted here.

Vieira: The Prophet

1. For details, see Oliveira Marques, I, 286–288, 390–396.

2. For some information on the controversy about the Order's "confirmation" by the Council of Trent, see Thomas J. Campbell, S.J., *The Jesuits, 1534–1921* (New York, 1921), 562–563; and E. Boyd Barrett, *The Jesuit Enigma* (New York, 1927), 271–273. Each author is an advocate of his outlook on the question; the latter directly attacks the former.

3. For clarity's sake it should be pointed out that there have been two somewhat distinguishable eras in the history of the Order. After having been expelled from various nations and territories in the eighteenth century—it was expelled from Portugal and Portuguese territories by Prime Minister Pombal in 1759—the Order was officially suppressed by Pope Clement XIV in 1773. The Order as reinstated in 1814, while maintaining many of the basic directions of Jesuitism, also manifested clear differences, in theory and practice, from its predecessor.

4. F.A. Ridley, *The Jesuits: A Study in Counter-Revolution* (London, 1938), 192. I feel that I should point out that this citing does not carry with it the sense that I agree with all of Ridley's analyses. Much of the nature of Jesuit "training" of belief is to be seen in the Order's initial document, Loyola's *Ejercicios espirituales*. For an analysis of that work—and of the accompanying instructions for its use by exercitants—that illuminates that aspect of Jesuit practice, see Roland Barthes, "Loyola," *Sade, Fourier, Loyola* (Paris, 1971), 43–80.

5. See Manoel Correa's page-long note on the stanza in his edition of *Os Lusíadas* (Lisbon, 1613), 296–298. The note is misleading in other ways that should not be allowed to distract attention from this central point.

6. Arthur Edward Waite, *The Brotherhood of the Rosy Cross* (London, 1924), 39–52.

7. For further discussion of the background sketched in this paragraph including treatment of the almost-continuous state of war in Europe and of competition among European nations for control of valuable territories in Asia, Africa, and America as a factor contributing to the general sense of anxiety, see Raymond Cantel, "Vieira e a Filosofia Política do Quinto Império," *Tempo Presente*, Ano 2, Nos. 17–18 (Sept.–Oct. 1960), 22–27. Some of the same remarks appear in the conclusion and elsewhere in Cantel, *Prophétisme et messianisme*.

8. João Lúcio de Azevedo, *A Evolução do Sebastianismo*, 2nd ed. (Lisboa, 1947), 9. A similar analysis is given by Eduardo Freitas da Costa, "O Sebastianismo Racional e Fernando Pessoa," *Revista de Literatura*, 11 (1957), 194–199. The Spanish origin of the prophecies is, of course, especially ironic in view of the anti-Spanish thrust of Sebastianism and its prominent role in stimulating popular support for the 1640 revolution.

9. All translations and glosses in this chapter are my own.

10. Bandarra, *Trovas* (Porto, 1866), 37. The survival of Bandarra's name and of his prophecies is largely a matter of chance. There were at the time many prophets, each in his own small area of the kingdom (Azevedo, *Evolução*, 18–19, 22, mentions especially one frei João de Rocacelsa; there were others).

Bandarra, almost surely because of what was viewed as his prediction of the revolution of 1640, came to be regarded by posterity as *the* prophet of Sebastianism. New "finds" of so-called "original Bandarra" prophetic poems dot ensuing ages. Fernando Pessoa, in his introduction to Augusto Ferreira Gomes's *Quinto Império* (Lisboa, 1934), could therefore say that he regarded "Bandarra" not as a proper name but as a generic one.

11. *História do Futuro*, I, (*Obras Escolhidas*, VIII [Lisboa, 1953]), 187–188.

12. Vieira touches on that notion often throughout his writings. See, for example, *História do Futuro*, II (*Obras Escolhidas*, IX [Lisboa, 1953]), 98–113 and his sermon "Sermão pelo Bom Sucesso das Armas de Portugal Contra as de Holanda," *Obras Escolhidas*, X (Lisboa, 1954), 42–79, at esp. 57–60.

13. Valuable on the subject of the place of typology in Christian thought are Erich Auerbach, "Figura," *Scenes from the Drama of European Literature* (Gloucester, Mass., 1973), 9–76, and A.C. Chárity, *Events and Their Afterlife; The Dialectics of Christian Typology in the Bible and in Dante* (Cambridge, 1966).

14. Another noteworthy Jesuit embodiment of such an attitude toward history is the work *Imago Primi Sæculi Societatis Iesv*, 6 vols. (Antwerpia, 1640) put out by a group of Belgian Jesuits to commemorate the centenary of the Order's founding. The work depicts the Order as a reincarnation in type of the Apostles and thus, ultimately, as both founded by God and predicted in the Scriptures.

15. Vieira's mania on the subject is treated by João Lúcio de Azevedo, *História de António Vieira*, 2nd ed. (Lisboa, 1931), I, 69.

16. A characteristic example is to be seen in Vieira's letter of April 29, 1659 to Bishop André Fernandes. That letter, since published under the title "Esperanças de Portugal, Quinto Império do Mundo, Primeira e Segunda Vida de El-Rei D. João IV, Escritas por Gonçalo Eanes Bandarra e Comentadas por pe. António Vieira," contains Vieira's most famous syllogism; I translate António Sérgio's reduction to a formal syllogism, to be found in his preface to Vol. I of Vieira's *Obras Escolhidas*, xxvi–xxvii:

> Bandarra announced certain accomplishments by King John IV (once we interpret him through allegorical correspondence);
> Now Bandarra had the gift of prophecy;
> Therefore the monarch will accomplish the things announced (through allegorical correspondence) by Bandarra;
> Nevertheless, the King did not accomplish those things during his lifetime;
> Therefore he will accomplish them after death;
> But to accomplish them after death he must return to life;
> Therefore King John IV will return to life.

The complete text of the letter is to be found on pp. 1–66 of *Obras Escolhidas*, VI. Cantel treats this famous letter in *Prophétisme*, 104–105, and it is also dealt with by Azevedo, *Evolução*, 81–82.

17. Cantel, "Vieira e a Filosofia Política," 22.

18. That is only to say that in their self-justification the traditional sectors of society relied heavily on elements of traditional faith. Nobiliarism is reconciled with it on most scores; conflict between the secular and the ecclesiastical ideological components—ongoing since much earlier times—came, in the era, in ways indicated by the Camões-Vieira contrast. Within *História do Futuro* Vieira clearly acknowledges the centrality of the hereditary nobility; see, for example, I, 36–37, 75.

19. Robert Ricard, "Prophecy and Messianism in the works of Antonio Vieira," *The Americas*, 17 (1961), 359, enumerates some specific points of contact and of correspondence that Vieira saw between the histories of the two nations, and then goes on to affirm that, in Vieira's mind, such comparisons pointed to a general conclusion: "The Jews had been propagators of the faith in ancient times. The Portuguese had been chosen to finish their work in modern times."

20. See the syllogism reproduced in n. 16.

21. See Azevedo, *História de António Vieira*, 2nd ed. (Lisboa, 1931), II, 24–25.

22. That aspect of his thought is patent in several passages; see, for example, *História*, I, 78. It is dealt with by Hernâni Cidade, in his Preface (pp. xxvii–xxix) to that volume.

Garrett: Return of a Poet, Rebirth of a Nation

1. For details on these aspects of pre-1820 Portugal, see Oliveira Marques, I, 538–547, 568–574.

2. In addition to treatment in the material referred to in n. 1, see, on this specific point, Norman M. Potter and Ronald W. Sousa, "Liberalismo e Romantismo em Portugal e no Brasil: Proposta para uma Correlação," *Ideologies and Literature*, 1, No. 3 (May–June 1977), 32-35.

3. See Oliveira Marques, II, 52–64.

4. Caio Prado Júnior, *História Económica do Brasil* (São Paulo, 1945), 127.

5. *O Dia Vinte Quatro d'Agosto*, pelo Cidadão J. B. S. L. A. Garett [sic] (Lisboa, 1821). The text of the pamphlet is reproduced in *Obras de Almeida Garrett* (Porto, 1963), I, 1043–1066. The initials refer to Garrett's full name: João Baptista da Silva Leitão de Almeida Garrett.

6. Oliveira Marques, II, 43–44, notes that a similar analysis of history and of the role of the *cortes* was propounded by the liberals of the era and was in fact incorporated into the Constitution of 1822. Note that I use the words "Liberal" and "Liberalism" to refer to general, Europe-wide "Liberal" thought, while "liberal" and "liberalism" refer to those Portuguese Constitutionalists—primarily the progressives—who adhered to a version of that thought applied to the Portuguese situation.

7. This many-sided question has been touched on in several ways.

R.A. Lawton, *Almeida Garrett: l'intime contrainte* (Paris, 1966), 176–177, explains that Garrett's "Muse" is a "political" one and, 361–362, describes Garrett as a "poet-citizen."

Teóphilo Braga touches on the matter in a historical context in *História do*

Romantismo em Portugal (Lisboa, 1880), 108–109 and in *Garrett e o Romantismo* (Porto, 1903), 7, 53, 242–246.

Francisco Gomes de Amorim, *Garrett: Memórias Biográphicas* (Lisboa, 1881), I, 167, 170–171, 210–211, touches on the matter from Garrett's viewpoint. Amorim's biography, it should be noted, approaches the status of autobiography, since it is based in great part on his friendship with Garrett in the last years of the poet's life, on conversations with Garrett with the understanding that a biography was being prepared, and on access to many of Garrett's papers. As a result, the validity of much of Amorim's work is questioned by Ofélia Milheiro Caldas Paiva Monteiro, *A Formação de Almeida Garrett: Experiência e Criação*, 2 vols. (Coimbra, 1971). She sees Garrett's own hand at work in Amorim's volumes and suggests that Garrett, with his flair for creating mythology with regard to himself, dramatized for Amorim many of the events in his life, and interpreted or reordered the sequence of other events.

8. Jacinto do Prado Coelho, in *Dicionário de Literatura*, ed. Jacinto do Prado Coelho, 2nd ed., rev. (Porto, 1969), I, 364. And Gomes de Amorim, III, 314, suggests that an article in resonant praise of Garrett published in a Lisbon periodical in 1851 was in fact written at least in part by Garrett himself. The text is reproduced in ibid., 311–314.

9. The division of a long poem into something akin to micro-poem and macro-poem dimensions as I use the terms is, to be sure, not a rare technique, and that technique was used in Garrett's time. In fact, Garrett had used it in poems written before *Camões*. Nevertheless, since Garrett clearly was very familiar with the contents of the micro-poem of *Os Lusíadas* and with the overall structure of Camões's epic, I find it difficult to suppose that he did not conceive his division of *Camões* into macro-poem and micro-poem to be one further parallel in a series of parallels with *Os Lusíadas*.

10. In the 1851 article that Gomes de Amorim suggests was written in part by Garrett himself (see n. 8), that concept is openly propounded: Camões and Garrett are described first as twin products of the national spirit and then, in a formula that clearly draws on similar formulae in *Os Lusíadas*, as the ancient Homer and the modern Homer of Portugal.

11. The text of *Camões* is reproduced in *Obras de Almeida Garrett*, II (Porto, 1963), 269–458. The text contained in *Obras* does not follow the 1825 version of *Camões*; rather, it reproduces textual revisions and additional notes that Garrett included in subsequent editions. The *Obras* text is used in this study because it represents the poet's definitive text, because it varies little from the 1825 version, and because reference to the notes added in later editions helps in establishing some of Garrett's concepts both in writing *Camões* and also in looking back upon it. References to the text are made to canto and section only. References to other areas of the *Obras* printing include page numbers.

12. For an English translation—one that renders Garrett's verse in prose paragraphs—I use [Almeida Garrett], "Camoëns," tr. Edgar C. Knowlton, Jr. (Macau, 1972). The volume is in fact a separata of the *Boletim do Instituto Luís de Camões* (Macau), 6 (1972), Nos. 1 and 2. The translation does not include renderings of Garrett's prologue or of all of the authorial notes accumulated in the various re-editions during the poet's lifetime. For some material, then, I

shall be unable to refer to an English text. On the occasions when Knowlton either does not translate a passage that I need to reproduce or takes directions in his translating that are not useful to my purposes, I shall include a translation of my own, noted as such.

13. Cf. Oliveira Marques, II, 63, and Potter and Sousa, 37–38.

14. Lawton, 469. This reference represents only one instance of Lawton's treatment of Garrett's use of the motif of the exile. The motif is referred to repeatedly throughout Lawton's analysis of Garrett as thinker and artist; it is, in fact, central to the analysis.

15. Luís de Sousa Rebelo, in Prado Coelho, ed., *Dicionário*, I, 489; João de Almeida Lucas, intro., *Camões*, by Garrett (Lisboa, 1946), xxviii–xxx; António José Saraiva, ed. and intro., *Camões e Dona Branca*, by Garrett (Lisboa, 1943), 12.

16. Garrett, *Doutrinas de Estética Literária* (Lisboa, 1938), 74–75.

Eça de Queiroz: The Social Critic and the End of Social Criticism

1. For background on Portugal at the end of the nineteenth century, see relevant passages in Oliveira Marques, II, 3–116. On Portuguese involvement in Africa, see the same work, 119–181.

2. See Oliveira Marques, II, 55–57, 241–242; João Gaspar Simões, *Vida e Obra de Eça de Queiroz* (Amadora, 1973), 278–287.

3. António Salgado Júnior, *História das Conferências do Casino (1871)* (Lisboa, 1930), 55–56; translation mine.

4. This observation, as the subsequent development of this chapter indicates, really applies only to the first (1875) and second (1876) versions of the novel. To my knowledge, the only treatment of the entire matter is to be found in brief remarks in my "Editorial," *Ideologies and Literature*, 2, No. 7 (May–June 1978), 6–7; and Carlos Felipe Moisés and Ronald W. Sousa, "Lendo Eça: Um Debate," ibid., 3, No. 15, in press.

5. See especially Hippolyte Taine's introductory essay to his *Histoire de la littérature anglaise* (1863–1869); available is the 12th ed. (Paris, 1905), in which the essay is to be found on pp. v–xliv. For Zola's theory, see the first essay of his highly idiosyncratic *Le Roman expérimental*, first published in France in 1880; available is the edition in *Collection des Œuvres Complètes [d'] Émile Zola*, [41] (Paris, [1928]), 11–50. Eça could not have known of the latter work in time for it to have had a role in his conception of his first two novels.

6. The Preface to *Thérèse Raquin* is to be found on pp. vii–xv of volume 34 in the *Collection des Œuvres Complètes*; see n. 5. It should be stated that in a letter of 8 April 1878 to his friend and collaborator Ramalho Ortigão, Eça, after mentioning Zola and several other French novelists, refers to his own use of "experimental methods" (my translation) in achieving the transition between observation of society and novel writing. The metaphor of the novel as a scientific "experiment" is linked specifically to Zola. See *Obras Completas de Eça de Queiroz* (Porto, n.d.), III, 519.

7. See, for example, Mário Sacramento, *Eça de Queiroz: Uma Estética da Ironia* ([Coimbra], 1945).

8. *O Crime do Padre Amaro* (Lisboa: Edição "Livros do Brasil," n.d.), 334; translation mine.

9. For my sense of the change in attitude after the 1876 version of *O Crime do Padre Amaro*, see the sources adduced in n. 4. The latter of the two titles mentioned in that note in fact constitutes a debate between Moisés and myself; his analysis, summarized in this chapter, is to be found in his portion of that debate.

10. The matter is complex, since it calls into consideration as well the fact of Eça's status as a member of a small intelligentsia speaking to the larger bourgeois public whose attention undoubtedly fell first upon its own economic well-being. For some further musing on the matter, see my two titles listed in n. 4, the latter more specifically.

11. *A Ilustre Casa de Ramires* (Lisboa: Edição "Livros do Brasil," n.d.), 254; quotations are identified by page and chapter numbers.

12. The English is quoted from *The Illustrious House of Ramires*, tr. Ann Stevens (Athens, Ohio, 1968), 217–218. All English translations and glosses in this chapter not noted as Stevens's are my own.

13. João Gaspar Simões, *Eça de Queiroz* (Lisboa, 1961), 193.

14. Edgard Marques, *Interpretação Espiritual de Eça de Queiroz* (Lisboa, [1946]), 185–201.

15. See, for example, René da Costa, "The Mythic Quest Theme in *A Cidade e as Serras*," *Luso-Brasilian Review*, 5, No. 2 (Dec. 1968), 76–77.

16. While it is true that an example from any other sector of society would not have provided the same kinds of possibilities of relating past and present in his text, there is no doubt that Eça is to some extent rehabilitating the traditional upper class in his presentation of Gonçalo Mendes Ramires in this novel, complete with ancestral lands and so on. It is relevant that Eça's marriage, in 1886, was one into the hereditary nobility—indeed into a family that predates the nationhood of Portugal. Nonetheless, the nature of the novel's development makes it clear that Eça does not envision a return to any sort of traditionalist social system.

17. For an evaluation of Eça's pessimistic view of the status of Portuguese society, see João Medina, *Eça Político* (Lisboa, 1974); also, I am indebted to Medina's chapter "Gonçalo Mendes Ramires, Personagem Hamlético" (89–112) for aspects of my analysis of *A Ilustre Casa de Ramires*.

Pessoa: The Messenger

1. My remarks presuppose that Eça would have published the novel in more or less the form in which it now exists—a form unrevised by the author, with a text that was in fact finished by acquaintances of his. This is an especially debatable supposition with Eça, who would procrastinate for years between finishing a draft of a novel and its publication and for whom "revision" could

mean wholesale recasting. Nonetheless, one can safely presume that the content of what is essentially a rough draft of *A Cidade e as Serras* is indicative of a trajectory in Eça's outlook and practice—even if it might later have been rejected by its author or had never seen print.

2. In 1890 Britain issued to Portugal an ultimatum concerning the boundaries of certain African territories and sovereignty over them. In Portuguese eyes the terms of the ultimatum were arbitrary and unfair, but the pronouncement effectively threatened confrontation between the two nations and led to Portugal's yielding to British occupation of lands around Lake Nyasa, which Portugal had considered its own.

3. Those remarks recapitulate and continue my analysis in the chapter on Eça de Queiroz; see above, p. 105–6 and the sources thereto noted.

4. For background on the Revolution and on the Republic, see Oliveira Marques, II, 185–263.

5. *Páginas Íntimas e de Auto-Interpretação* (Lisboa, [1966]), 4–6.

6. A general work that discusses many of the aspects of the phenomenon—unfortunately, in ways with which I do not always agree—is Renato Poggioli, *The Theory of the Avant-Garde* (Cambridge, 1968).

7. Pessoa, *Cartas a Armando Côrtes-Rodrigues* (Lisboa, 1944), 69–70. All English translations in this chapter are mine.

8. I analyze Pessoa's "scientism" in greater detail, within the framework created by other, similar facets of Pessoa's work, in "Estruturas para uma Imagem do 'Eu'," *Persona*, No. 3, 51–59, esp. at 56. In that article I do not touch on the comparison with Eça de Queiroz.

9. João Gaspar Simões, *Vida e Obra de Fernando Pessoa* (Amadora, [1970]), 535–536.

10. From his letter of 6 Dec. 1915 to Mário de Sá-Carneiro, reproduced, with minor differences in reading, both in Simões, 543–544, and in Pessoa, *Hyram* (Porto, n.d.), 97–98. My text follows the reading in the latter source.

11. *Athena*, I, No. 1 (Oct. 1924), 7. This is one of the small journals Pessoa founded.

12. Formulations of the "depersonalization scale" are to be found in *Páginas Íntimas*, 106–109, 394–398; and in Pessoa, *Páginas de Estética e de Teoria e Crítica Literárias* (Lisboa, [1967]), 67–69, 299–300. My treatment in "Estruturas" carries the present analysis further.

13. Information about the gestation of *Mensagem* is to be found in the following sources: Jacinto do Prado Coelho, "Cronologia e Variantes da *Mensagem*," *A Letra e o Leitor* ([Lisboa], [1969]), 309–319; Jorge Nemésio, *A Obra Poética de Fernando Pessoa: Estrutura das Futuras Edições* ([Salvador (da Bahia)], 1958); João Gaspar Simões, *Vida e Obra*, 630–642; and Pessoa, *Obra Poética*, 3rd ed. (Rio de Janeiro, 1969), 671–676.

14. *Interregno: Defesa e Justificação da Ditadura Militar em Portugal* (Lisboa, 1928).

15. Further analysis of the evolution of Pessoa's stance, seen in concert with social and economic change and, especially, change in political attitudes on the part of sectors of the Portuguese public, is to be found in Neil Larsen and

Ronald W. Sousa, "From Whitman (to Marinetti) to Álvaro de Campos: A Case Study in Materialist Approaches to Literary Influence," unpublished.

16. It is not the point of this remark to suggest that Pessoa was a supporter of Salazarism. Indeed, if Pessoa's authorship is accepted, we even have several bits of anti-Salazar doggerel verse from his pen: Jorge de Sena, "Quatro Poemas Anti-Salazaristas de Fernando Pessoa," *Seara Nova*, No. 1545 (July 1974), 18–20. Nonetheless, the position vis-a-vis society implicit in his work, his defense of the Dictatorship of 1926, and other public pronouncements scattered through his writings make it clear that he participated in the orientation of that sector of the bourgeoisie that grew to oppose the 1910 Republic. As we shall see, *Mensagem* is a piece with that orientation and came to be used by Salazar's Estado Novo.

17. "The Structure of Pessoa's *Mensagem*," *Bulletin of Hispanic Studies*, 59, No. 1, forthcoming in 1982.

18. The seven remaining poems of *Mensagem*'s total of forty-four should be dealt with. The structure common to those seven poems does create some difficulty for the argument that there is a consistent speaker throughout the book, for in those poems—the five "Shields," "Portuguese Sea" III, and the first poem of "The Symbols"—there is no foreground speaker at all. The subjects themselves do the speaking. What is said, however, is similar both in content and in syntax to what Pessoa, as the speaker, relates in those poems in which he deals in his own voice with a poetized subject. Thus the seven exceptions do not stand out as radically different from the other poems of the book. What difference there is seems only technical; the words are Pessoa's words put in the mouths of the subjects of the poems. The reader-neophyte still receives Pessoa's interpretation of the subject under consideration in each poem—still receives, then, his initiation—but a part of that initiation is presented to him in dramatic fashion through the mouths of the historical figures involved.

19. H.P. Blavatsky, *A Voz do Silêncio* (Lisboa, 1916).

20. The readings used in this chapter basically follow the text of *Obra Poética*, in which pp. 69–89 reproduce *Mensagem*. For the rationale for the small changes that I make, see the Introduction to this study. The reader is directed to my *Da Mensagem, Do Mensageiro* (Lisboa, 1981) for information about that question as well as for a reading of *Mensagem* in its entirety, though one that goes beyond the regenerationist focus of the present work.

21. There is a comparison to be made with Camões, *Os Lusíadas* X.145.5–8:

> O favor com que mais se acende o engenho,
> Não no dá a Pátria, não, que está metida
> No gosto da cobiça e na rudeza
> Dũa austera, apagada e vil tristeza.

Bacon, apparently rendering *vil* as 'gross', translates:

> The favor which sets genius all on fire
> My land grants not to song, but runs perforce

> After its envious lusts and brutishness,
> Sunken in harsh, depraved, and gross distress.
>
> (p. 385)

The following quotation is characteristic of Pessoa's use of the term:

> Ficamos no estado vil de inteligência, servil e mimético, em que desde esse tempo [a Idade dos Descobrimentos] temos vegetado.
>
> [We remain in the base state of intelligence, servile and mimetic, in which since that time [the Age of the Discoveries] we have vegetated.]

The Portuguese comes from Pessoa, *Análise da Vida Mental Portuguesa* (Porto, n.d.), 81. *Vil*, for both poets, is a term resulting from an idealistic orientation toward experience. Indeed, the uses to which they put it are similar in many ways: for both poets it denotes mere materialism, which Camões accepts only as a reflex of idealism and Pessoa not at all. By contrast, they propose an idealism that is linked to artistic vision. Pessoa's position on those scores will become clear as this chapter proceeds.

22. I deal in "Estruturas" with some locations in Pessoa's writing where the definition is worked out; see too Georg Rudolf Lind, *Teoria Poética de Fernando Pessoa* (Porto, 1970), 95–127.

23. The source is p. 11 of the separately paginated "Addenda" to *Análise da Vida Mental Portuguesa*.

24. See, for example, his introduction to Augusto Ferreira Gomes, *Quinto Império* (Lisboa, 1943), xvii–xx. A part of that introduction is reproduced and analyzed in my "The Structure of Pessoa's *Mensagem*."

25. "Paganism" is in fact the system rooted in Pessoa's definition of "God" or "Gods" referred to in n. 22. The references there apply equally to this juncture.

26. See, for example, Douglas Wheeler, *Republican Portugal: A Political History, 1910–1926* (Madison, 1978), 208. In addition to documentation of the term "desnacionalização," Wheeler, in chapters 10–14 of his book, documents the sectors of society for which "nationalism" became an anti-Republic rallying point.

27. Indeed, at times Pessoa makes "denationalization" a criterion for good modern art in general, see *Páginas Íntimas*, 114, 143–144.

28. See, for example, his introduction to Gomes's *Quinto Império*, referred to in n. 24.

29. *Portugal, Vasto Império: Um Inquérito Nacional*, comp. Augusto da Costa (Lisboa, 1934), 36.

30. Once again, for an analysis of the presence in Pessoa of the notion that myth is all, a notion usually centered in his use of the verb *fingir* 'to pretend' or 'to create', see my "Estruturas," 54–56.

The Rediscoverers: A Retrospect

1. On the formation of those agencies and their place within the developing

structures of Salazar's Estado Novo, see Oliveira Marques, II, 303–333, 363–365. An irony, but not a coincidence, is to be seen in the fact that the Director of the Secretariat of National Information, António Ferro, was, in 1915, at age twenty, the youngest member of the *Orpheu* group, indeed the nominal Director of the journal.

2. "O Mundo Português," *O Mundo Português*, No. 1, 1. The Pessoa poems appear in I, Nos. 7–8, 249–252. More *Mensagem* poems (in fact, all twelve of "Mar Portuguez") appear in II, No. 24 (Dec. 1935), 401–408; the Latin epigraph to the section is not reproduced, but there appears a note informing the reader of Pessoa's death on 30 Nov. of that year.

Bibliography

General

(Note: The following titles represent—some in ways different from others—general works on aspects of Portuguese cultural history. They constitute the sources primarily consulted in the formulation of the notion of history embodied in this study. As such, they are not always referred to in textual notes. Moreover, even where one or more may be cited, publication information is not reiterated in the corresponding section of this Bibliography, this initial reference being considered sufficient.)

Azevedo, João Lúcio de. *Elementos Para a História Económica de Portugal (Séculos XII a XVII)*. Estudos Documento. Lisboa: Gabinete de Investigações Económicas do Instituto Superior de Ciências Económicas e Financeiras, 1967.
―――. *A Evolução do Sebastianismo*. 2nd ed., rev. Lisboa: Livraria Clássica Editora, 1947.
Cantel, Raymond. *Prophétisme et messianisme dans l'œuvre d'António Vieira*. Paris: Ediciones Hispano-Americanas, 1960.
Cerejeira, M. Gonçalves. *Clenardo e a Sociedade Portuguesa*. 4th ed. O Renascimento em Portugal, Vol. I. [Coimbra]: Coimbra Editora, Limitada, 1974.
Dicionário de História de Portugal. Ed. Joel Serrão. 2nd ed., 6 vols. Lisboa: Iniciativas Editoriais, 1975-1978.
Godinho, Vitorino de Magalhães. *Os Descobrimentos e a Economia Mundial*. 2 vols. Lisboa: Editora Arcádia, 1963-1965.
―――. *A Estrutura da Antiga Sociedade Portuguesa*. Lisboa: Editora Arcádia, 1971.
Oliveira Marques, António Henrique de. *História de Portugal*. 4th ed., 2 vols. Lisboa: Palas Editores, 1974-1976. (This general work on the major aspects of Portuguese history exists in an English version that has not had benefit of the author's latest revisions: *History of Portugal*. 2 vols. New York and London: Columbia University Press, 1972.)
Saraiva, António José. *História da Cultura em Portugal*. 3 vols. Lisboa: Jornal do Fôro, 1950-1962. Vol. II "em colaboração com Óscar Lopes e Luís de Albuquerque."
Saraiva, António José, and Óscar Lopes. *História da Literatura Portuguesa*. 7th ed., revised and brought up to date. Porto: Porto Editora, Lda., n.d.

Serrão, Joel. *Do Sebastianismo ao Socialismo em Portugal*. 3rd ed., rev. and ampl. Lisboa: Livros Horizonte, 1973.

Introduction and Retrospect

Bataillon, Marcel. "Novo Mundo e Fim do Mundo." Tr. Ana Leonísia Ferreira Aratangy. *Revista de História* (São Paulo), Ano V (1954), No. 18, 343–351.
Castro, Américo. *La realidad histórica de España*. Mexico City: Editorial Porrua, S.A., 1954.
———. *The Structure of Spanish History*. Tr. Edmund L. King. Princeton: Princeton University Press, 1954.
O Mundo Português (Lisboa: Agência Geral das Colónias e Secretariado de Propaganda Nacional), I–II (1934–1935).
Sá de Miranda, Francisco de. *Poesias de Francisco de Sá de Miranda*. Ed. Carolina Michaëlis de Vasconcellos. Halle: Max Niemeyer, 1885.

Camões

Actas [da I Reunião Internacional de Camonistas]. Lisboa: Comissão Executiva do IV Centenário da Publicação de "Os Lusíadas," 1973. Frank Pierce, "The Structure and the Style of 'Os Lusíadas'," 301–316; Jorge de Sena, "Aspectos do Pensamento de Camões Através da Estrutura Linguística de 'Os Lusíadas'," 45–58.
Berardinelli, Cleonice. "Os Excursos do Poeta n'*Os Lusíadas*." *Ocidente*, 83, No. 415 (Nov. 1972), 246–258.
Bowra, Cecil Maurice. *From Virgil to Milton*. London: Macmillan & Co. Ltd., 1945.
Brasil, Reis (pseud. of José Gomes Bras). *Os Lusíadas; Comentários e Estudo Crítico*. 6 vols. in 7. Lisboa: [Editorial Minerva], 1960–1967.
Calmon, Pedro. *O Estado e o Direito n'os Lusíadas*. Rio de Janeiro: Edições Dois Mundos, 1945.
Camões, Luís de. *Os Lusíadas*. Ed. Emanuel Paulo Ramos. Porto: Porto Editora Lda., 1974.
———. *The Lusiads of Luiz de Camões*. Tr. Leonard Bacon. New York: The Hispanic Society of America, 1950.
———. *Obras Completas*. Ed. Hernâni Cidade. Colecção de Clássicos Sá da Costa. Lisboa: Livraria Sá da Costa Editora, 1946–1947.
Enciclopedia Dantesca. 5 vols. Roma: Instituto dell'Enciclopedia Italiana, 1970.
Giamatti, A. Bartlett. *The Earthly Paradise and the Renaissance Epic*. Princeton: Princeton University Press, 1966.
Holanda, Francisco de. *Diálogos de Roma. Da Pintura Antiga*. Ed. Manuel Mendes. Colecção de Clássicos Sá da Costa. Lisboa: Livraria Sá da Costa Editora, 1955.
Le Gentil, Georges. *Camoëns, L'œuvre épique et lyrique*. Connaissance des lettres. Paris: Hatier-Boivin, 1954.
Lopes, Fernão. *Crónica de D. João I*. Ed. M. Lopes de Almeida and A. de

Magalhães Bastos. *Biblioteca Histórica—Série Régia.* 2 vols. Porto: Livraria Civilização Editora, [1945].
Maravall, José Antonio. *La cultura del barroco.* Esplugues de Llobregat: Ariel, 1975.
Mendes, João. "Camões e o seu Mito Pessoal." *Brotéria,* 86, No. 5 (May 1968), 621–642; 87, No. 7 (July 1968), 10–27.
Peixoto, Afrânio, and Pedro A. Pinto. *Dicionário d'*Os Lusíadas. Rio de Janeiro: Livraria Francisco Alves, 1924.
Scantimburgo, João de. *Interpretação de Camões à Luz de Santo Tomás de Aquino.* São Paulo: Edições Melhoramentos, 1979.
Sena, Jorge de. *A Estrutura de* Os Lusíadas *e Outros Estudos Camonianos e de Poesia Peninsular do Século XVI.* Colecção Problemas, No. 31. Lisboa: Portugália Editora, [1970].
Seznec, Jean. *La Survivance des dieux antiques; essai sur le rôle de la tradition mythologique dans l'humanisme et dans l'art de la Renaissance.* London: Warburg Institute, 1939.
Sousa, Ronald W. "Os Lusíadas: Voz Poética/Leitura." *Estudos Ibero-Americanos* (Porto Alegre), in press.
———. "Philosophical Implications of Camões' Use of the Classical Mythological Tradition in the Adamastor Episode of *Os Lusíadas.*" *Garcia de Orta* (Lisbon), Número Especial, 1972, 535–546.
———. "A Poet and His Nation: The Foreground Myth of *Os Lusíadas.*" *The Texas Quarterly,* 15, No. 4 (Winter 1972), 19–31.
———. "The View of the Artist in Francisco de Holanda's *Dialogues*: A Clash of Feudal Models." *Luso-Brazilian Review,* 15, Supplementary Issue (Summer 1978), 43–58.
Vergilius Maro, Publius. *Opera.* Ed. and intro. (in Latin) Frederic Arthur Hirtzel. Scriptorum Classicorum Bibliotheca Oxoniensis. Oxford: Clarendon Press, 1964.
Visages de Luís de Camões: *Conférences.* Série Histórica & Literária, X. Paris: Fundação Calouste Gulbenkian, 1972. Eduardo Lourenço de Faria, "Camões et le temps ou la raison oscillante," 109–124; Jorge de Sena "Camões: Quelques vues nouvelles sur son épopée et sa pensée," 145–169.
Weinberg, Bernard. *A History of Literary Criticism in the Italian Renaissance.* 2 vols. Chicago: University of Chicago Press, 1961.
Woodward, William Harrison. *Desiderius Erasmus Concerning the Aim and Method of Education.* Classics in Education, No. 19. 1904; rpt. New York: Teacher's College, Columbia University, 1964.

Vieira

Auerbach, Erich. "Figura." *Scenes from the Drama of European Literature.* Gloucester, Mass.: Peter Smith, 1973, 9–76.
Azevedo, João Lúcio de. *História de António Vieira.* 2nd ed., 2 vols. Porto: Livraria Clássica Eidtora, 1931.
Bandarra, Gonçalo Anes. *Trovas.* Porto: Imprensa Popular de J. L. de Sousa, 1866.
Barrett, E. Boyd. *The Jesuit Enigma.* New York: Boni & Liveright, 1927.
Barthes, Roland. *Sade, Fourier, Loyola.* Paris: Éditions du Seuil, 1971.

Camões, Luís de. *Os Lvsiadas do Grande Lvis de Camoens... Commentados pelo Licenciado Manoel Correa....* Lisboa: Pedro Crasbeek, 1613.
Cambell, Thomas J., S.J. *The Jesuits, 1534–1921.* New York: The Encyclopedia Press, 1921.
Cantel, Raymond. "Vieira e a Filosofia Política do Quinto Império." *Tempo Presente* (Lisboa), Ano 2, Nos. 17–18 (Sept.–Oct. 1960), 22–27.
Charity, A[lan] C. *Events and Their Afterlife; The Dialectics of Christian Typology in the Bible and Dante.* Cambridge: Cambridge University Press, 1966.
Costa, Eduardo Freitas da. "O Sebastianismo Racional e Fernando Pessoa." *Revista de Literatura* (Madrid), 11 (1957), 194–199.
Imago Primi Sæcvli Societatis Iesv a Provincia Flandro-Belgica Eivsdem Societatis Repræsentata. 6 vols. Antwerpia: Ex Officina Plantiniana Balthasaris Moreti, 1640.
Ricard, Robert. "Prophecy and Messianism in the Works of Antonio Vieira." *The Americas* (Academy of American Franciscan History), 17 (1961), 357–368.
Ridley, F[rancis] A. *The Jesuits: A Study in Counter-Revolution.* London: Secker and Warburg, 1938.
Vieira, António. *Defesa Perante o Tribunal do Santo Oficio.* Intro. Hernâni Cidade. Biblioteca de Autores Clássicos. 2 vols. Salvador [da Bahia]: Livraria Progresso Editora, 1957.
———. *Obras Escolhidas.* Ed. António Sérgio and Hernâni Cidade. Colecção de Clássicos Sá da Costa. 12 vols. Lisboa: Sá da Costa [1951–1954].
———. *Sermões.* Ed. Jamil Almansur Haddad. São Paulo: Companhia Editora Nacional. 1957.
Waite, Arthur Edward. *The Brotherhood of the Rosy Cross, Being Records of the House of the Holy Spirit in its Inward and Outward History.* London: William Rider & Son Limited, 1924.

Garrett

Braga, Theóphilo. *Garrett e o Romantismo.* História da Litteratura Portugueza. Porto: Livraria Chardron, 1903 [on cover, 1904].
———. *História do Romantismo em Portugal.* História da Litteratura Portugueza. Lisboa: Nova Livraria Internacional, 1880.
Dicionário de Literatura. Ed. Jacinto do Prado Coelho. 2nd ed., rev. 2 vols., paged continuously. Porto: Livraria Figueirinhas, 1969–1971. "'Camões'," by Jacinto do Prado Coelho, 139; "Garrett," by Jacinto do Prado Coelho, 363–367; "Influência Inglesa na Literatura Portuguesa," by Luís de Sousa Rebelo, 481–487.
Garrett, João Baptista da Silva Leitão de Almeida. "Camoëns." Tr. Edgar C. Knowlton, Jr. *Boletim do Instituto Luís de Camões* (Macau), 6 (1972), Nos. 1 and 2.
———. *Camões.* Ed. João de Almeida Lucas. Lisboa: Livraria Popular, 1946.
———. *Camões e Dona Branca* (selected passages). Ed. António José Saraiva. Colecção Clássicos Portugueses. Lisboa: Livraria Clássica Editora, 1943.
———. *Doutrinas de Estética Literária.* Ed. Agostinho da Silva. Lisboa: Textos Literários, 1938.
———. *Obras de Almeida Garrett.* 2 vols. Porto: Lello e Irmão Editores, 1963.

———. *O Dia Vinte Quatro d'Agosto*. Lisboa: Typographia Rollandiana, 1821.
Gomes de Amorim, Francisco. *Garrett: Memórias Biográphicas*. 3 vols. Lisboa: Imprensa Nacional, 1881.
Lawton, R. A. *Almeida Garrett: l'intime contrainte*. Paris: Didier, 1966.
Monteiro, Ofélia Milheiro Caldas Paiva. *A Formação de Almeida Garrett: Experiência e Criação*. Universidade de Coimbra. Centro de Estudos Românicos. 2 vols. Coimbra: [Atlântida Editora], 1971.
Potter, Norman M. and Ronald W. Sousa. "Liberalismo e Romantismo em Portugal e no Brasil: Proposta para uma Correlação. *Ideologies and Literature*, 1, No. 3 (May–June 1977), 32–52.
Prado Júnior, Caio. *História Económica do Brasil*. São Paulo: Editora Brasiliense Limitada, 1945.
Romanticism. Ed. John B. Halsted. The Documentary History of Western Civilization. New York: Walker and Company, 1969.

Eça de Queiroz

Chamberlain, Bobby J. "Eça e Jung: Uma Análise do Onírico e da Arte n'*A Ilustre Casa de Ramires*." *Mester*, 8, No. 1 (Jan. 1979), 5–17.
Cirurgião, António. "A Estrutura de *A Ilustre Casa de Ramires* de Eça de Queiroz." *Ocidente* (Lisboa), 77 (1969), 137–170.
Cortesão, Jaime. *Eça de Queiroz e a Questão Social*. Lisboa: Seara Nova, 1949.
Costa, René da. "The Mythic Quest Theme in *A Cidade e as Serras*." *Luso-Brazilian Review*, 5, No. 2 (Dec. 1968), 71–79.
Eça de Queiroz, José Maria de. *O Crime do Padre Amaro*. Obras de Eça de Queiroz, ed. Helena Cidade Moura. Lisboa: Edição "Livros do Brasil," n.d.
———. *The Illustrious House of Ramires*. Tr. Ann Stevens. Athens, Ohio: Ohio University Press, 1968.
———. *A Ilustre Casa de Ramires*. De acordo com a primeira edição (1900). Obras de Eça de Queiroz, ed. Helena Cidade Moura. Lisboa: Edição "Livros do Brasil," n.d.
———. *Obras Completas de Eça de Queiroz*. 3 vols. Porto: Lello & Irmão, Editores, n.d.
Goldmann, Lucien. *The Philosophy of the Enlightenment: The Christian Burgess and the Enlightenment*. Tr. Henry Maas. Cambridge, Mass.: The MIT Press, 1973.
Kolakowski, Leszek. *The Alienation of Reason; A History of Positivist Thought*. Tr. Norbert Guterman. Garden City, N.Y.: Doubleday & Company, Inc., 1968.
Lins, Álvaro. *História Literária de Eça de Queiroz*. 6th ed. Rio de Janeiro: Edições O Cruzeiro, 1966.
Marques, Edgard. *Interpretação Espiritual de Eça de Queiroz*. Lisboa: Livraria Editora Guimarães & C.ª, [1946].
Medina, João. *Eça Político (Ensaios sobre Aspectos Político-Ideológicos da Obra de Eça de Queiroz)*. Lisboa: Seara Nova, 1974.
Menezes, Djacir. *Crítica Social de Eça de Queiroz*. 2nd ed. Pref. Galeão Coutinho. Fortaleza: Imprensa Universitária do Ceará, [1962].
Moisés, Carlos Felipe, and Ronald W. Sousa. "Lendo Eça: Um Debate." *Ideologies and Literature*, 3, No. 15, in press.

Sacramento, Mário. *Eça de Queiroz: Uma Estética da Ironia.* [Coimbra]: Coimbra Editora, Limitada, 1945.
Salgado Júnior, António. *História das Conferências do Casino (1871).* Lisboa: Tipografia da Cooperativa Militar, 1930.
Saraiva, António José. *As Ideias de Eça de Queiroz.* Lisboa: Centro Bibliográfico, [1947].
Simões, João Gaspar. *Eça de Queiroz.* Colecção A Obra e o Homem, No. 4. Lisboa: Editora Arcádia Limitada, 1961.
———. *Vida e Obra de Eça de Queirós.* Amadora: Livraria Bertrand, 1973.
Sousa, Ronald W. "Editoral." *Ideologies and Literature*, 2, No. 7 (1978), 3–8.
Taine, Hippolyte. *Histoire de la littérature anglaise.* 12th ed. 5 vols. Paris: Librairie Hachette et Cie., 1905.
Zola, Émile. *Le Roman expérimental*, in *Collection des Œuvres Complètes* [d'] *Emile Zola*, [41]. Paris: Typographie François Bernouard, [1928].
———. *Thérèse Raquin*, in *Collection des Œuvres Complètes* [d'] *Emile Zola*, [34]. Paris: Typographie François Bernouard, [1928].

Fernando Pessoa

Athena; Revista de Arte (Lisboa). I, Nos. 1–5 (Oct. 1924–Feb. 1925).
B[lavatsky], H[elena] P[etrovna]. *The Voice of the Silence and Other Chosen Fragments from the Book of the Golden Precepts.* London: Theosophical Publishing Society, 1913.
———. *A Voz do Silêncio.* Tr. Fernando Pessoa. Lisboa: Livraria Clássica Editora, 1916.
Coelho, Jacinto do Prado. *Diversidade e Unidade em Fernando Pessoa.* 3rd ed. Lisboa: Editorial Verbo Lda., 1969.
———. *A Letra e o Leitor.* Colecção Problemas, No. 27. [Lisboa]: Portugália Editora, [1969]. Several essays in the volume deal with Pessoa; most valuable are "Fernando Pessoa e Teixeira de Pascoaes," 239–270; "O Nacionalismo Utópico de Fernando Pessoa," "Cronologia e Variantes da 'Mensagem'," 309–319.
Galvão, José. *Fontes Impressas da Obra de Fernando Pessoa.* Lisboa: n.n., [1965?].
Gomes, Augusto Ferreira. *Quinto Império.* Lisboa: Parceria António Maria Pereira, 1934.
Larsen, Neil, and Ronald W. Sousa. "From Whitman (to Marinetti) to Álvaro de Campos:" A Case Study in Materialist Approaches to Literary Influence. Unpublished manuscript.
Lind, Georg Rudolf. *Teoria Poética de Fernando Pessoa.* Colecção Civilização Portuguesa, No. 8. Porto: Editorial Inova, [1970].
Monteiro, Adolfo Casais. "Teoria da Impersonalidade: Fernando Pessoa e T. S. Eliot." *O Tempo e o Modo* (Lisboa), No. 68 (1969), 204–209.
Monteiro, Maria da Encarnação. *Incidências Inglesas na Poesia de Fernando Pessoa.* Coimbra, 1956. Reprinted from *Biblos* (Coimbra), 31 (1955), 21–123.
Nemésio, Jorge. *A Obra Poética de Fernando Pessoa: Estrutura das Futuras Edições.* Publicações da Universidade da Bahia. Sér. 2, No. 13. 1958. Also issued independently—[Salvador (da Bahia)]: Aguiar e Sousa, [1958].
Nunes, Benedito. *O Dorso do Tigre.* São Paulo: Perspectiva, 1969.
Pessoa, Fernando. *Análise da Vida Mental Portuguesa.* Ed. Petrus. Porto: Edições Cultura, n.d.

———. *Apologia do Paganismo*. Ed. Petrus. Porto: Editorial Cultura, n.d.
———. *Apreciações Literárias*. Ed. Petrus. Porto: Editorial Cultura, n.d.
———. "Cartas." *Presença* (Coimbra), No. 48 (July 1936), 3.
———. *Cartas a Armando Côrtes-Rodrigues*. Ed. Joel Serrão. Lisboa: Editorial Confluência, 1944.
———. *Crónicas Intemporais*. Ed. Petrus. Colecção "Tendências." [Porto?]: n.n., n.d.
———. *Hyram: Filosofia Religiosa e Ciências Ocultas*. Ed. Petrus. "Tendências." [Porto?]: n.n., n.d.
———. *Interregno: Defesa e Justificação da Ditadura Militar em Portugal*. Manifesto do Núcleo de Acção Nacional. Lisboa, 1928.
———. "Mar Portuguez." *Contemporânea*, No. 4 ([Oct.] 1922), 9–14.
———. *Mensagem*. Lisboa: Parceria António Maria Pereira, 1934.
———. ———. 6th ed. Ed. David Mourão-Ferreira. Lisboa: Edições Ática, 1959.
———. *Obra Poética*. Ed. Maria Aliete Galhoz. Biblioteca Luso-Brasileira, Série Portuguesa, No. 5. 3rd ed. Rio de Janeiro: Companhia José Aguilar Editora, 1969.
———. *Páginas de Doutrina Estética*. Ed. Jorge de Sena. Lisboa: Inquérito, 1946.
———. *Páginas de Estética e de Teoria e Crítica Literárias*. Ed. Georg Rudolf Lind and Jacinto do Prado Coelho. Lisboa: Edições Ática, [1967].
———. *Páginas Íntimas e de Auto-Interpretação*. Ed. Georg Rudolf Lind and Jacinto do Prado Coelho. Lisboa: Edições Ática, [1966].
———. *Textos Filosóficos*. Ed. António de Pina Coelho. 2 vols. Lisboa: Edições Ática, 1968.
———. *Ultimatum*, by Álvaro de Campos. Ed. Petrus. Porto: Editorial Cultura, n.d.
Poggioli, Renato. *The Theory of the Avant-Garde*. Tr. Gerald Fitzgerald. Cambridge: Harvard University Press, 1968.
Portugal, Vasto Império: Um Inquérito Nacional. Comp. Augusto da Costa. Lisboa: Imprensa Nacional, 1934.
Quadros, António. *Fernando Pessoa*. Colecção A Obra e o Homem, 3. 2nd ed. Lisboa: Arcádia, n.d.
Sena, Jorge de. "Quatro Poemas Anti-Salazaristas de Fernando Pessoa." *Seara Nova*, No. 1545 (July, 1974), 18–20.
Senior, John. *The Way Down and Out: The Occult in Symbolist Literature*. Ithaca, N.Y.: Cornell University Press, [1959].
Simões, João Gaspar. *Vida e Obra de Fernando Pessoa: História duma Geração*. 2nd ed., rev. Amadora: Livraria Bertrand, [1970].
Sousa, Ronald W. *Da Mensagem, Do Mensageiro*. Lisboa: Sá da Costa, 1981.
———. "Estruturas para uma Imagem do 'Eu'," *Persona* (Porto), No. 3 (July 1979), 51–59.
———. "The Structure of Pessoa's *Mensagem*." *Bulletin of Hispanic Studies*, 59, No. 1, forthcoming in 1982.
Waite, Arthur Edward. *The Brotherhood of the Rosy Cross, Being Records of the House of the Holy Spirit in its Inward and Outward History*. London: William Rider & Son Limited, 1924.
Wheeler, Douglas. *Republican Portugal: A Political History, 1910–1926*. Madison: University of Wisconsin, 1978.

Index

Absolutism, 22, 78, 79, 80, 89, 94, 141
Adamastor, 30, 82–83, 89–90, 93
Africa, Portugal in, 1, 3, 19, 50, 74, 83, 101, 109–110, 111, 124, 126, 128, 172 (n. 7), 178 (n. 2); *see also* "Alcácer-Kebir"
Alcácer-Kebir, 3, 51, 54, 82, 84, 89, 91, 108, 147
aristocratic tendency. *See* "noble class, ascendancy of"

Bandarra, Gonçalo Anes, 53, 55, 61, 66, 70, 71–72, 98, 142, 150, 152, 172–173 (n. 10), 173 (n. 16)
bourgeois intelligentsia. *See* "Generation of 1870"
bourgeoisie. *See* "middle class, middle groups, in social structure"
Brazil, 50, 51, 56, 77, 78–79, 101

Camões, Luís Vaz de, 5, 11-45 (chapter), 161-168 passim; in literature, 82–99, 107, 165; Garrett's identification with, 83, 84, 86, 87-88, 91, 92, 95, 165
censorship, 22, 28, 35, 41, 47, 49, 77
chosen nation, or chosen people, Portugal as, 35–36, 52, 55, 59, 70, 174 (n. 19)
Church, as institution, 21, 23, 48, 56, 57, 58, 68, 70, 102, 103, 104–105, 136, 174 (n. 18)
converts. *See* "New Christians"
Counter Reformation, 13, 18, 19, 20, 21, 22, 24, 42, 47, 48, 52, 58, 59, 67, 78

"devil figure," in *A Ilustre Casa de Ramires*, 110–111, 117, 118–119, 122, 124
Discoveries, Age of the, 1–3, 11–13, 14, 19, 21, 35, 73, 88, 91, 142, 144, 149, 156, 163, 165, 180 (n. 21)

Eça de Queiroz, José Maria de, 5, 101-129 (chapter), 131-132, 136, 161-168 passim
empiricism, in sixteenth and seventeenth centuries, 21–22, 23, 29, 30, 37, 38–43, 45, 67, 68
Estado Novo, 141, 161–162, 167, 179 (n. 16), 180–181 (n. 1)
expansion, political and cultural. *See* "Discoveries, Age of the"

failure, sense of, after Age of the Discoveries, 2–3, 12–13, 17, 21–22, 24, 52
Fifth Empire. *See* "Quinto Império"

Gama, Vasco da, 1, 14, 16, 25, 27, 29, 30, 31, 33, 34, 37, 38, 51, 74, 89, 147
Garrett, Almeida, 5, 77-99 (chapter), 101, 132, 134, 155, 161-168 passim
Generation of 1870, 102, 106, 165, 177 (n. 10)

Humanism, 2, 12, 13, 21, 22–24, 25–31, 35, 37, 38–43, 45, 47, 48, 171 (n. 10)

India, Portugal in, 1, 2, 14, 20, 26, 28, 34, 47, 50, 74, 93
Inquisition, 13, 22, 24, 47–48, 51, 56, 58, 67, 77, 93

Jesuit Order, 13, 22, 24, 48–51, 55, 58, 59, 68, 73, 77, 164, 172 (nn. 3, 4), 173 (n. 14)

Liberalism, 79–80, 81, 82, 87, 88, 89, 93, 94, 95, 101–105, 111, 120, 127, 138, 155, 174 (n. 6)

middle class, or middle groups, in social structure, 11–12, 21, 22, 47, 48, 55,

INDEX

77–79, 101, 102, 103, 106, 128, 131, 132, 133, 134, 135, 165, 179 (n. 16)

"national spirit," or "national psyche," 81–82, 83, 93, 94–98, 107, 126, 128–129, 146, 155, 157–158, 160, 162, 164–165, 166, 175 (n. 10)

New Christians, 47, 56, 77

noble class: ascendancy of, 12, 51, 77, 78, 81–82, 87, 88, 101, 167, 174 (n. 18); history and ideology of, 2, 11, 12, 13, 18, 19–21, 22, 27, 31–37, 38, 40–43, 45, 47, 48, 50, 51, 68, 78, 79, 86, 88, 108, 110, 118, 127, 163, 164, 171 (n. 10), 174 (n. 18), 177 (n. 16)

Pessoa, Fernando Nogueira, 5, 131-160 (chapter), 161-168 passim

prophecy, prophet(s), in Portuguese history, 2, 52, 53, 55, 56, 57, 60–67, 70, 72, 73, 74–75, 98, 152, 165, 166, 172–173 (n. 10); *see also* "Bandarra"

Quinto Império, 69, 70–73, 150, 152, 154, 157–158, 162, 173 (n. 16)

regenerationism: in Camões, 43–47, 163–164; in Eça de Queiroz, 124–129, 165–166; in Garrett, 81, 94–95, 98–99, 164–165; in Pessoa, 156–157, 160, 166–167; in Vieira, 68–75, 77, 164; symbols of, and definition of, 3–4, 163, 167–168

Republic of 1910, or First Republic. *See* "Republicanism"

Republicanism, 111, 133, 134, 141, 153, 162, 179 (n. 16), 180 (n. 26)

Revolution of 1640, 3, 51, 52, 53, 55, 68, 70, 77, 95, 172, (n. 8), 173 (n. 10)

Revolution of 1820, 79, 80, 81, 95

Revolution of 1910, 133, 134, 141, 162

Scholasticism, 48, 64, 67, 68

Sebastian, King, 3, 13, 15, 37, 42, 45, 50, 51–56, 61, 69, 71–72, 83–84, 86, 89, 91, 93, 108, 141, 146–148, 149–152, 154, 157–158, 160, 163, 164, 169 (n. 5), 172 (n. 8), 173 (n. 10)

Sebastianism. *See* "Sebastian"

Spanish accession to the throne (1580), 3, 51, 54, 80

Thomism, 18–19, 21, 22, 23, 24, 27, 28, 29, 31, 35, 37, 39–42, 45, 48, 64, 67, 75, 171 (n. 8)

typological reasoning, 59–61, 67, 69–70, 72, 152

Vieira, Padre António, 5, 47-75 (chapter), 77, 149, 152, 161-168 passim